JACKED

ERIC KRIPKE WRITER

JOHN HIGGINS
WITH SALLY JANE HURST
AND MARC OLIVENT
ARTISTS

John Higgins SotoColor
Colorists

Clem Robins
Letterer

Glenn Fabry and Ryan Brown
Cover Art and Original Series Covers

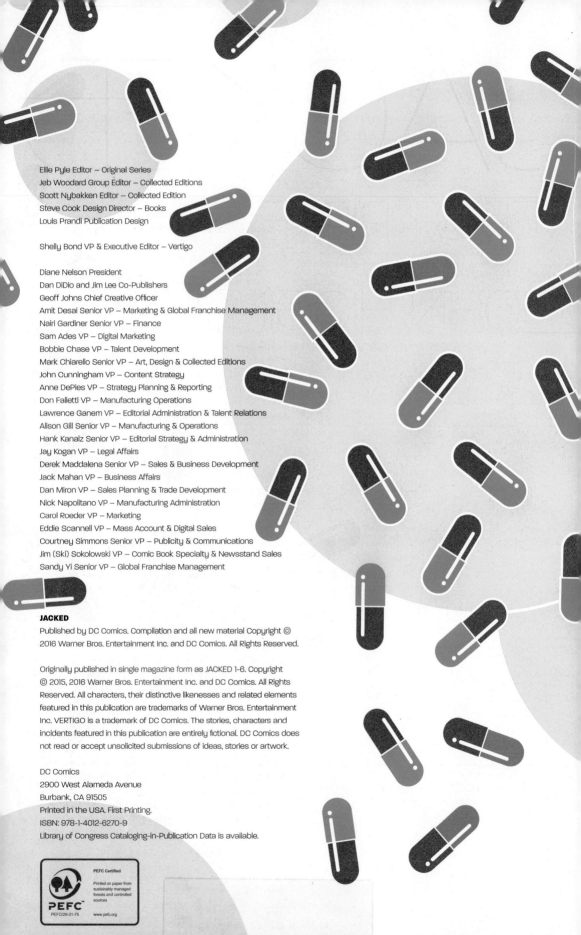

Ellie Pyle Editor – Original Series
Jeb Woodard Group Editor – Collected Editions
Scott Nybakken Editor – Collected Edition
Steve Cook Design Director – Books
Louis Prandi Publication Design

Shelly Bond VP & Executive Editor – Vertigo

Diane Nelson President
Dan DiDio and Jim Lee Co-Publishers
Geoff Johns Chief Creative Officer
Amit Desai Senior VP – Marketing & Global Franchise Management
Nairi Gardiner Senior VP – Finance
Sam Ades VP – Digital Marketing
Bobbie Chase VP – Talent Development
Mark Chiarello Senior VP – Art, Design & Collected Editions
John Cunningham VP – Content Strategy
Anne DePies VP – Strategy Planning & Reporting
Don Falletti VP – Manufacturing Operations
Lawrence Ganem VP – Editorial Administration & Talent Relations
Alison Gill Senior VP – Manufacturing & Operations
Hank Kanalz Senior VP – Editorial Strategy & Administration
Jay Kogan VP – Legal Affairs
Derek Maddalena Senior VP – Sales & Business Development
Jack Mahan VP – Business Affairs
Dan Miron VP – Sales Planning & Trade Development
Nick Napolitano VP – Manufacturing Administration
Carol Roeder VP – Marketing
Eddie Scannell VP – Mass Account & Digital Sales
Courtney Simmons Senior VP – Publicity & Communications
Jim (Ski) Sokolowski VP – Comic Book Specialty & Newsstand Sales
Sandy Yi Senior VP – Global Franchise Management

JACKED

DC Comics
2900 West Alameda Avenue
Burbank, CA 91505
Printed in the USA. First Printing.
ISBN: 978-1-4012-6270-9
Library of Congress Cataloging-in-Publication Data is available.

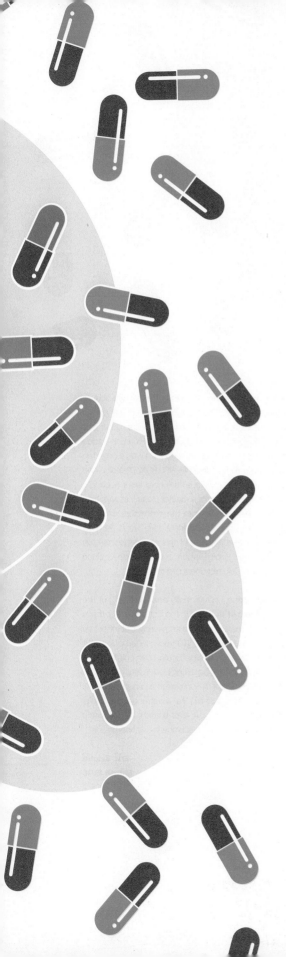

FOREWORD

Okay, so I had a mid-life crisis about a year or two ago. It's a cliché, I'm aware, but I had one. I was working too hard. Not seeing nearly enough of my family. I was coming off a failed TV show. I felt out of balance and depressed. And it got me thinking—was I living the life I wanted to live? (No. No, I wasn't.) On top of that, I felt my meat-suit slowly going rancid. Bald. Bad knee. Acid reflux. Time was contracting; gut was expanding. But was it too late? Could I still course correct? Do something—be someone—great? (And what does "*great*" even *mean*?)

I told you. What an asshole. A goddamn cliché.

But one day—I think I was looking at some online porn—all of this churning Semitic angst suddenly coalesced into a single idea: what if I got super powers? Not the square-jawed, mildly fascist Aryan type that usually gets them—but me, a neurotic, balding, reasonably selfish Jew? For one thing, I'd get all my physical ailments under control. Then I'd show up all those toned and tanned sonsofbitches I see every day. And I'd have sex like a champ. About the very last thing I'd do is *fight crime*. And, on a deeper, emotional level: what if mid-life-crisis-me suddenly had the chance to do something—be someone—great? Would I be fulfilled? Happy? Or would I just make a mess out of the whole thing?

I was excited and a little scared by this idea. I've never been quite so personal, quite so honest, in my writing before. But what to do with it? It occurred to me that a superhero story might best be told as a comic book. And, ultimately, I was able to pitch it to the sharp, supportive and talented Geoff Johns, Hank Kanalz, Shelly Bond and Ellie Pyle. Insanely, they actually bought the thing. Even more insanely, they bought it for VERTIGO, my all-time favorite imprint. (Confession: I've never really been into superhero comics—but PREACHER? HELLBLAZER? SANDMAN? That's my shit.) I have dozens of VERTIGO trade paperbacks on my bookshelf, so this was a check off the bucket list for sure. Now, I'm not a comic book writer, and never have been, but I've read hundreds of them. How hard could it be?

The answer: really fucking hard. I think if I knew just how hard, I doubt I would've done it. I'm here to tell you: the comic books you've been casually reading on the shitter? Their writers bust their asses. Each script is something like 30 pages of carefully mapped-out prose. You have to use entirely new muscles. Learn a whole new language. I'm not gonna lie, I bitched and grumbled through the whole process. But Ellie Pyle was a patient editor and quietly cajoled me into the light.

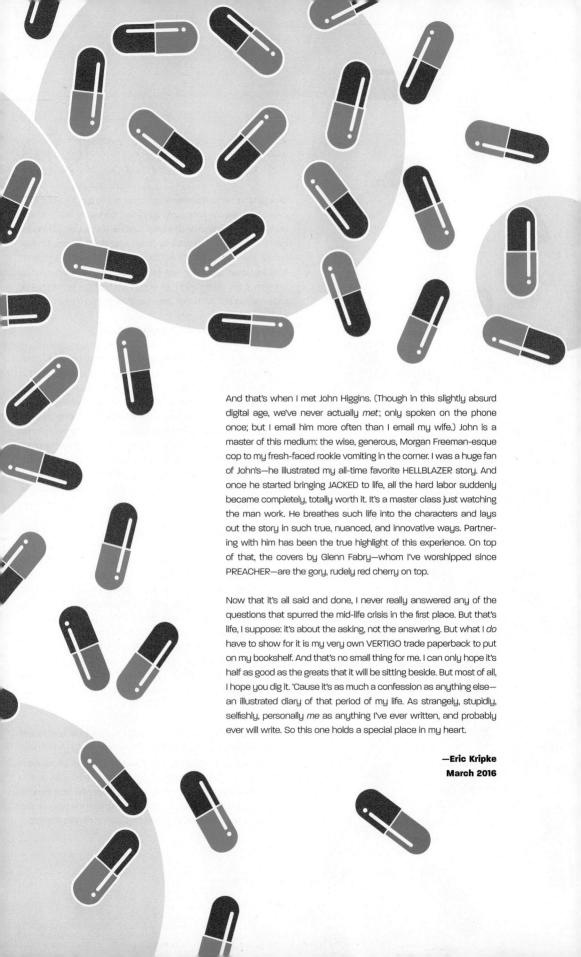

And that's when I met John Higgins. (Though in this slightly absurd digital age, we've never actually *met*; only spoken on the phone once; but I email him more often than I email my wife.) John is a master of this medium: the wise, generous, Morgan Freeman-esque cop to my fresh-faced rookie vomiting in the corner. I was a huge fan of John's—he illustrated my all-time favorite HELLBLAZER story. And once he started bringing JACKED to life, all the hard labor suddenly became completely, totally worth it. It's a master class just watching the man work. He breathes such life into the characters and lays out the story in such true, nuanced, and innovative ways. Partnering with him has been the true highlight of this experience. On top of that, the covers by Glenn Fabry—whom I've worshipped since PREACHER—are the gory, rudely red cherry on top.

Now that it's all said and done, I never really answered any of the questions that spurred the mid-life crisis in the first place. But that's life, I suppose: it's about the asking, not the answering. But what I *do* have to show for it is my very own VERTIGO trade paperback to put on my bookshelf. And that's no small thing for me. I can only hope it's half as good as the greats that it will be sitting beside. But most of all, I hope you dig it. 'Cause it's as much a confession as anything else— an illustrated diary of that period of my life. As strangely, stupidly, selfishly, personally *me* as anything I've ever written, and probably ever will write. So this one holds a special place in my heart.

—Eric Kripke
March 2016

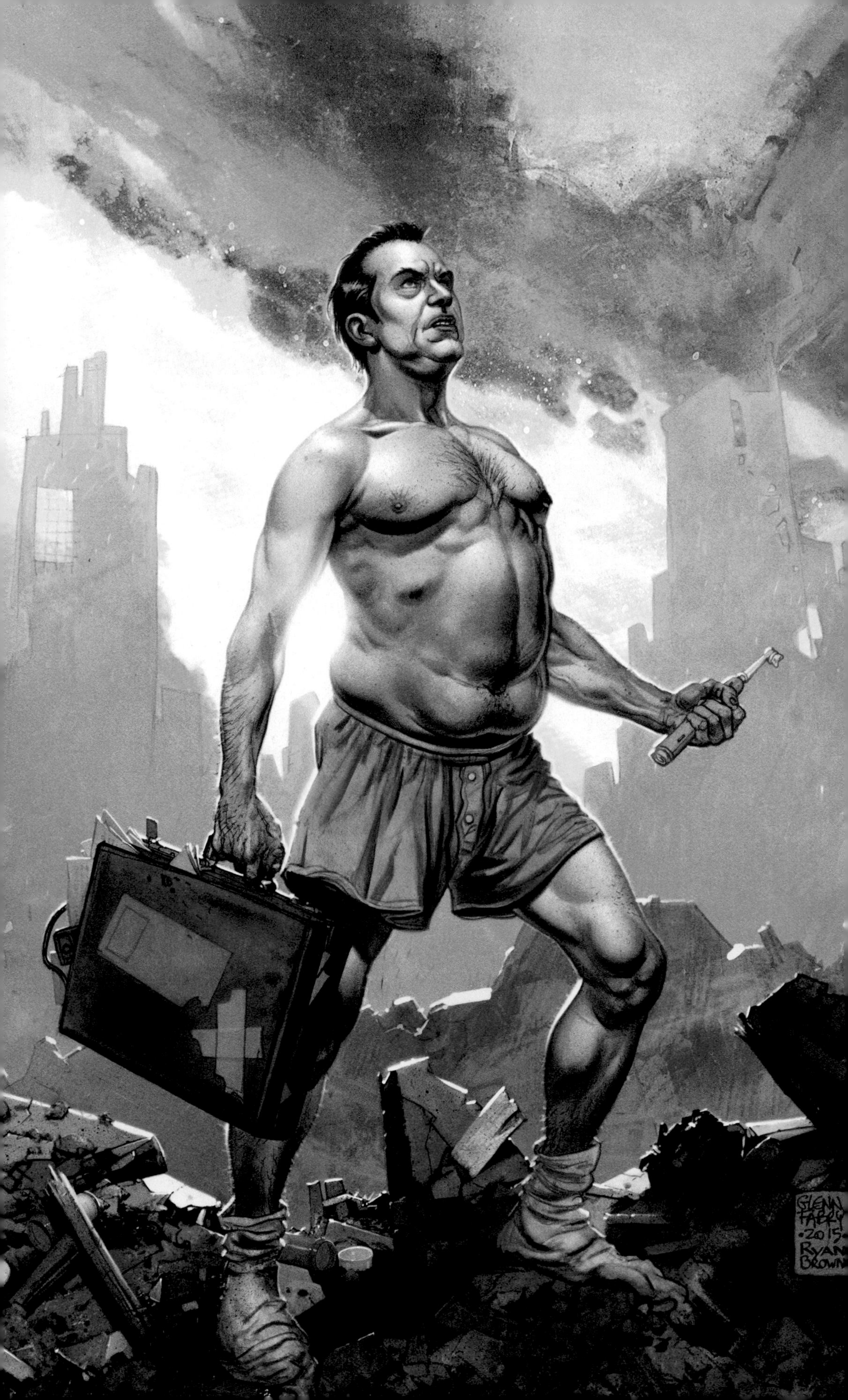
GLENN FABRY
·2015·
RYAN BROWN

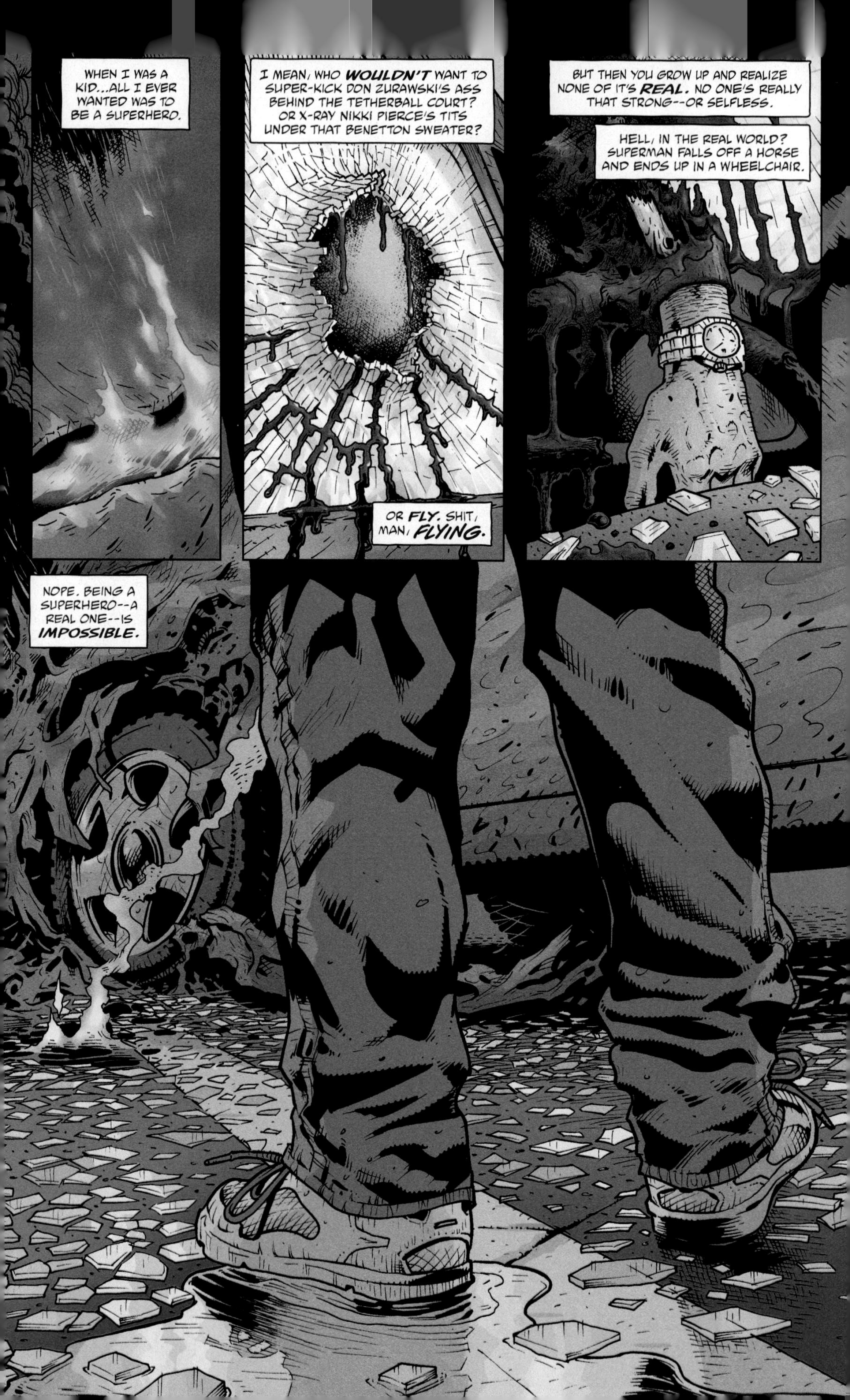
WHEN I WAS A KID...ALL I EVER WANTED WAS TO BE A SUPERHERO.
I MEAN, WHO WOULDN'T WANT TO SUPER-KICK DON ZURAWSKI'S ASS BEHIND THE TETHERBALL COURT? OR X-RAY NIKKI PIERCE'S TITS UNDER THAT BENETTON SWEATER?
OR FLY. SHIT, MAN, FLYING.
BUT THEN YOU GROW UP AND REALIZE NONE OF IT'S REAL. NO ONE'S REALLY THAT STRONG--OR SELFLESS.
HELL, IN THE REAL WORLD? SUPERMAN FALLS OFF A HORSE AND ENDS UP IN A WHEELCHAIR.
NOPE. BEING A SUPERHERO--A REAL ONE--IS IMPOSSIBLE.

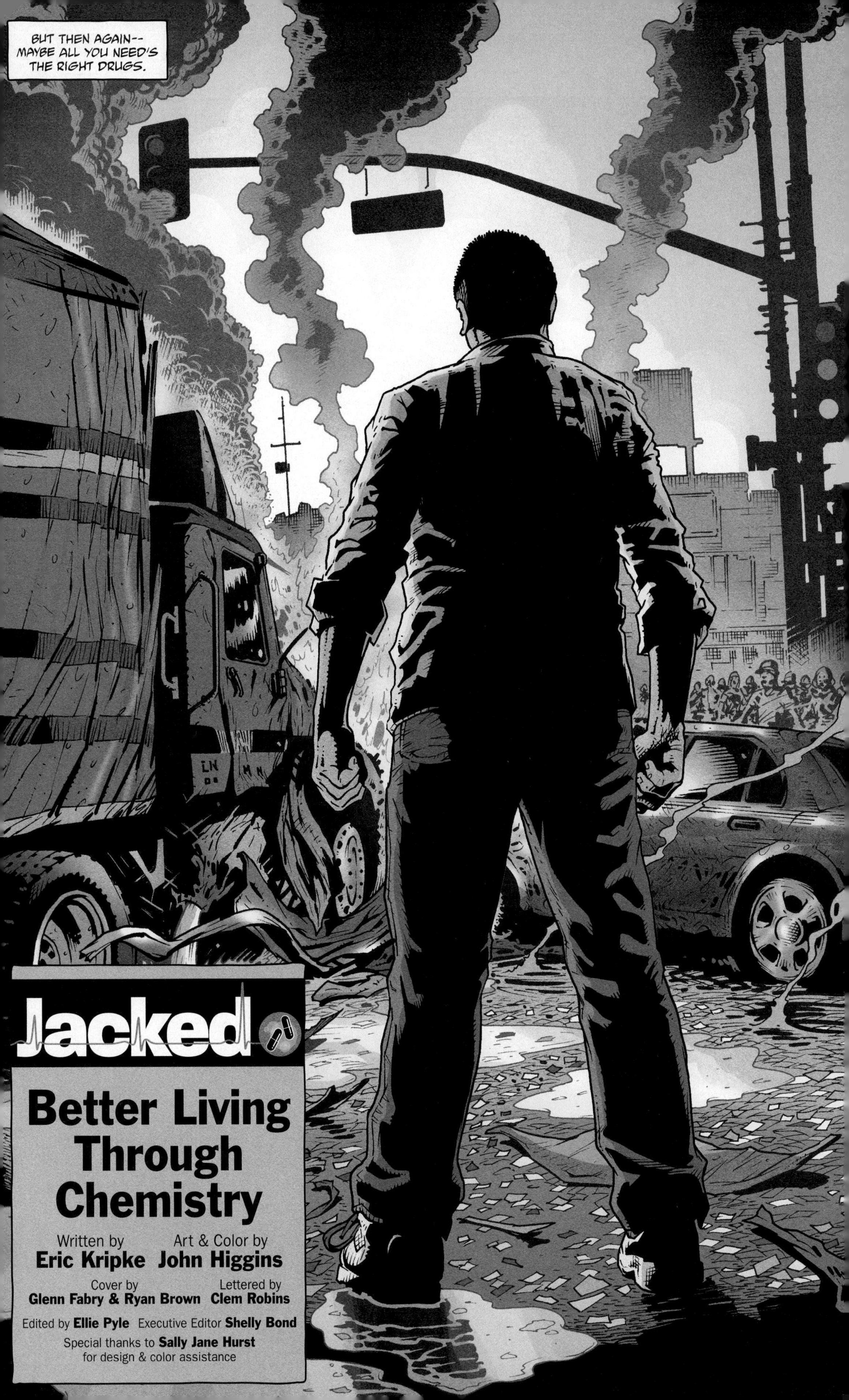
BUT THEN AGAIN--
MAYBE ALL YOU NEED'S
THE RIGHT DRUGS.

Jacked

Better Living Through Chemistry

Written by **Eric Kripke** Art & Color by **John Higgins**

Cover by **Glenn Fabry & Ryan Brown** Lettered by **Clem Robins**

Edited by **Ellie Pyle** Executive Editor **Shelly Bond**

Special thanks to **Sally Jane Hurst** for design & color assistance

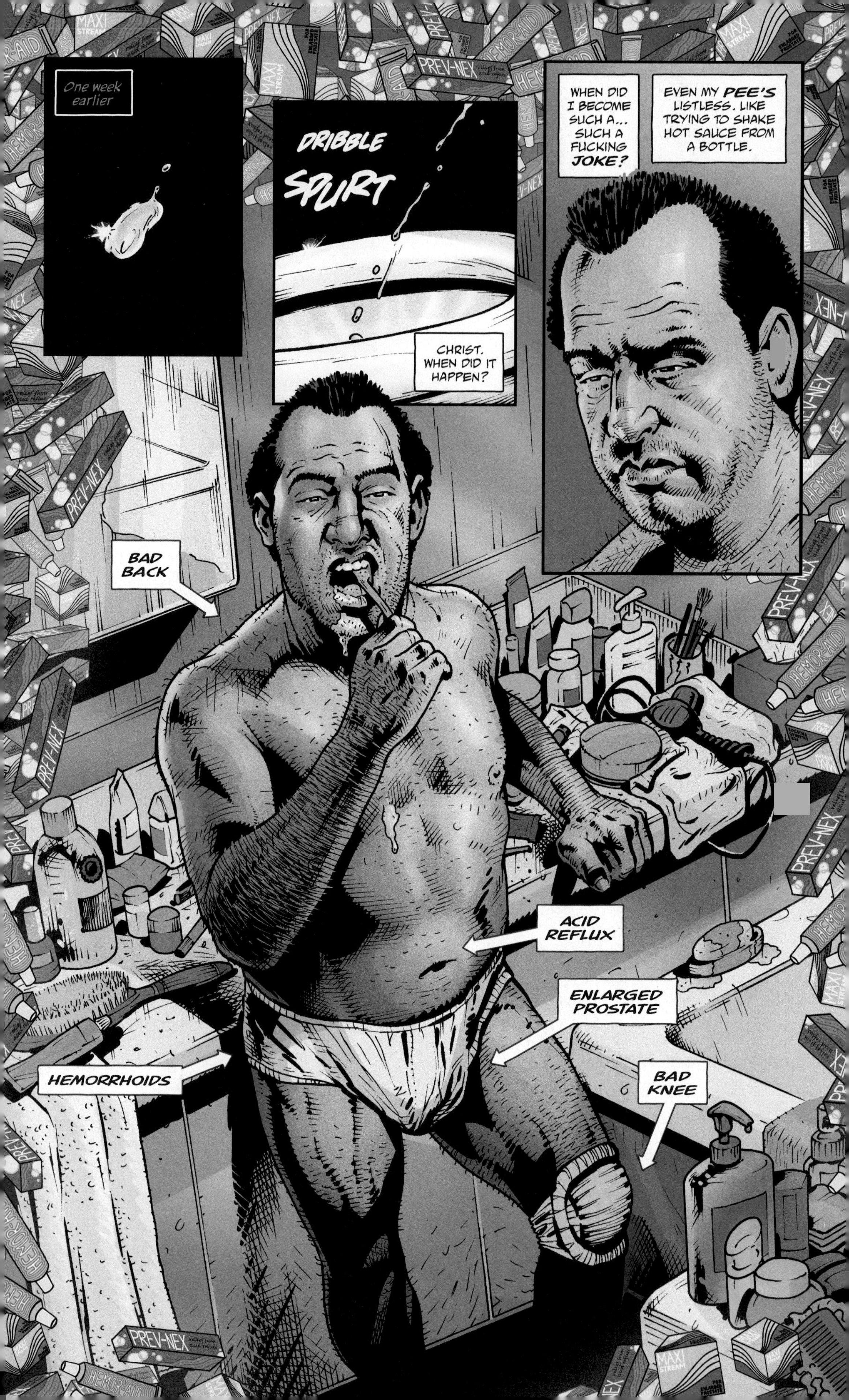
One week earlier
DRIBBLE
SPURT
CHRIST. WHEN DID IT HAPPEN?
WHEN DID I BECOME SUCH A... SUCH A FUCKING JOKE?
EVEN MY PEE'S LISTLESS. LIKE TRYING TO SHAKE HOT SAUCE FROM A BOTTLE.
BAD BACK
ACID REFLUX
ENLARGED PROSTATE
HEMORRHOIDS
BAD KNEE

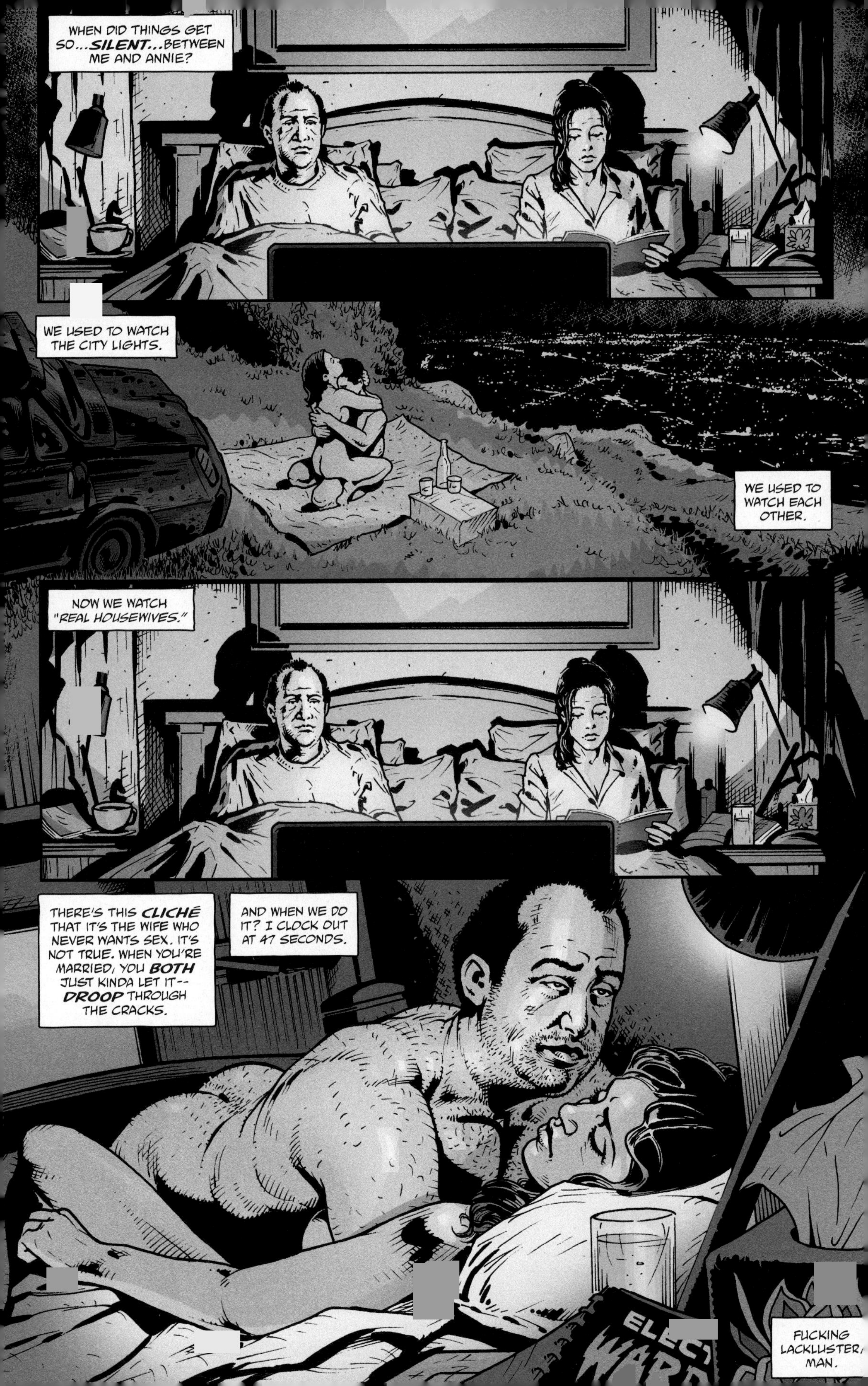
WHEN DID THINGS GET SO...SILENT...BETWEEN ME AND ANNIE?
WE USED TO WATCH THE CITY LIGHTS.
WE USED TO WATCH EACH OTHER.
NOW WE WATCH "REAL HOUSEWIVES."
THERE'S THIS CLICHÉ THAT IT'S THE WIFE WHO NEVER WANTS SEX. IT'S NOT TRUE. WHEN YOU'RE MARRIED, YOU BOTH JUST KINDA LET IT--DROOP THROUGH THE CRACKS.
AND WHEN WE DO IT? I CLOCK OUT AT 47 SECONDS.
FUCKING LACKLUSTER, MAN.

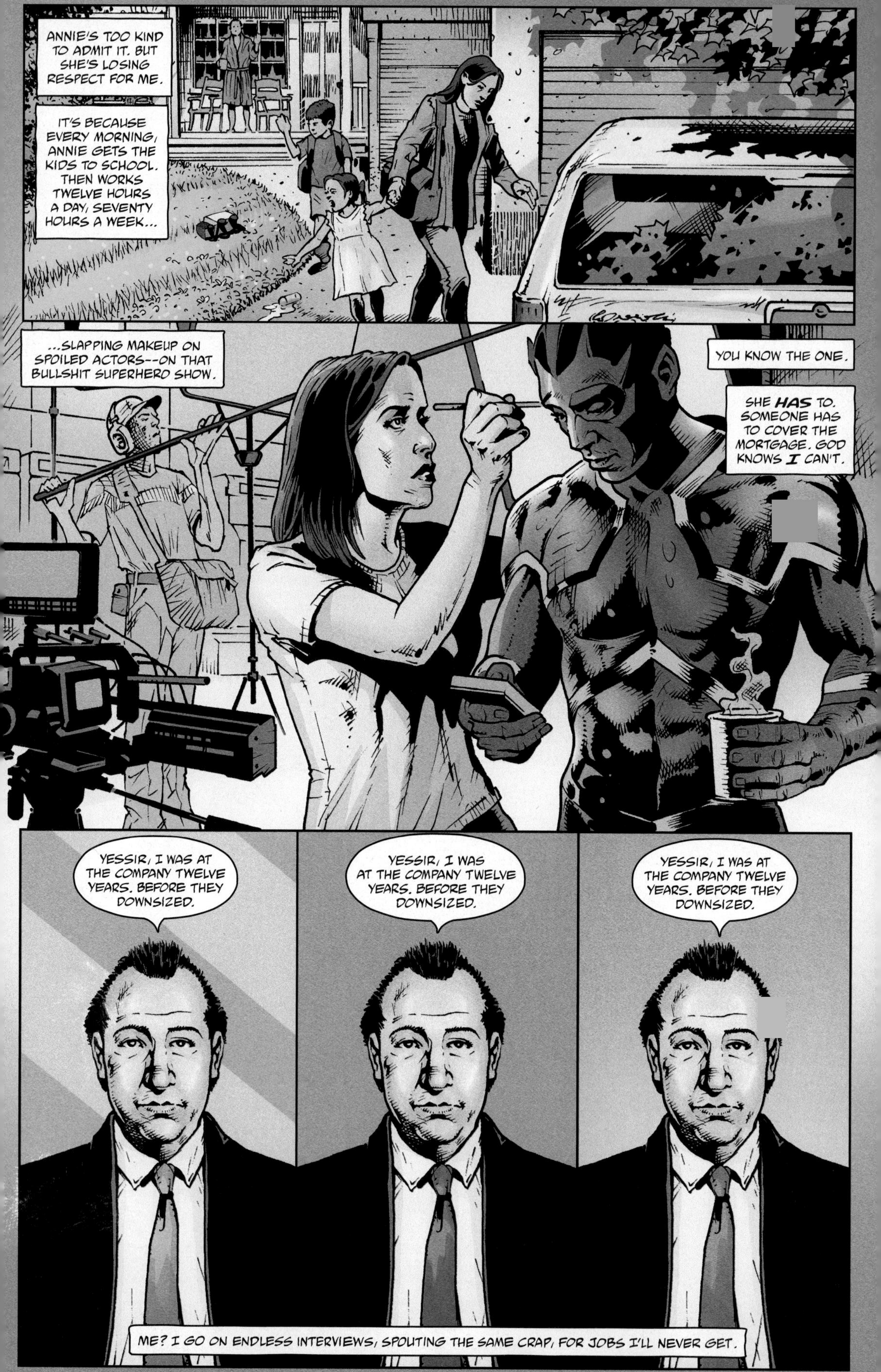
ANNIE'S TOO KIND TO ADMIT IT. BUT SHE'S LOSING RESPECT FOR ME.
IT'S BECAUSE EVERY MORNING, ANNIE GETS THE KIDS TO SCHOOL. THEN WORKS TWELVE HOURS A DAY, SEVENTY HOURS A WEEK...
...SLAPPING MAKEUP ON SPOILED ACTORS--ON THAT BULLSHIT SUPERHERO SHOW.
YOU KNOW THE ONE.
SHE HAS TO. SOMEONE HAS TO COVER THE MORTGAGE. GOD KNOWS I CAN'T.
YESSIR, I WAS AT THE COMPANY TWELVE YEARS. BEFORE THEY DOWNSIZED.
YESSIR, I WAS AT THE COMPANY TWELVE YEARS. BEFORE THEY DOWNSIZED.
YESSIR, I WAS AT THE COMPANY TWELVE YEARS. BEFORE THEY DOWNSIZED.
ME? I GO ON ENDLESS INTERVIEWS, SPOUTING THE SAME CRAP, FOR JOBS I'LL NEVER GET.

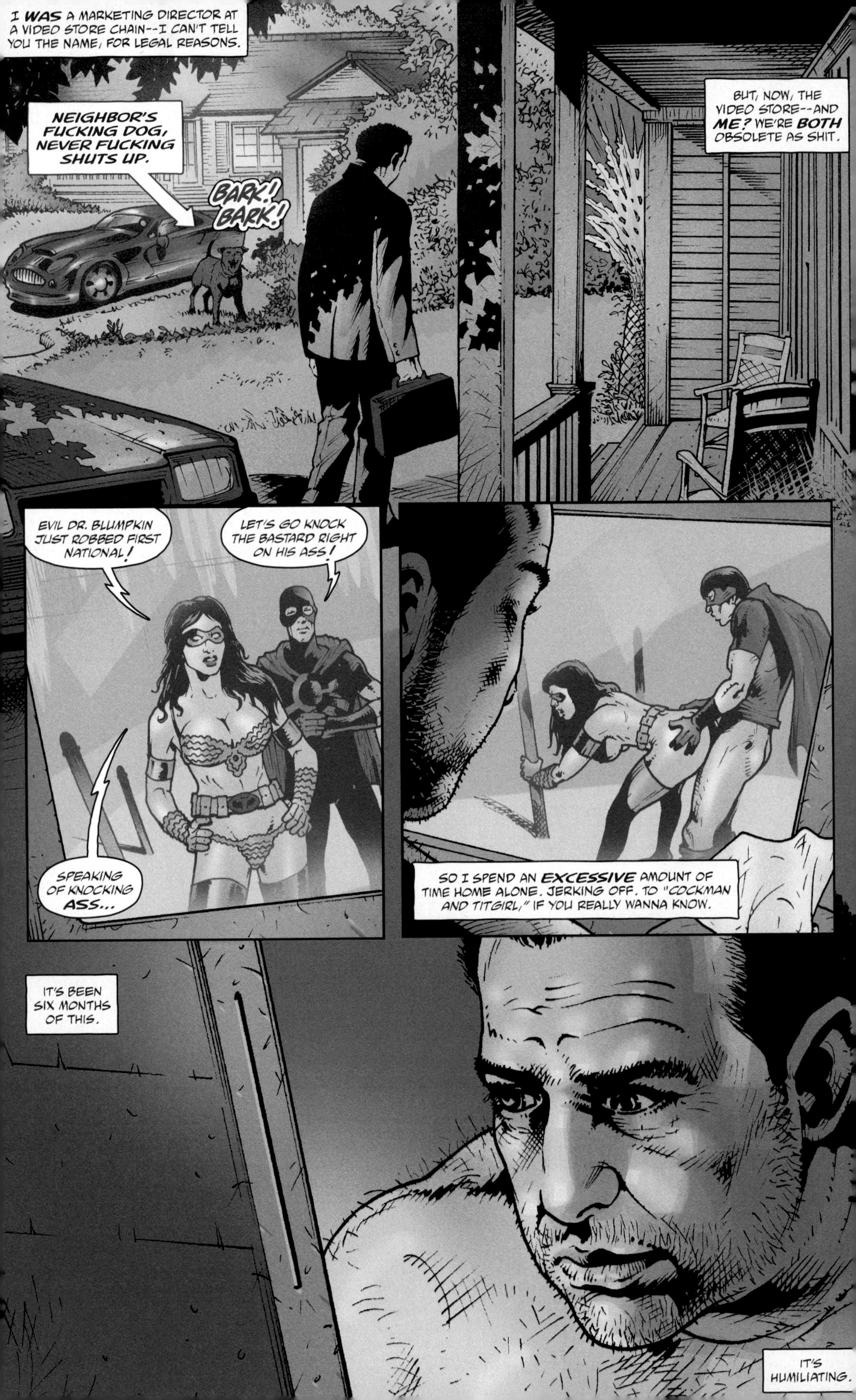
I WAS A MARKETING DIRECTOR AT A VIDEO STORE CHAIN--I CAN'T TELL YOU THE NAME, FOR LEGAL REASONS.
NEIGHBOR'S FUCKING DOG, NEVER FUCKING SHUTS UP.
BARK! BARK!
BUT, NOW, THE VIDEO STORE--AND ME? WE'RE BOTH OBSOLETE AS SHIT.
EVIL DR. BLUMPKIN JUST ROBBED FIRST NATIONAL!
LET'S GO KNOCK THE BASTARD RIGHT ON HIS ASS!
SPEAKING OF KNOCKING ASS...
SO I SPEND AN EXCESSIVE AMOUNT OF TIME HOME ALONE. JERKING OFF. TO "COCKMAN AND TITGIRL," IF YOU REALLY WANNA KNOW.
IT'S BEEN SIX MONTHS OF THIS.
IT'S HUMILIATING.

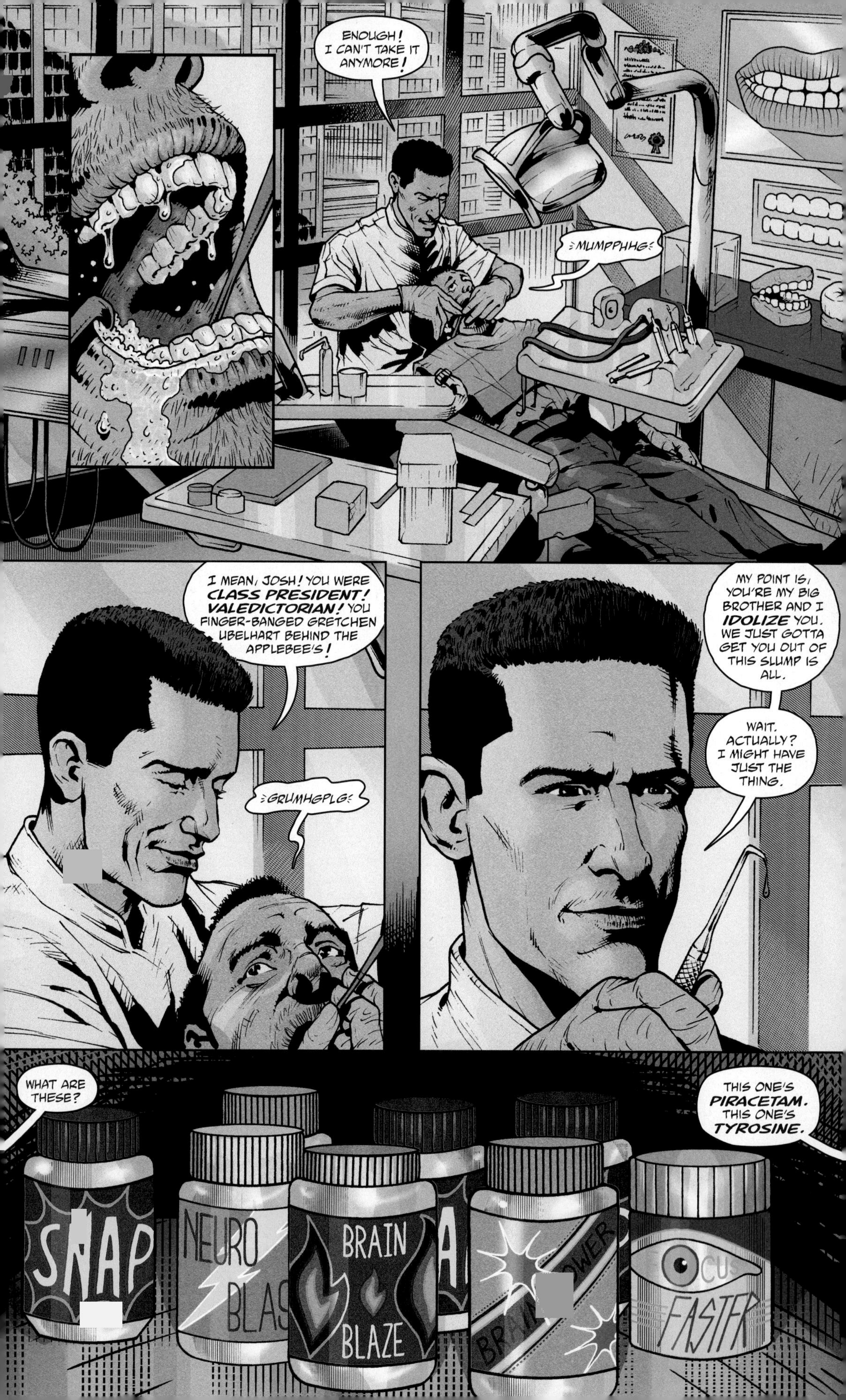

ENOUGH! I CAN'T TAKE IT ANYMORE!
MUMPPHHG
I MEAN, JOSH! YOU WERE **CLASS PRESIDENT! VALEDICTORIAN!** YOU FINGER-BANGED GRETCHEN UBELHART BEHIND THE APPLEBEE'S!
GRUMHGPLG
MY POINT IS, YOU'RE MY BIG BROTHER AND I **IDOLIZE** YOU. WE JUST GOTTA GET YOU OUT OF THIS SLUMP IS ALL.
WAIT. ACTUALLY? I MIGHT HAVE JUST THE THING.
WHAT ARE THESE?
THIS ONE'S **PIRACETAM.** THIS ONE'S **TYROSINE.**
NEURO
BRAIN BLAZE
FASTER

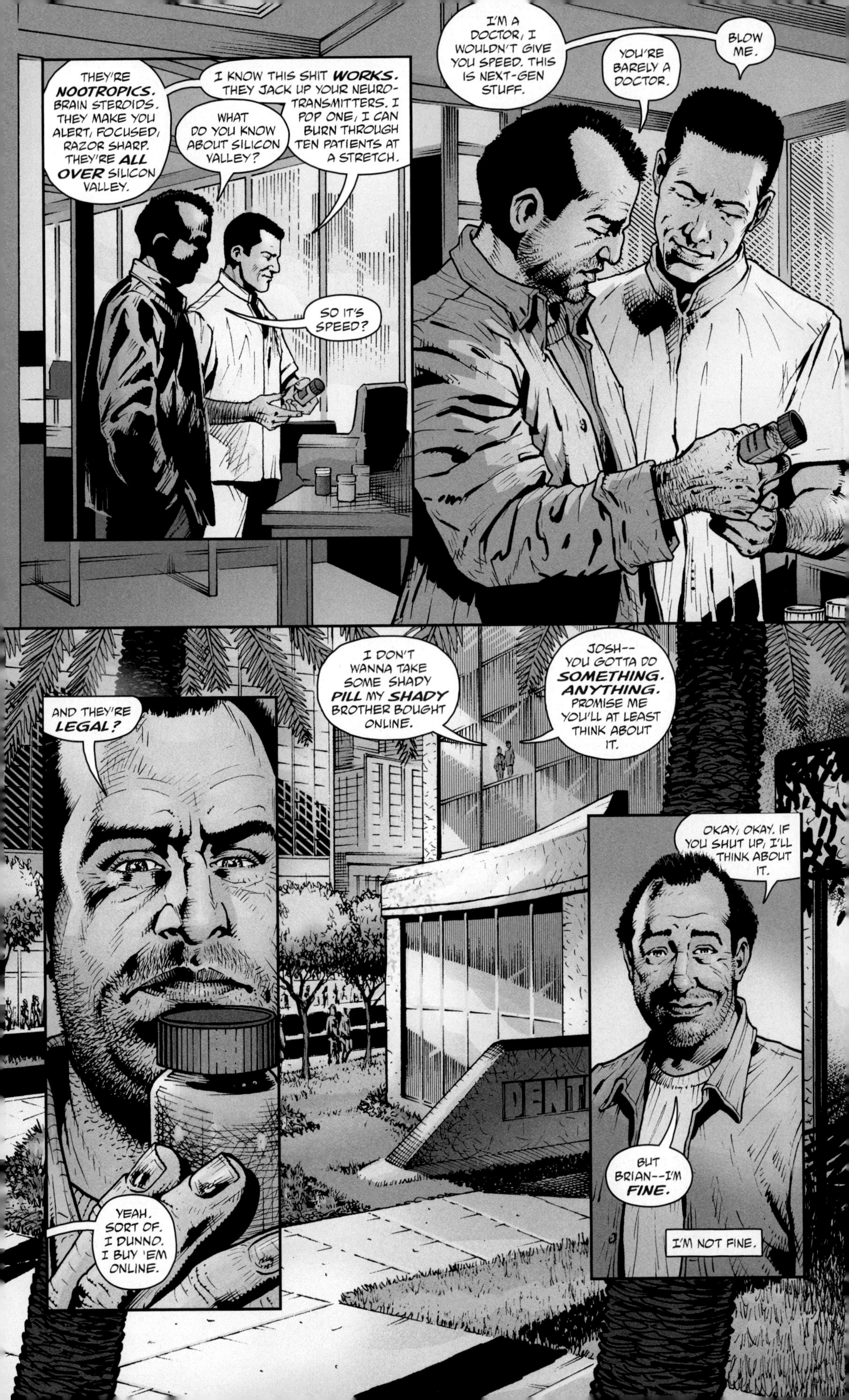
THEY'RE **NOOTROPICS.** BRAIN STEROIDS. THEY MAKE YOU ALERT, FOCUSED, RAZOR SHARP. THEY'RE **ALL OVER** SILICON VALLEY.
WHAT DO YOU KNOW ABOUT SILICON VALLEY?
I KNOW THIS SHIT **WORKS.** THEY JACK UP YOUR NEURO-TRANSMITTERS. I POP ONE, I CAN BURN THROUGH TEN PATIENTS AT A STRETCH.
SO IT'S SPEED?
I'M A DOCTOR, I WOULDN'T GIVE YOU SPEED. THIS IS NEXT-GEN STUFF.
YOU'RE BARELY A DOCTOR.
BLOW ME.
AND THEY'RE **LEGAL?**
YEAH. SORT OF. I DUNNO. I BUY 'EM ONLINE.
I DON'T WANNA TAKE SOME SHADY **PILL** MY **SHADY** BROTHER BOUGHT ONLINE.
JOSH-- YOU GOTTA DO **SOMETHING. ANYTHING.** PROMISE ME YOU'LL AT LEAST THINK ABOUT IT.
OKAY, OKAY. IF YOU SHUT UP, I'LL THINK ABOUT IT.
BUT BRIAN--I'M **FINE.**
I'M NOT FINE.

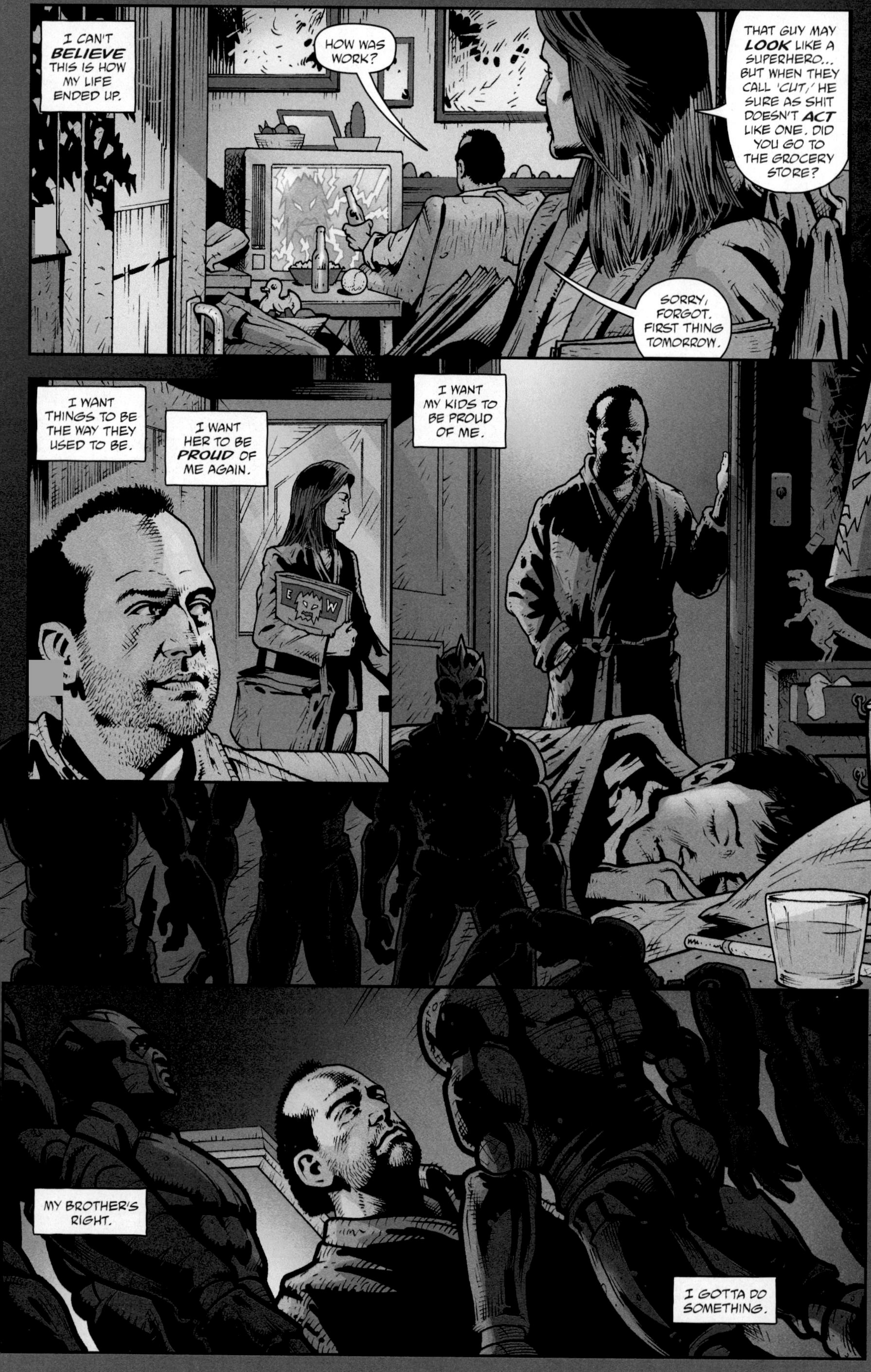
I CAN'T **BELIEVE** THIS IS HOW MY LIFE ENDED UP.
HOW WAS WORK?
THAT GUY MAY **LOOK** LIKE A SUPERHERO... BUT WHEN THEY CALL 'CUT,' HE SURE AS SHIT DOESN'T **ACT** LIKE ONE. DID YOU GO TO THE GROCERY STORE?
SORRY, FORGOT. FIRST THING TOMORROW.
I WANT THINGS TO BE THE WAY THEY USED TO BE.
I WANT HER TO BE **PROUD** OF ME AGAIN.
I WANT MY KIDS TO BE PROUD OF ME.
MY BROTHER'S RIGHT.
I GOTTA DO SOMETHING.

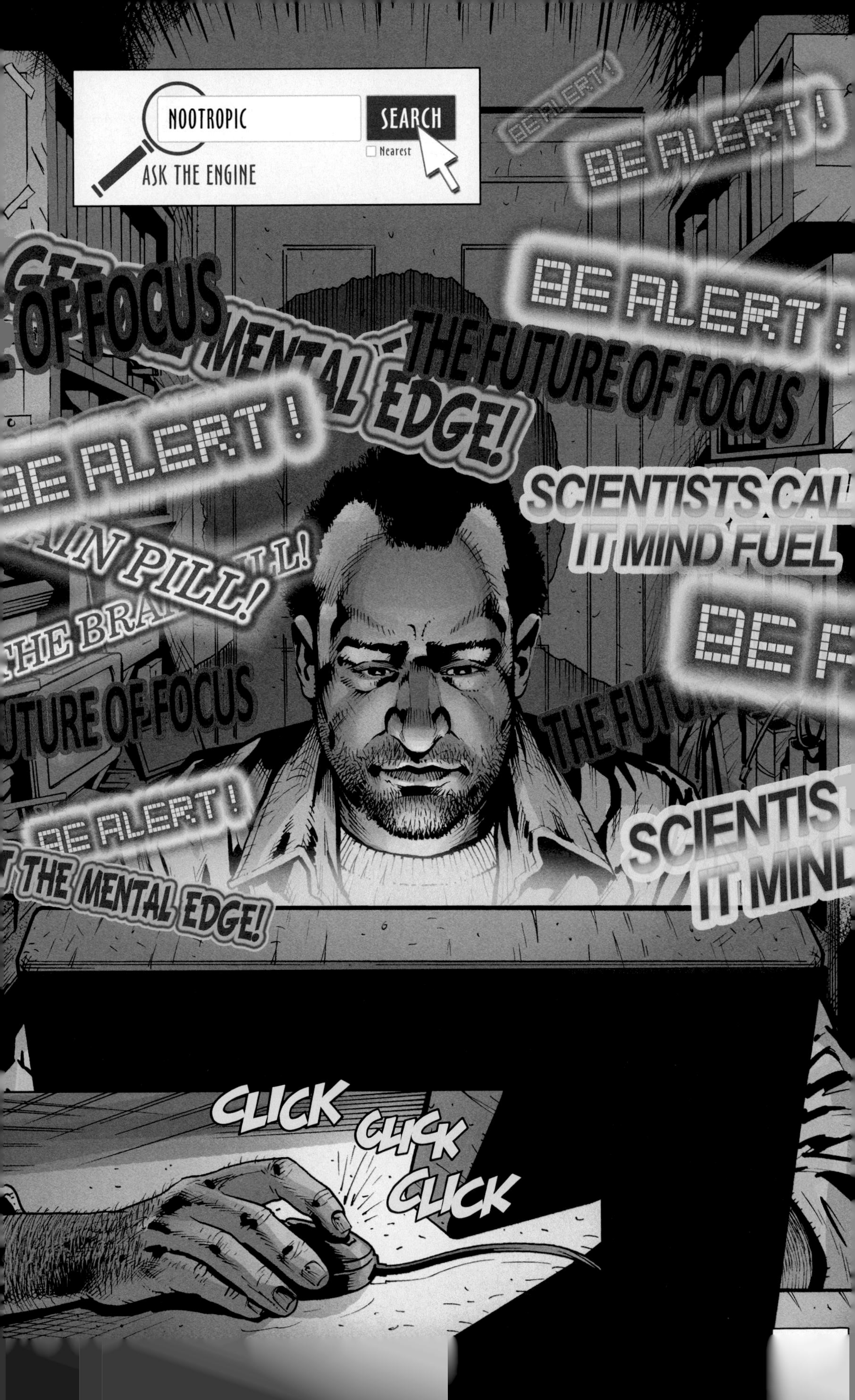
NOOTROPIC
SEARCH
Nearest
ASK THE ENGINE
BE ALERT!
BE ALERT!
OF FOCUS
BE ALERT!
MENTAL EDGE!
THE FUTURE OF FOCUS
BE ALERT!
SCIENTISTS CAL
IT MIND FUEL
IN PILL!
THE BRA
UTURE OF FOCUS
THE FUTU
BE ALERT!
THE MENTAL EDGE!
SCIENTIS
IT MIND
CLICK
CLICK
CLICK

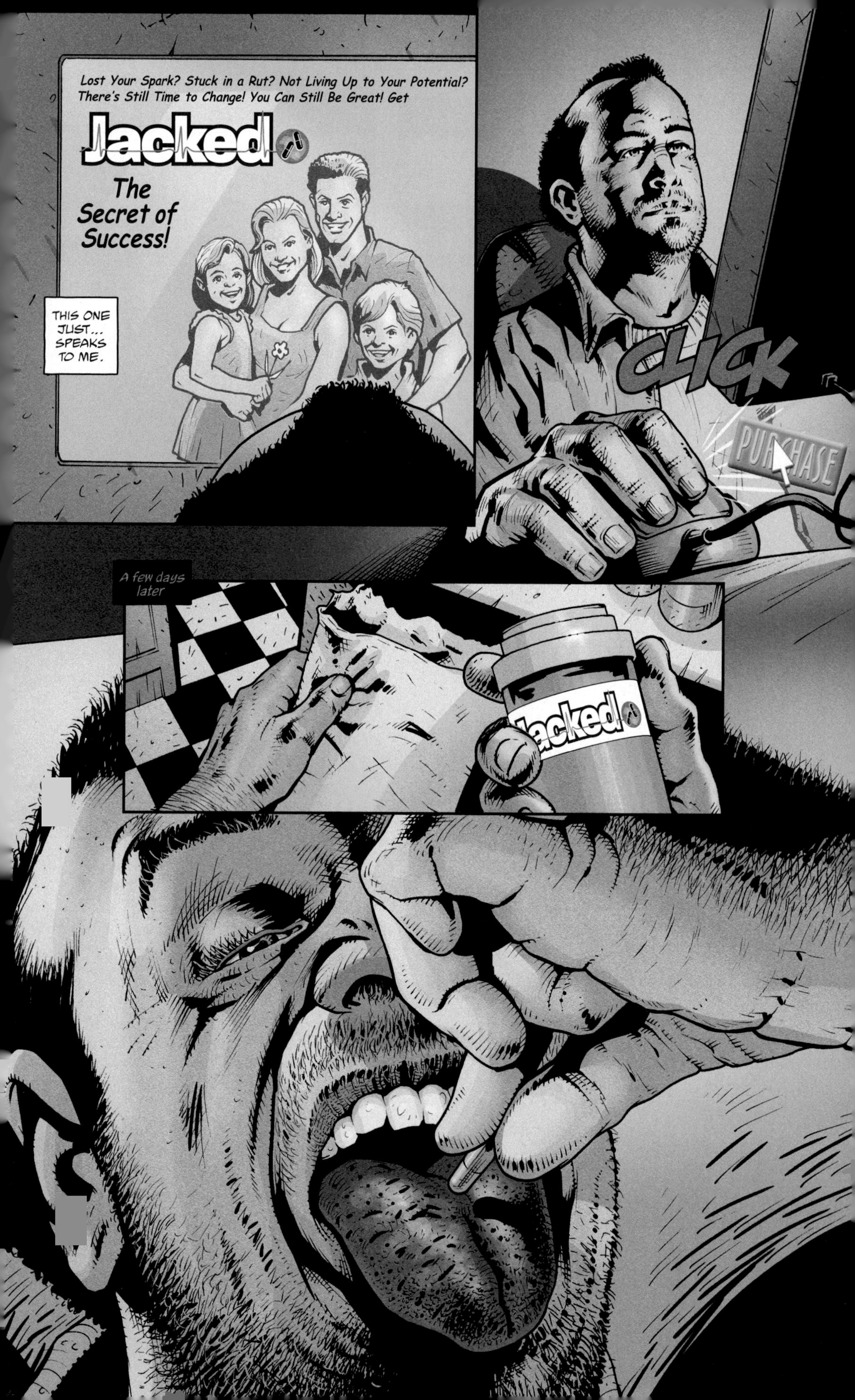
Lost Your Spark? Stuck in a Rut? Not Living Up to Your Potential?
There's Still Time to Change! You Can Still Be Great! Get
Jacked
The Secret of Success!
THIS ONE JUST... SPEAKS TO ME.
CLICK
PURCHASE
A few days later
Jacked

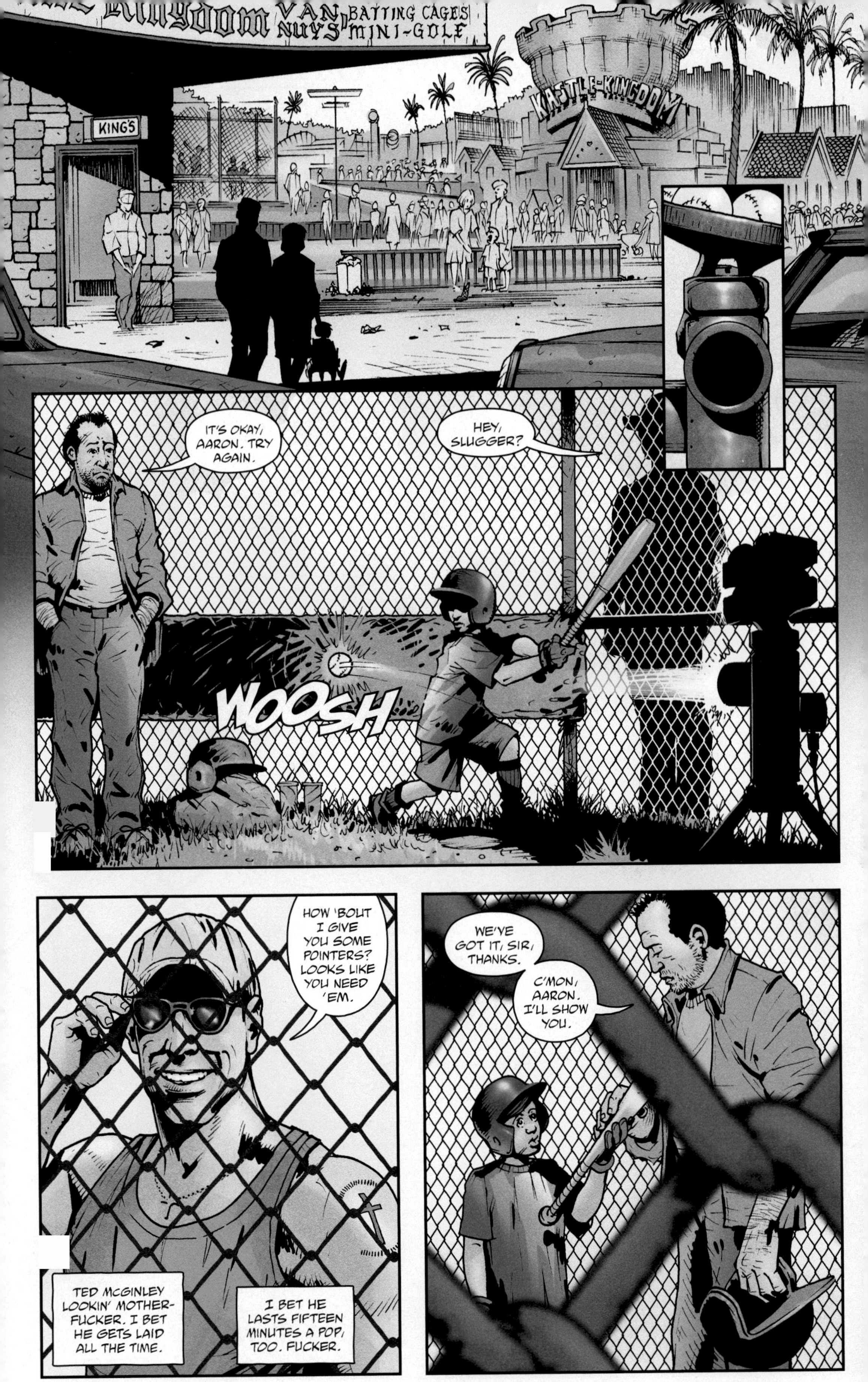
KINGDOM VAN NUYS BATTING CAGES MINI-GOLF
KING'S
KASTLE-KINGDOM
IT'S OKAY, AARON. TRY AGAIN.
HEY, SLUGGER?
WOOSH
HOW 'BOUT I GIVE YOU SOME POINTERS? LOOKS LIKE YOU NEED 'EM.
TED MCGINLEY LOOKIN' MOTHER-FUCKER. I BET HE GETS LAID ALL THE TIME.
I BET HE LASTS FIFTEEN MINUTES A POP, TOO. FUCKER.
WE'VE GOT IT, SIR, THANKS.
C'MON, AARON. I'LL SHOW YOU.

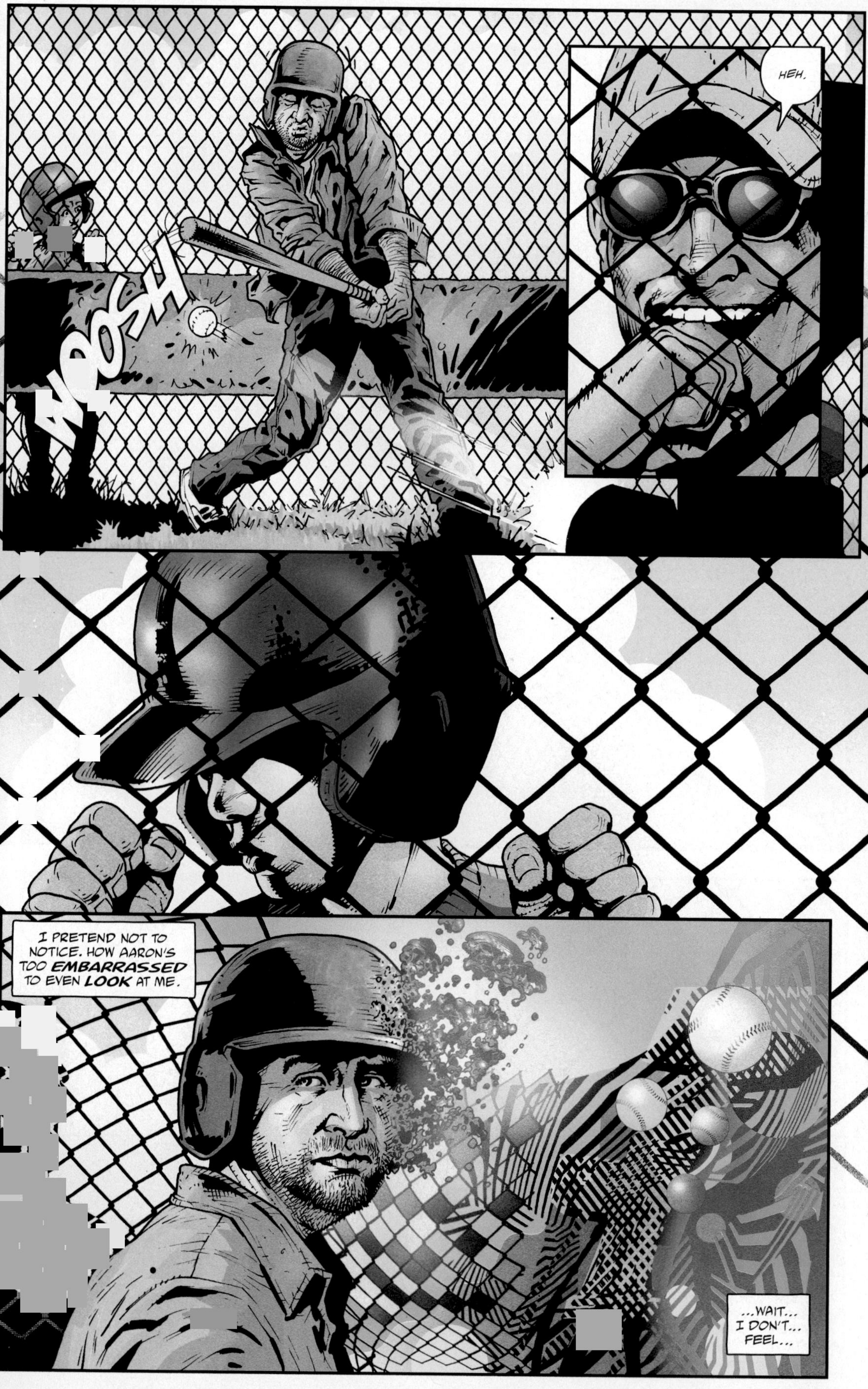
WOOSH
HEH.
I PRETEND NOT TO NOTICE. HOW AARON'S TOO EMBARRASSED TO EVEN LOOK AT ME.
...WAIT... I DON'T... FEEL...

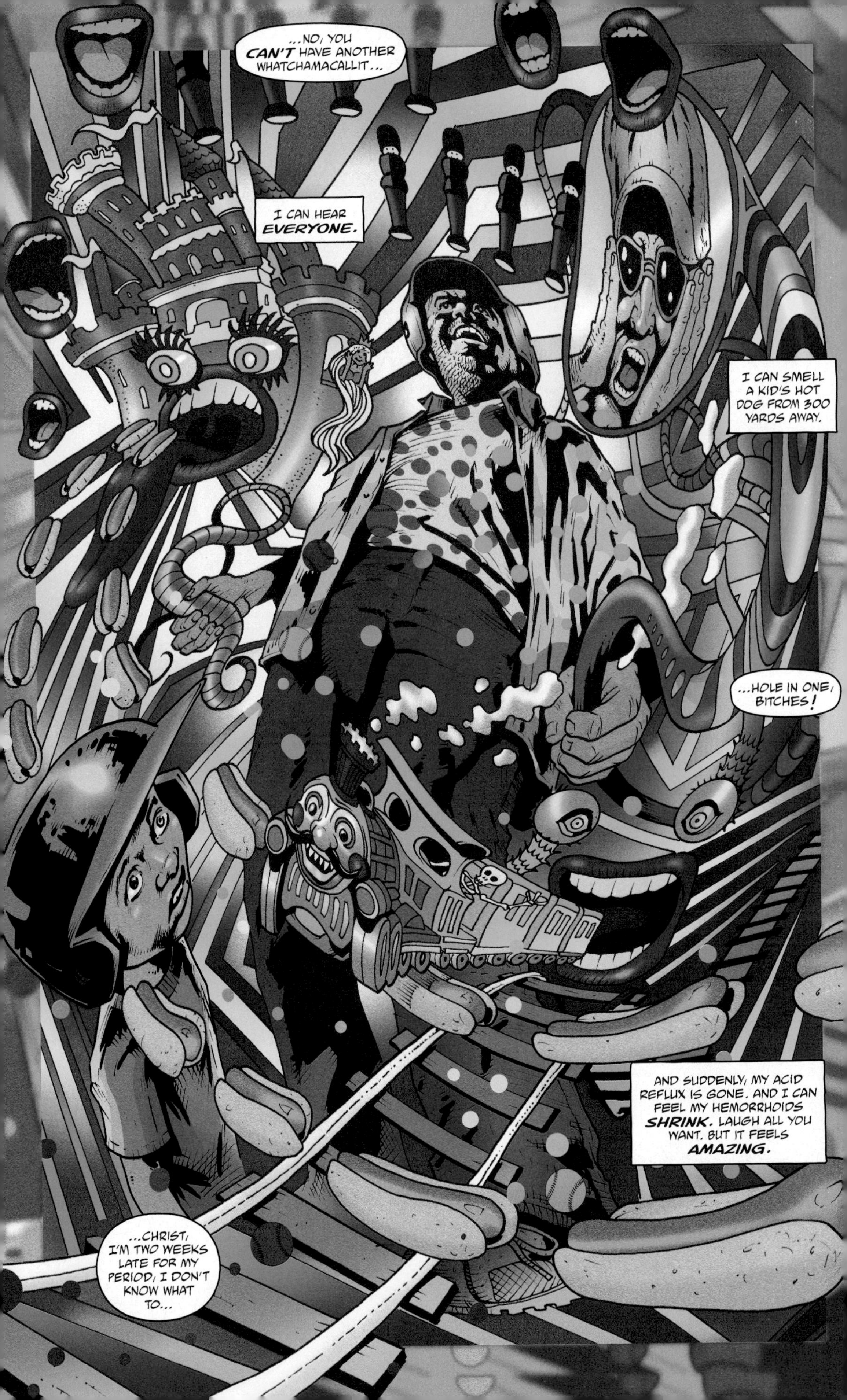

...NO, YOU CAN'T HAVE ANOTHER WHATCHAMACALLIT...
I CAN HEAR EVERYONE.
I CAN SMELL A KID'S HOT DOG FROM 300 YARDS AWAY.
...HOLE IN ONE, BITCHES!
AND SUDDENLY, MY ACID REFLUX IS GONE. AND I CAN FEEL MY HEMORRHOIDS SHRINK. LAUGH ALL YOU WANT. BUT IT FEELS AMAZING.
...CHRIST, I'M TWO WEEKS LATE FOR MY PERIOD, I DON'T KNOW WHAT TO...

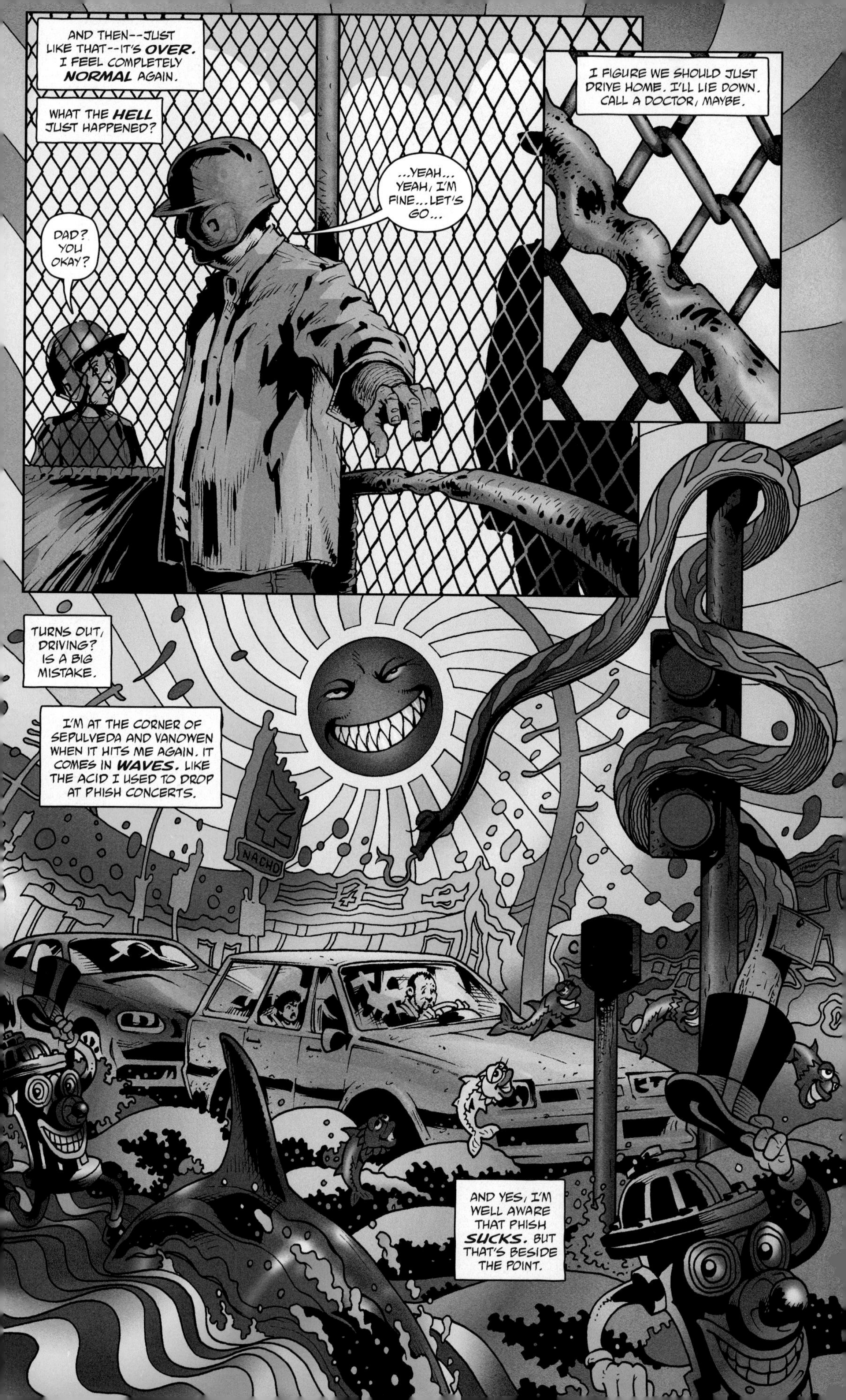
AND THEN--JUST LIKE THAT--IT'S OVER. I FEEL COMPLETELY NORMAL AGAIN.
WHAT THE HELL JUST HAPPENED?
DAD? YOU OKAY?
...YEAH... YEAH, I'M FINE...LET'S GO...
I FIGURE WE SHOULD JUST DRIVE HOME. I'LL LIE DOWN. CALL A DOCTOR, MAYBE.
TURNS OUT, DRIVING? IS A BIG MISTAKE.
I'M AT THE CORNER OF SEPULVEDA AND VANOWEN WHEN IT HITS ME AGAIN. IT COMES IN WAVES. LIKE THE ACID I USED TO DROP AT PHISH CONCERTS.
NACHO
AND YES, I'M WELL AWARE THAT PHISH SUCKS. BUT THAT'S BESIDE THE POINT.

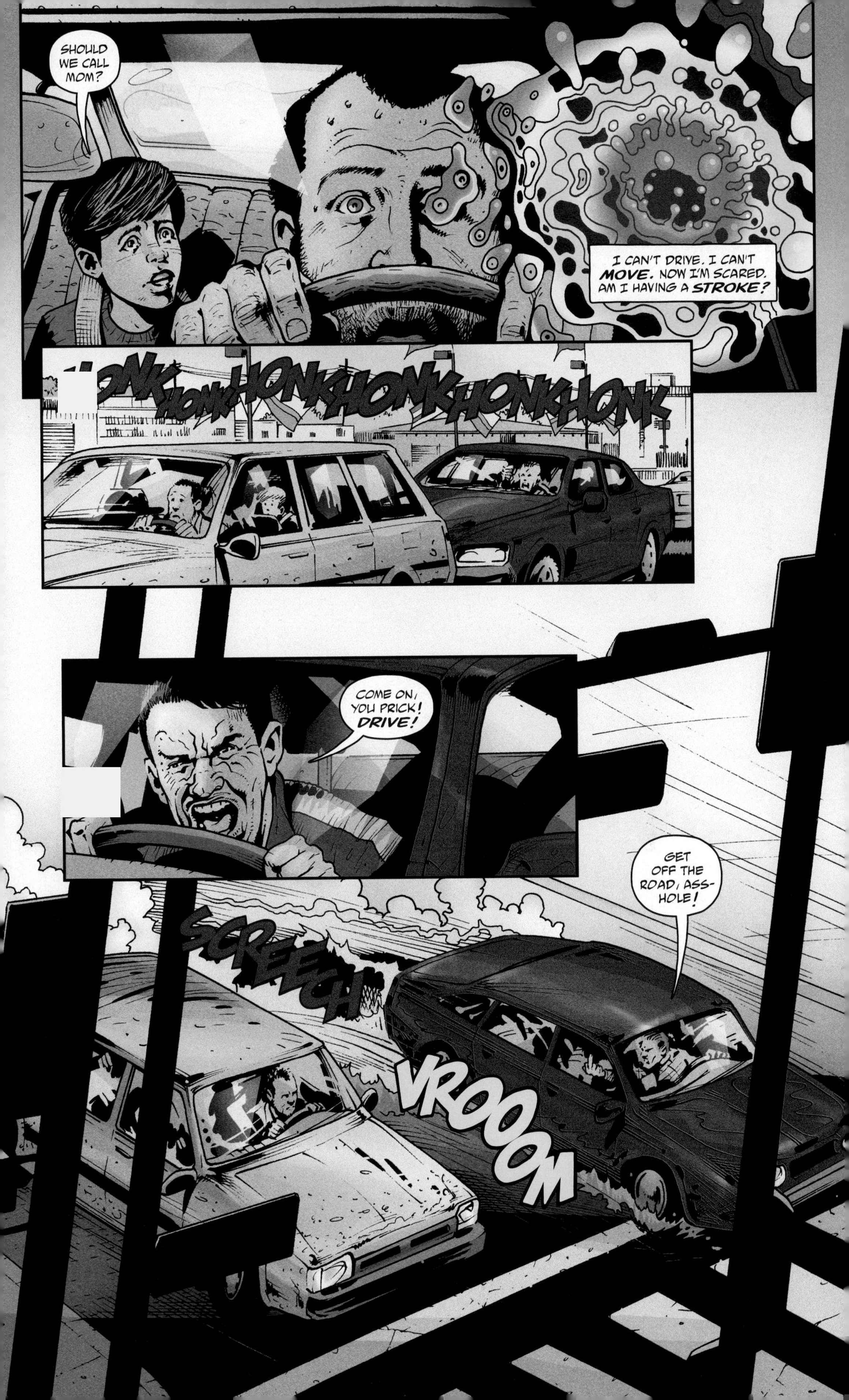
SHOULD WE CALL MOM?
I CAN'T DRIVE. I CAN'T MOVE. NOW I'M SCARED. AM I HAVING A STROKE?
HONK HONK HONK HONK HONK HONK
COME ON, YOU PRICK! DRIVE!
GET OFF THE ROAD, ASS-HOLE!
SCREECH
VROOOM

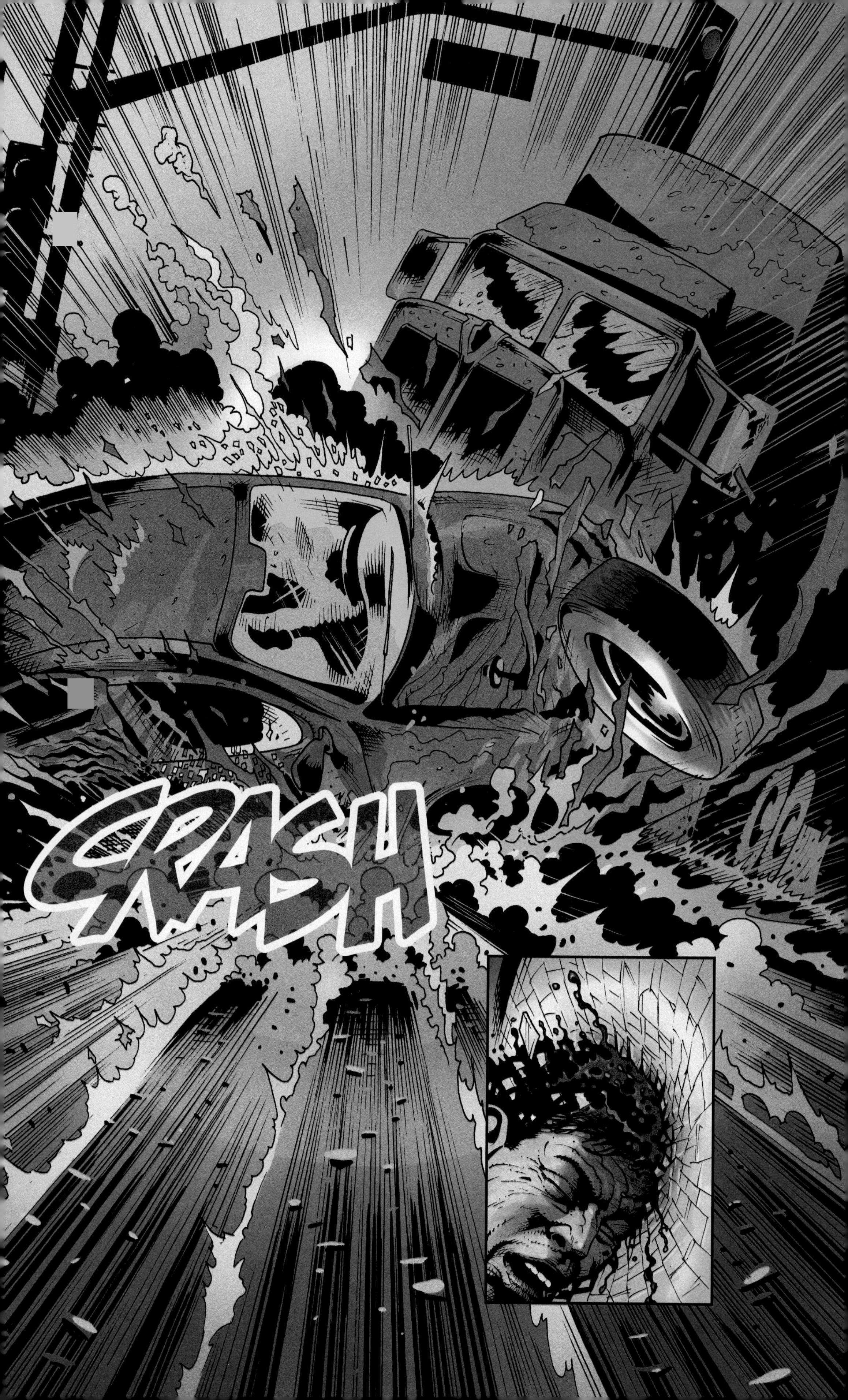
CRASH

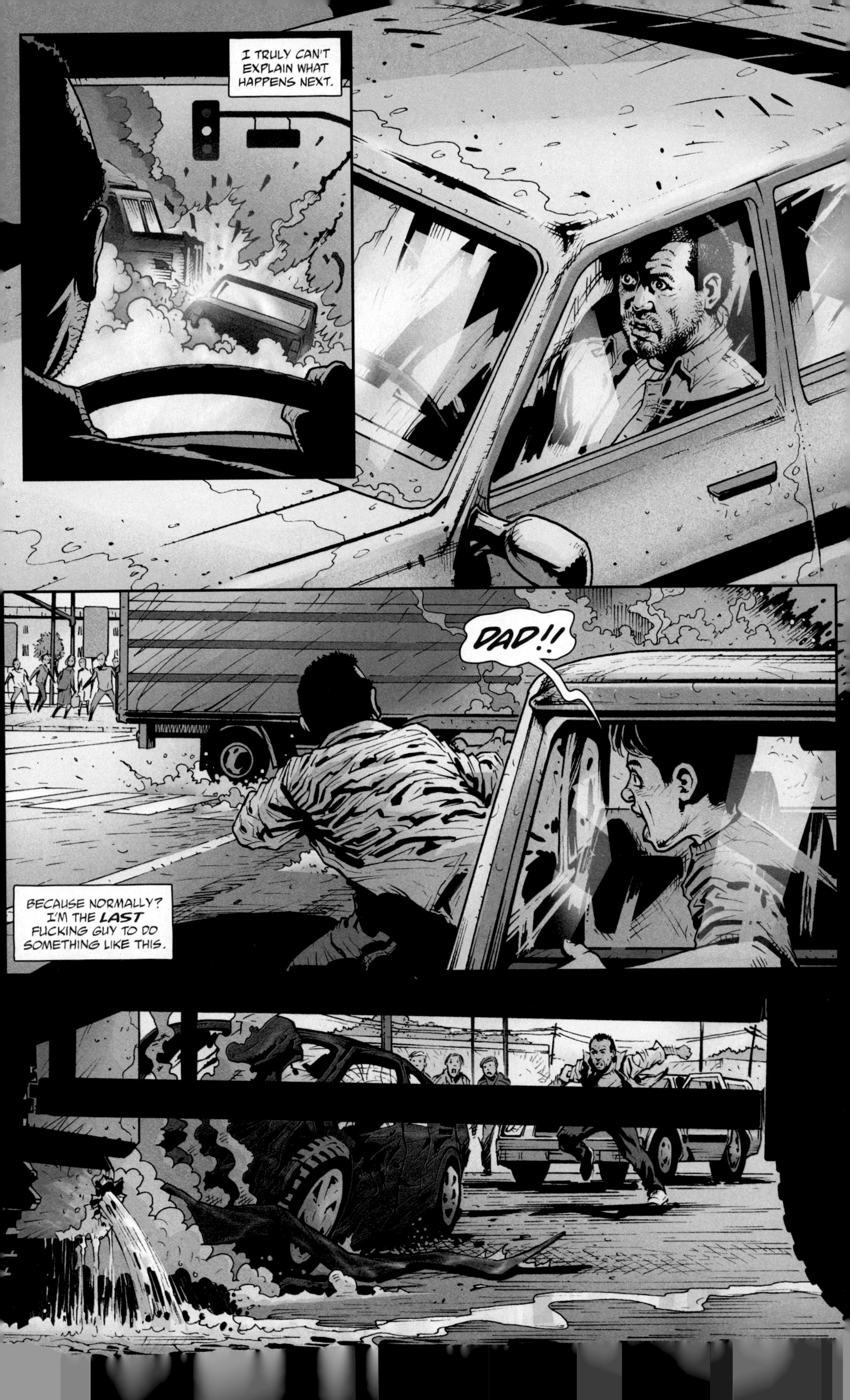
I TRULY CAN'T EXPLAIN WHAT HAPPENS NEXT.
DAD!!
BECAUSE NORMALLY? I'M THE **LAST** FUCKING GUY TO DO SOMETHING LIKE THIS.

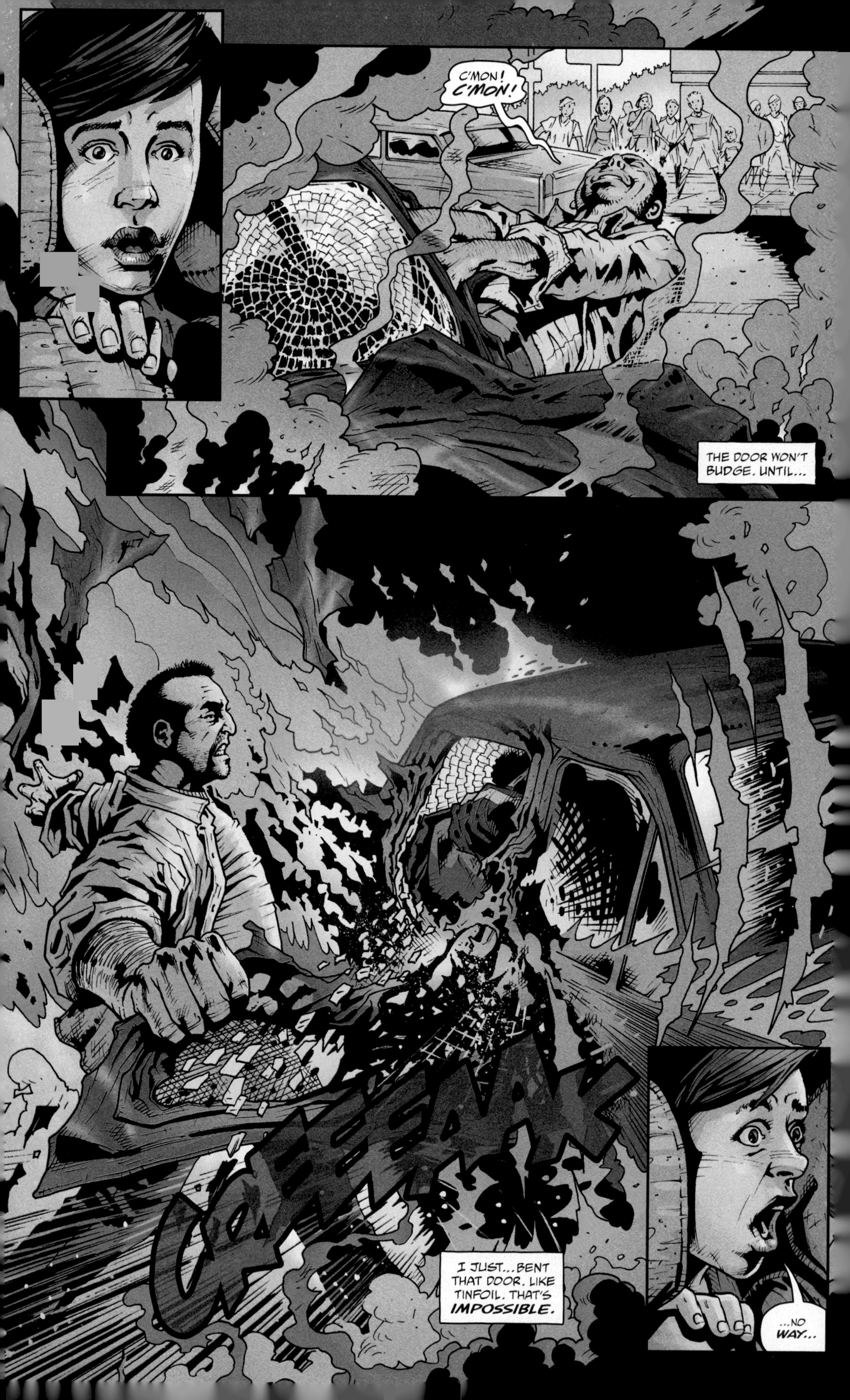
C'MON! C'MON!
THE DOOR WON'T BUDGE. UNTIL...
I JUST...BENT THAT DOOR. LIKE TINFOIL. THAT'S IMPOSSIBLE.
...NO WAY...

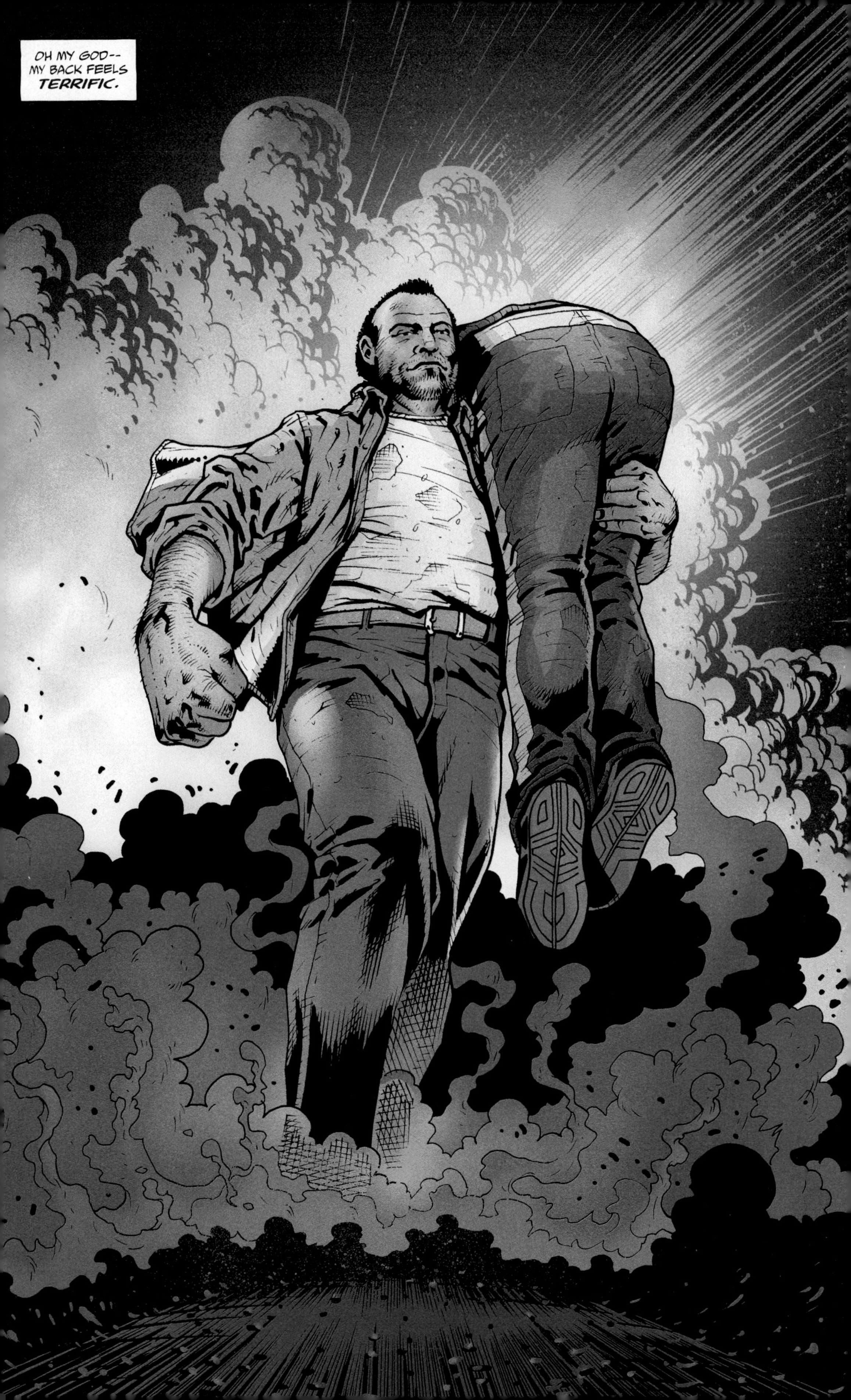
OH MY GOD--
MY BACK FEELS
TERRIFIC.

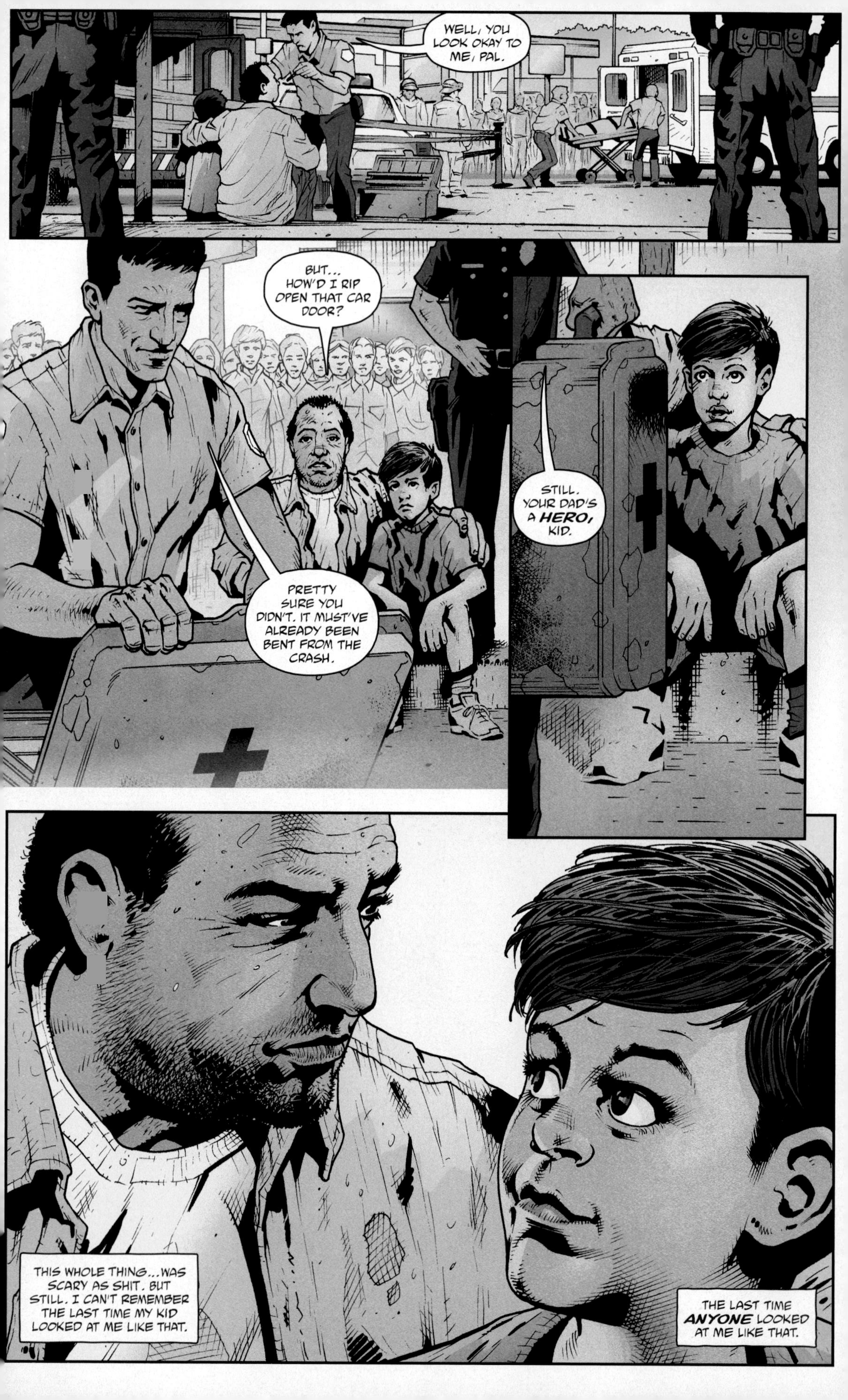
WELL, YOU LOOK OKAY TO ME, PAL.
BUT... HOW'D I RIP OPEN THAT CAR DOOR?
PRETTY SURE YOU DIDN'T. IT MUST'VE ALREADY BEEN BENT FROM THE CRASH.
STILL. YOUR DAD'S A **HERO,** KID.
THIS WHOLE THING...WAS SCARY AS SHIT. BUT STILL. I CAN'T REMEMBER THE LAST TIME MY KID LOOKED AT ME LIKE THAT.
THE LAST TIME **ANYONE** LOOKED AT ME LIKE THAT.

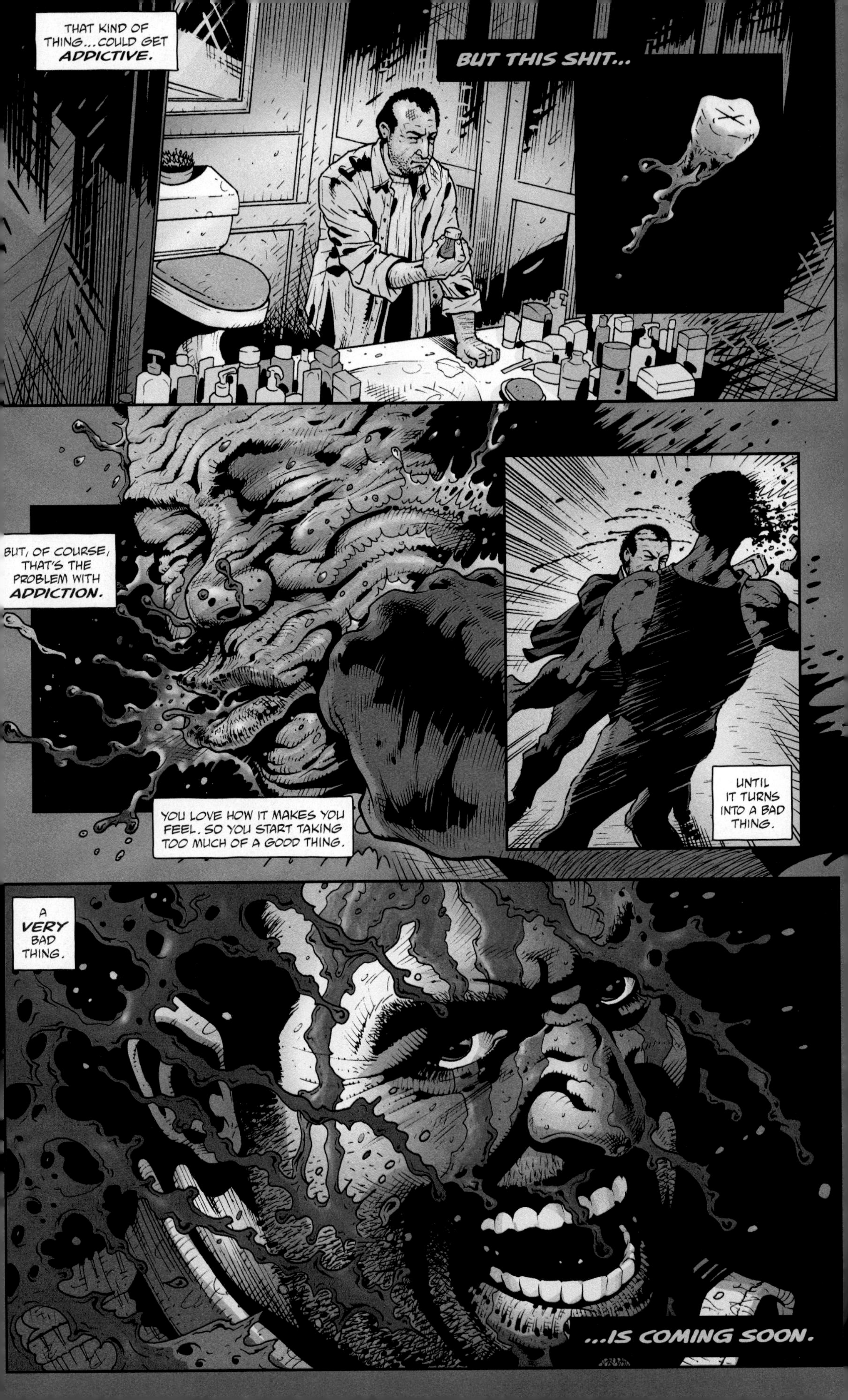
THAT KIND OF THING... COULD GET ADDICTIVE.
BUT THIS SHIT...
BUT, OF COURSE, THAT'S THE PROBLEM WITH ADDICTION.
YOU LOVE HOW IT MAKES YOU FEEL. SO YOU START TAKING TOO MUCH OF A GOOD THING.
UNTIL IT TURNS INTO A BAD THING.
A VERY BAD THING.
...IS COMING SOON.

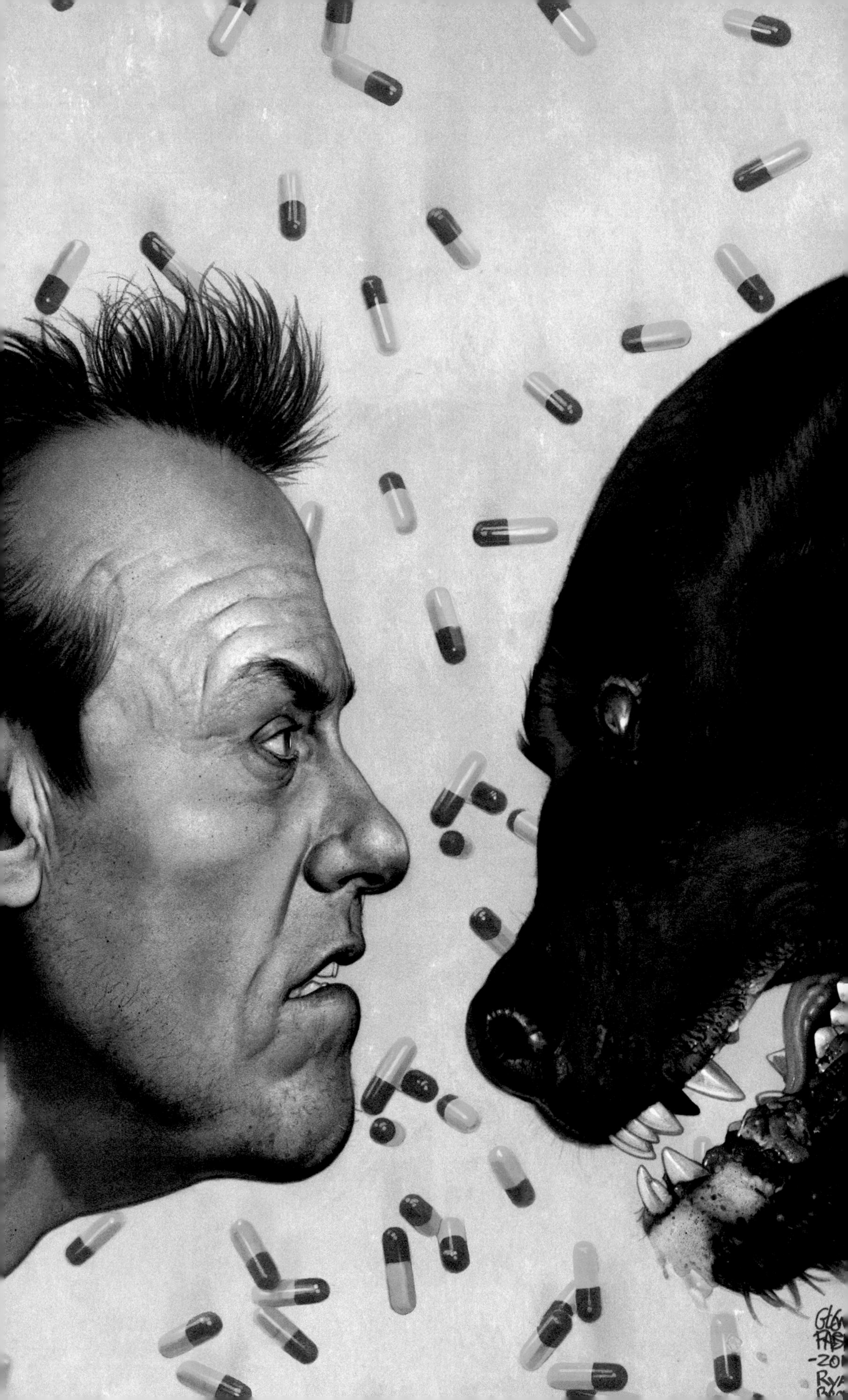

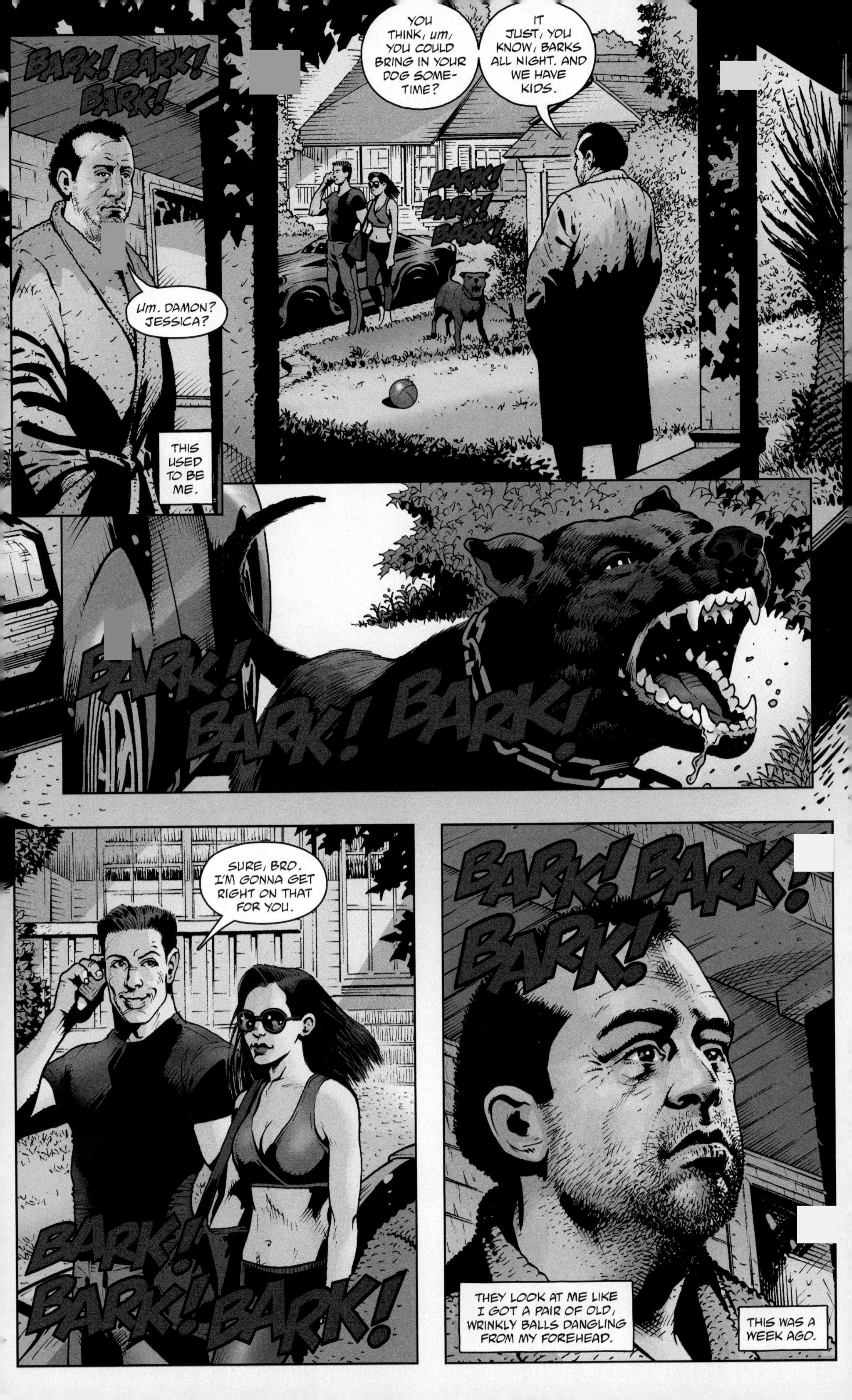
BARK! BARK! BARK!
UM. DAMON? JESSICA?
THIS USED TO BE ME.
YOU THINK, UM, YOU COULD BRING IN YOUR DOG SOMETIME?
IT JUST, YOU KNOW, BARKS ALL NIGHT. AND WE HAVE KIDS.
BARK! BARK! BARK!
BARK! BARK! BARK!
SURE, BRO. I'M GONNA GET RIGHT ON THAT FOR YOU.
BARK! BARK! BARK!
BARK! BARK! BARK!
THEY LOOK AT ME LIKE I GOT A PAIR OF OLD, WRINKLY BALLS DANGLING FROM MY FOREHEAD.
THIS WAS A WEEK AGO.

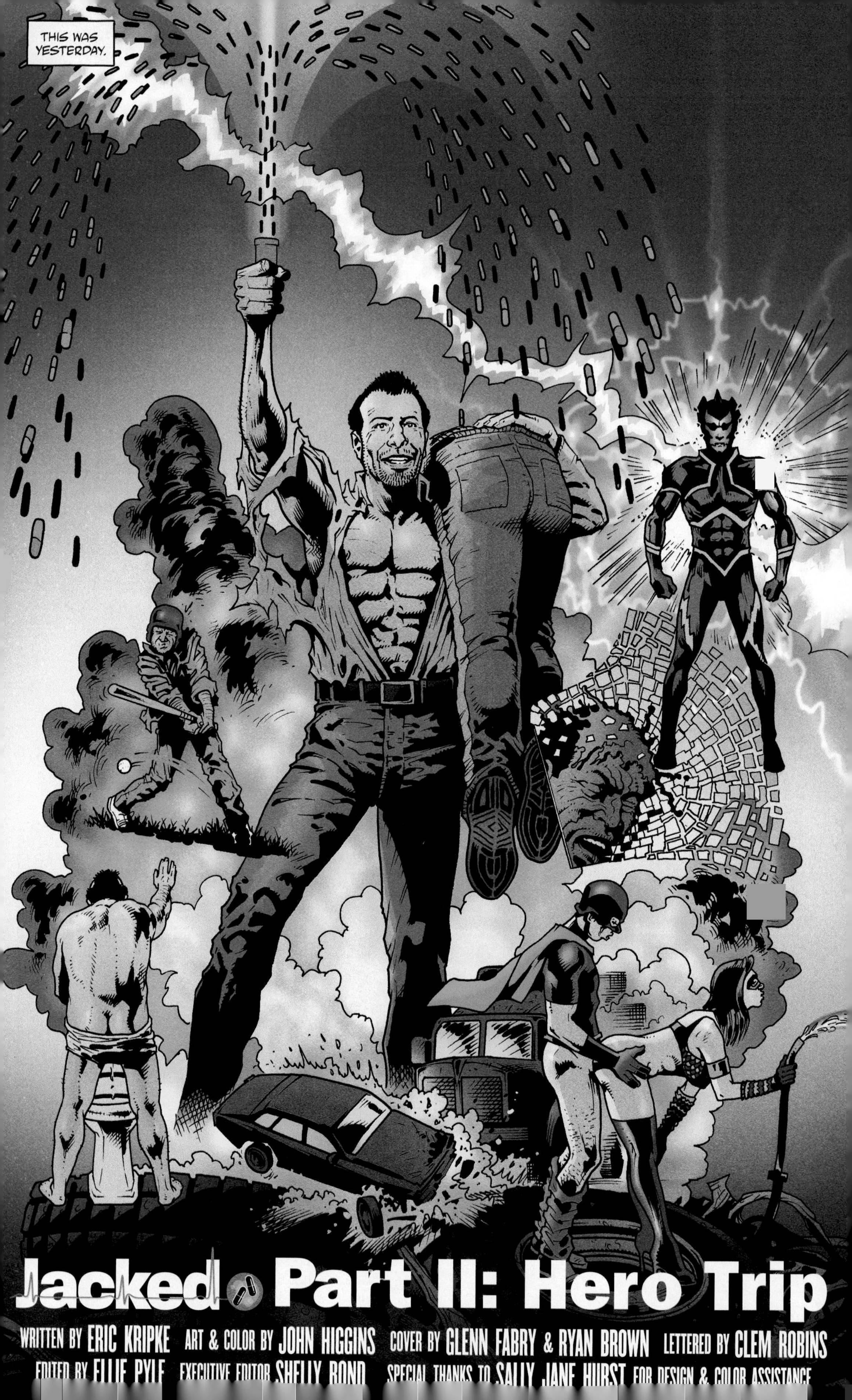
THIS WAS YESTERDAY.
Jacked • Part II: Hero Trip
WRITTEN BY ERIC KRIPKE ART & COLOR BY JOHN HIGGINS COVER BY GLENN FABRY & RYAN BROWN LETTERED BY CLEM ROBINS
EDITED BY ELLIE PYLE EXECUTIVE EDITOR SHELLY BOND SPECIAL THANKS TO SALLY JANE HURST FOR DESIGN & COLOR ASSISTANCE

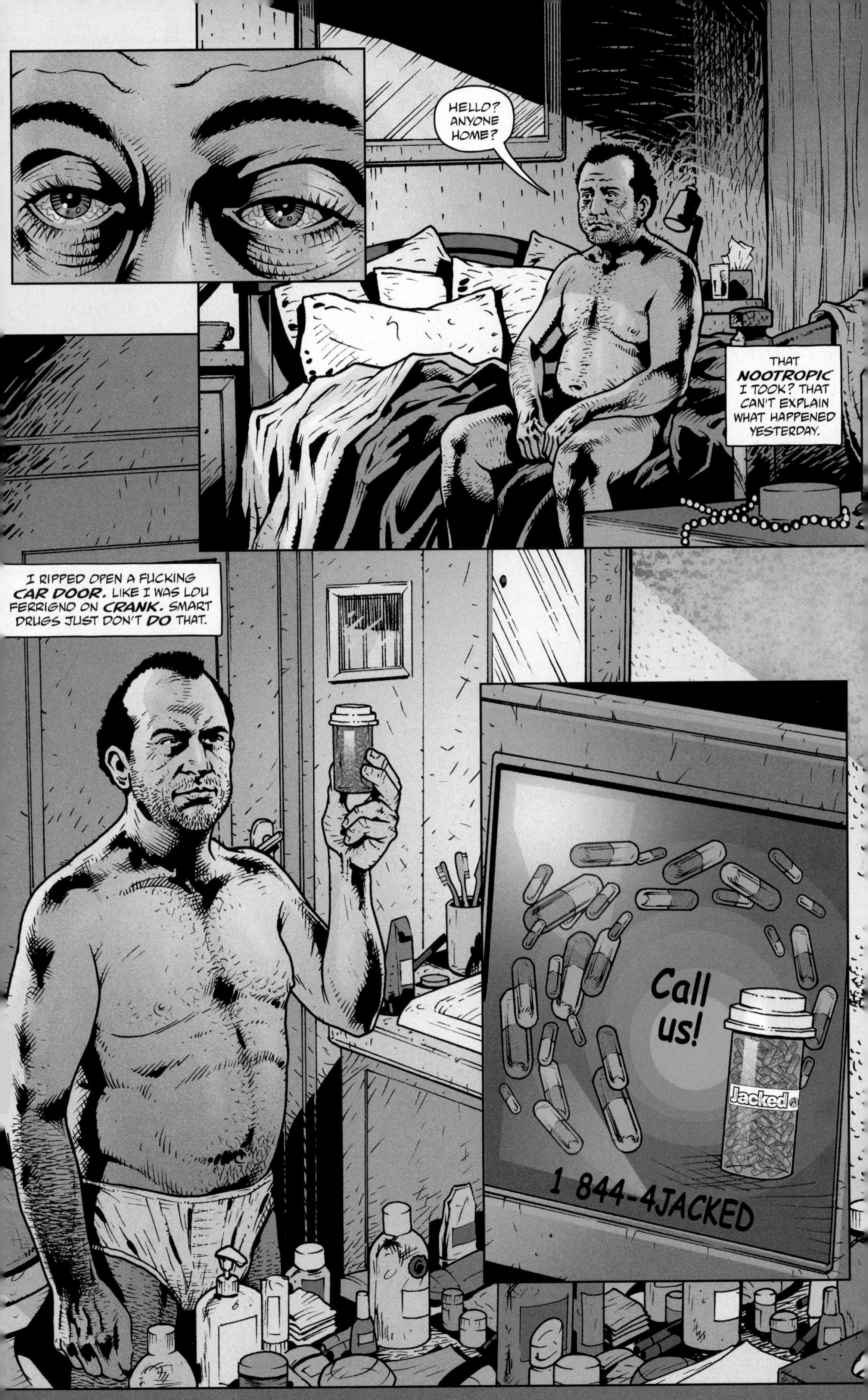
HELLO? ANYONE HOME?
THAT NOOTROPIC I TOOK? THAT CAN'T EXPLAIN WHAT HAPPENED YESTERDAY.
I RIPPED OPEN A FUCKING CAR DOOR. LIKE I WAS LOU FERRIGNO ON CRANK. SMART DRUGS JUST DON'T DO THAT.
Call us!
Jacked
1 844-4JACKED

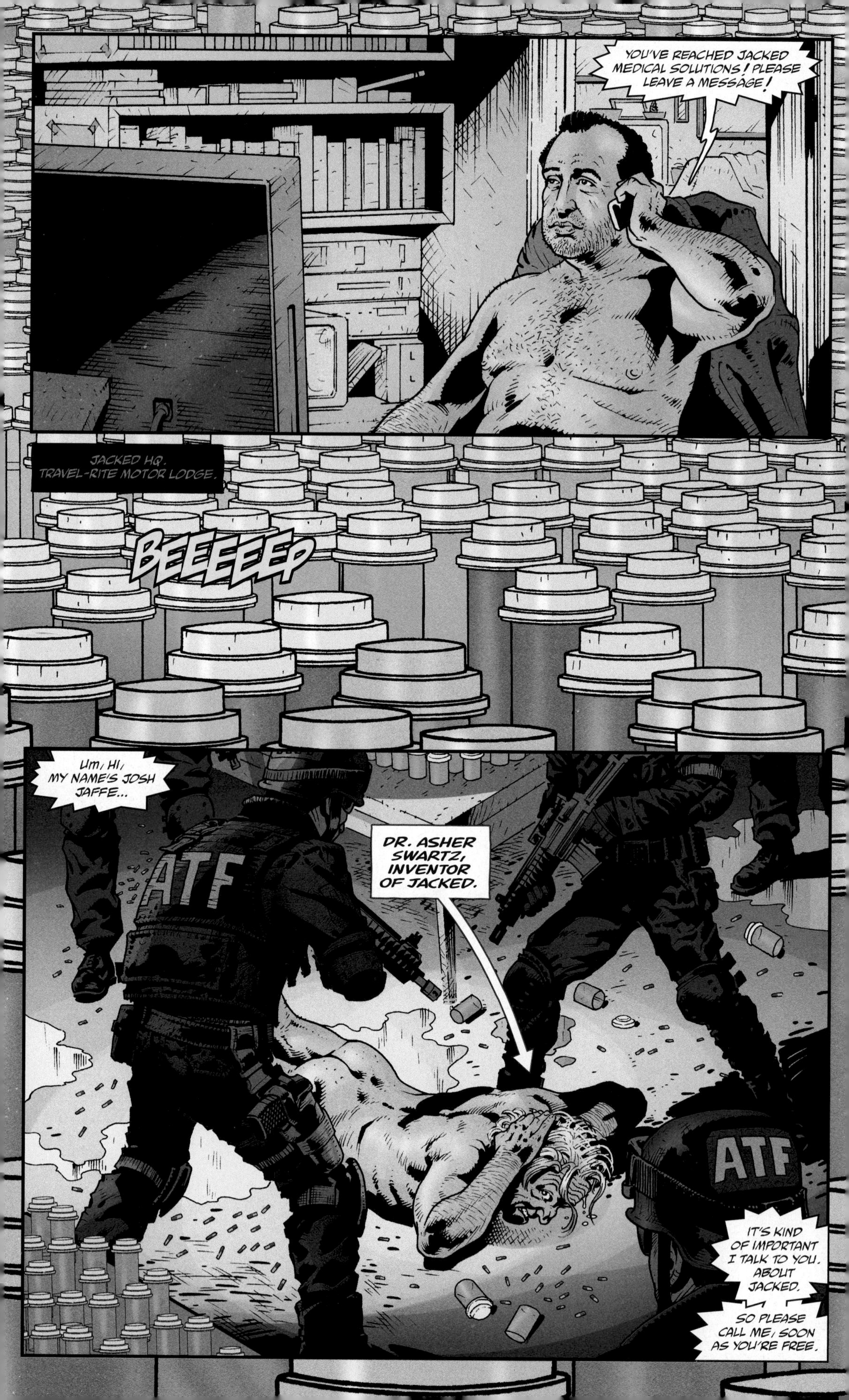
YOU'VE REACHED JACKED MEDICAL SOLUTIONS! PLEASE LEAVE A MESSAGE!
JACKED HQ. TRAVEL-RITE MOTOR LODGE.
BEEEEEEP
UM, HI, MY NAME'S JOSH JAFFE...
DR. ASHER SWARTZ, INVENTOR OF JACKED.
ATF
ATF
IT'S KIND OF IMPORTANT I TALK TO YOU. ABOUT JACKED.
SO PLEASE CALL ME, SOON AS YOU'RE FREE.

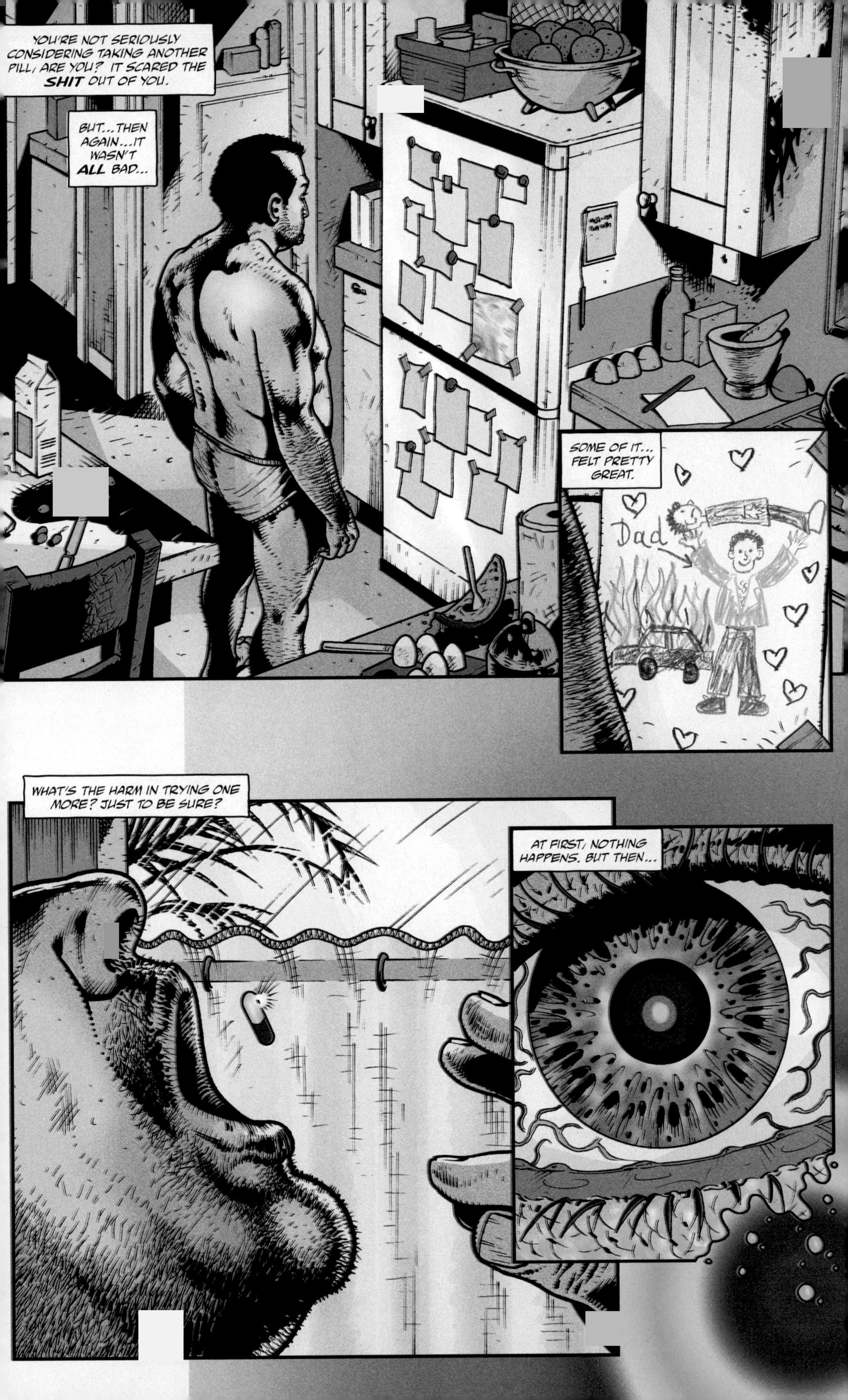
YOU'RE NOT SERIOUSLY CONSIDERING TAKING ANOTHER PILL, ARE YOU? IT SCARED THE SHIT OUT OF YOU.
BUT...THEN AGAIN...IT WASN'T ALL BAD...
SOME OF IT... FELT PRETTY GREAT.
Dad
WHAT'S THE HARM IN TRYING ONE MORE? JUST TO BE SURE?
AT FIRST, NOTHING HAPPENS. BUT THEN...

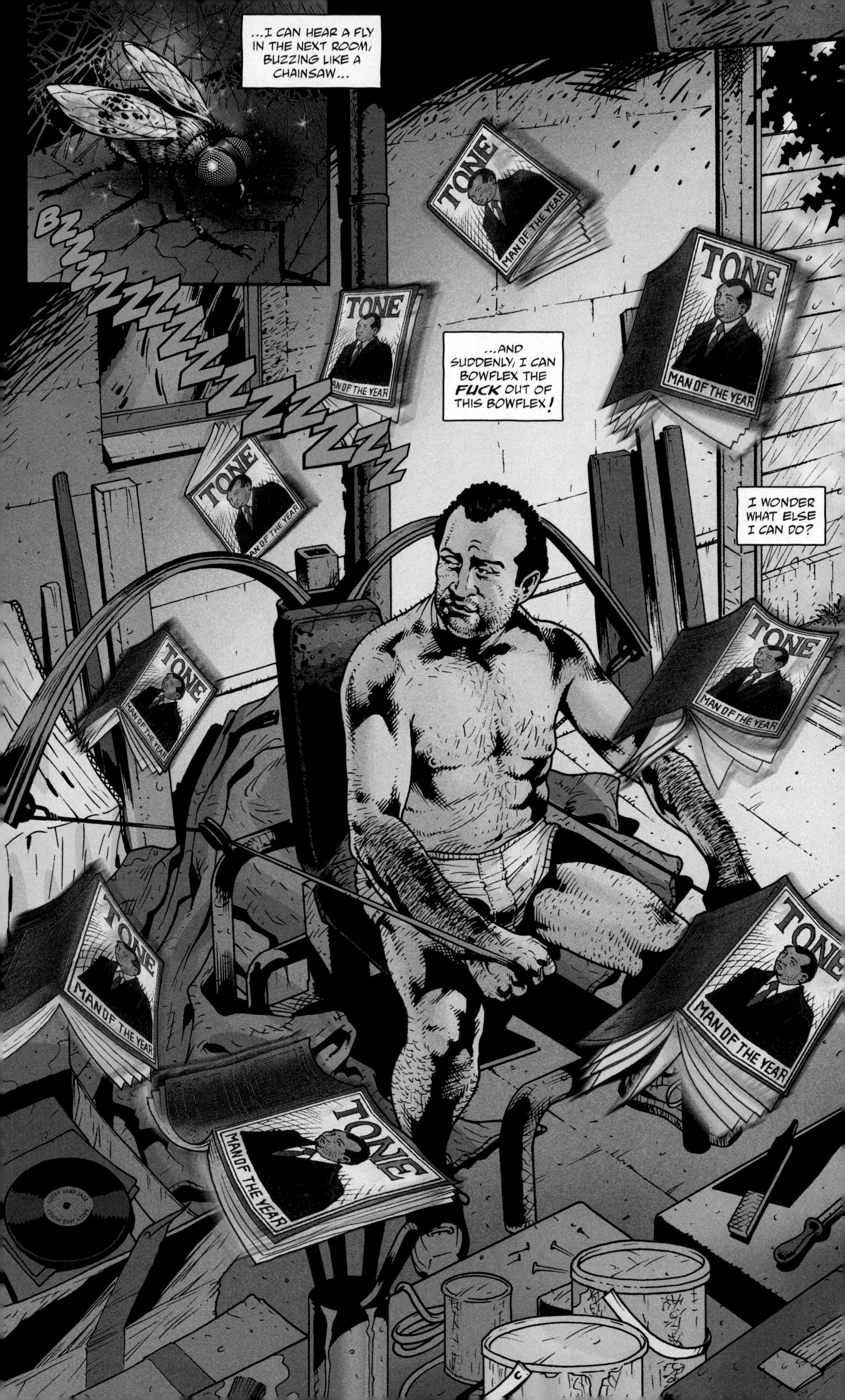
...I CAN HEAR A FLY IN THE NEXT ROOM, BUZZING LIKE A CHAINSAW...
BZZZZZZZZZZZZZZZZ
TONE
MAN OF THE YEAR
...AND SUDDENLY, I CAN BOWFLEX THE **FUCK** OUT OF THIS BOWFLEX!
I WONDER WHAT ELSE I CAN DO?

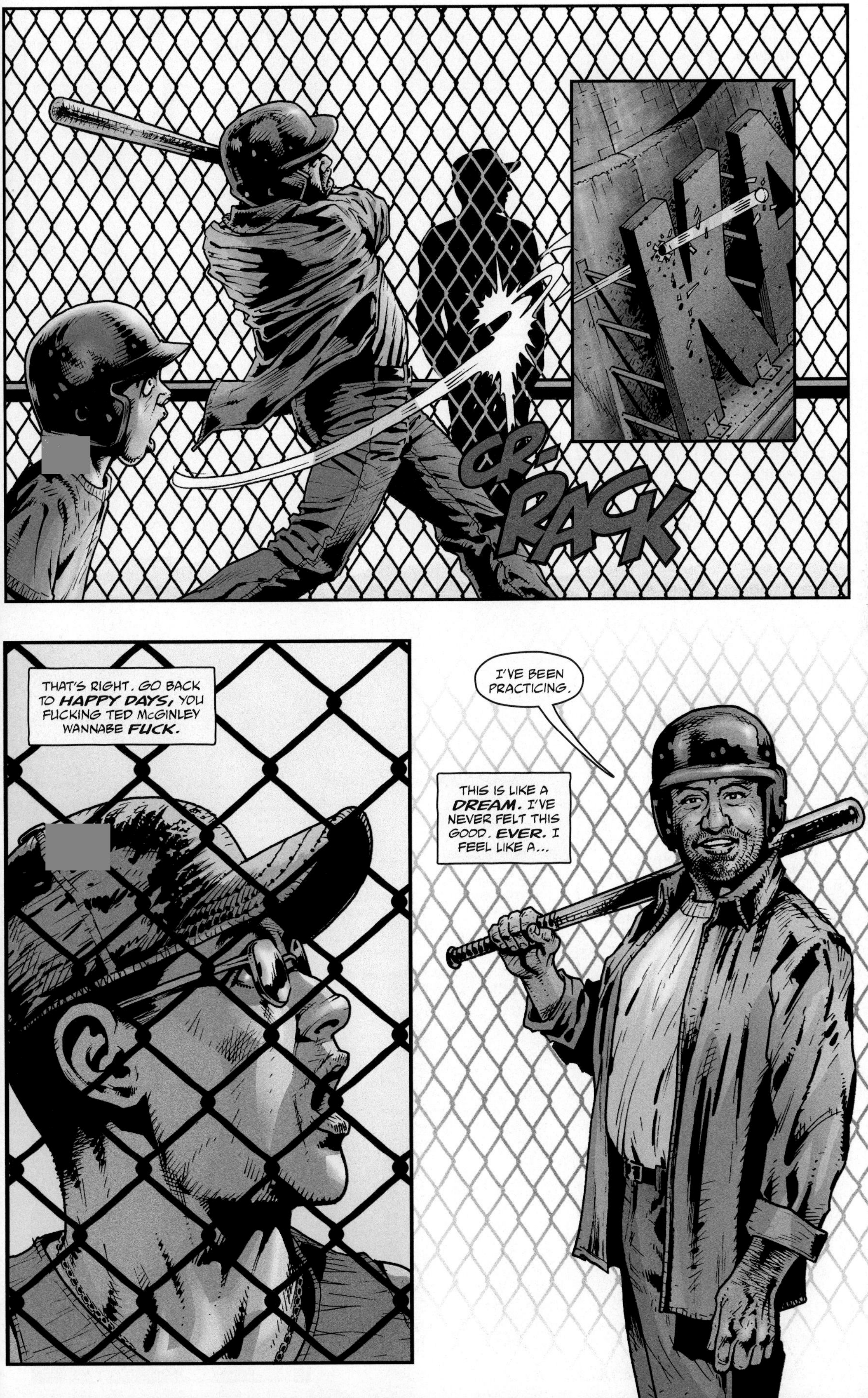
CR-RACK
THAT'S RIGHT. GO BACK TO HAPPY DAYS, YOU FUCKING TED McGINLEY WANNABE FUCK.
I'VE BEEN PRACTICING.
THIS IS LIKE A DREAM. I'VE NEVER FELT THIS GOOD. EVER. I FEEL LIKE A...

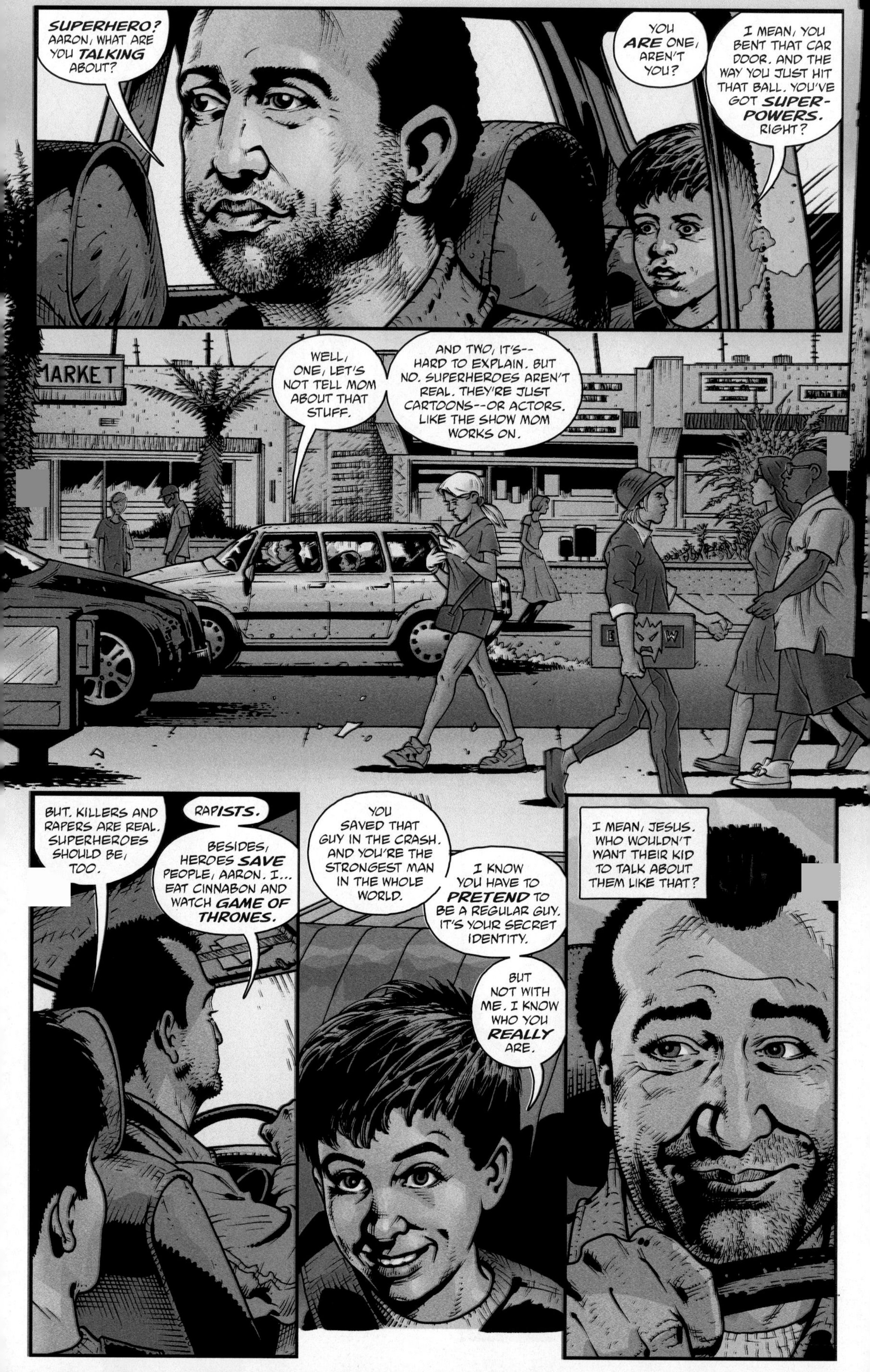
SUPERHERO? AARON, WHAT ARE YOU TALKING ABOUT?
YOU ARE ONE, AREN'T YOU?
I MEAN, YOU BENT THAT CAR DOOR. AND THE WAY YOU JUST HIT THAT BALL. YOU'VE GOT SUPER-POWERS. RIGHT?
MARKET
WELL, ONE, LET'S NOT TELL MOM ABOUT THAT STUFF.
AND TWO, IT'S-- HARD TO EXPLAIN. BUT NO. SUPERHEROES AREN'T REAL. THEY'RE JUST CARTOONS--OR ACTORS. LIKE THE SHOW MOM WORKS ON.
BUT, KILLERS AND RAPERS ARE REAL. SUPERHEROES SHOULD BE, TOO.
RAPISTS.
BESIDES, HEROES SAVE PEOPLE, AARON. I... EAT CINNABON AND WATCH GAME OF THRONES.
YOU SAVED THAT GUY IN THE CRASH. AND YOU'RE THE STRONGEST MAN IN THE WHOLE WORLD.
I KNOW YOU HAVE TO PRETEND TO BE A REGULAR GUY. IT'S YOUR SECRET IDENTITY.
BUT NOT WITH ME. I KNOW WHO YOU REALLY ARE.
I MEAN, JESUS. WHO WOULDN'T WANT THEIR KID TO TALK ABOUT THEM LIKE THAT?

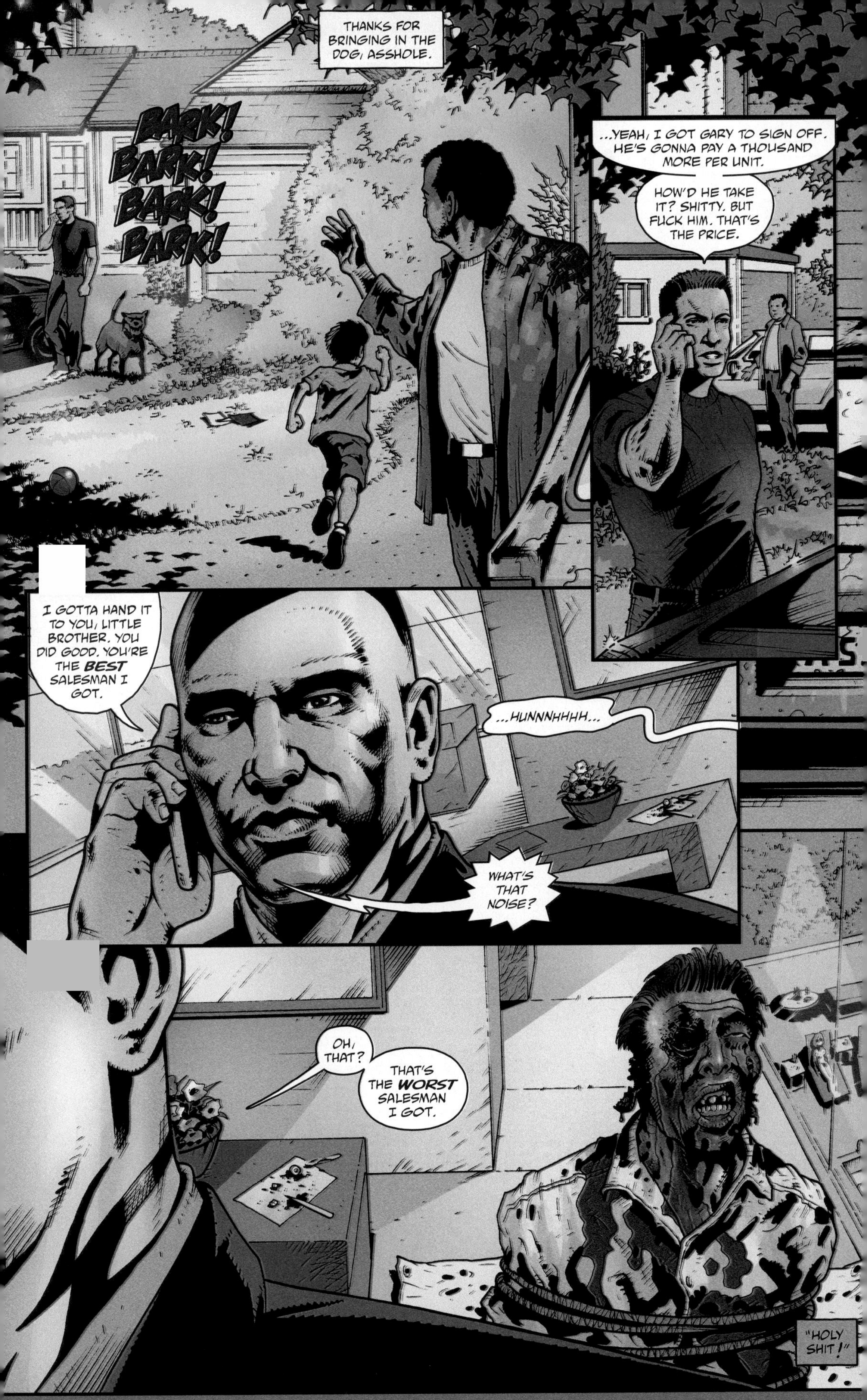
THANKS FOR BRINGING IN THE DOG, ASSHOLE.
BARK! BARK! BARK! BARK!
...YEAH, I GOT GARY TO SIGN OFF. HE'S GONNA PAY A THOUSAND MORE PER UNIT.
HOW'D HE TAKE IT? SHITTY. BUT FUCK HIM. THAT'S THE PRICE.
I GOTTA HAND IT TO YOU, LITTLE BROTHER. YOU DID GOOD. YOU'RE THE **BEST** SALESMAN I GOT.
...HUNNNHHHH...
WHAT'S THAT NOISE?
OH, THAT?
THAT'S THE **WORST** SALESMAN I GOT.
"HOLY SHIT!"

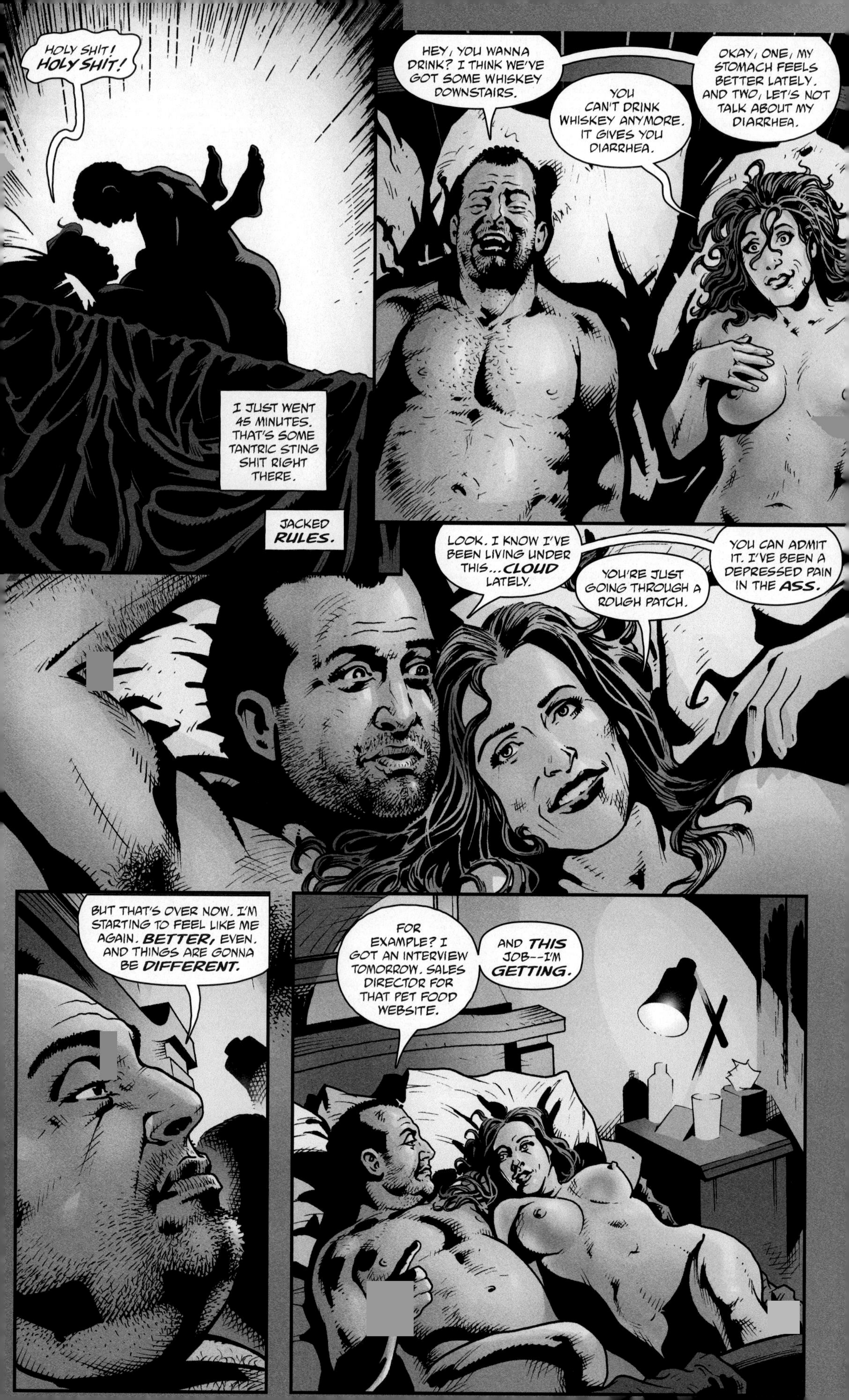
HOLY SHIT! HOLY SHIT!
I JUST WENT 45 MINUTES. THAT'S SOME TANTRIC STING SHIT RIGHT THERE.
JACKED RULES.
HEY, YOU WANNA DRINK? I THINK WE'VE GOT SOME WHISKEY DOWNSTAIRS.
YOU CAN'T DRINK WHISKEY ANYMORE. IT GIVES YOU DIARRHEA.
OKAY, ONE, MY STOMACH FEELS BETTER LATELY. AND TWO, LET'S NOT TALK ABOUT MY DIARRHEA.
LOOK. I KNOW I'VE BEEN LIVING UNDER THIS...CLOUD LATELY.
YOU'RE JUST GOING THROUGH A ROUGH PATCH.
YOU CAN ADMIT IT. I'VE BEEN A DEPRESSED PAIN IN THE ASS.
BUT THAT'S OVER NOW. I'M STARTING TO FEEL LIKE ME AGAIN. BETTER, EVEN. AND THINGS ARE GONNA BE DIFFERENT.
FOR EXAMPLE? I GOT AN INTERVIEW TOMORROW. SALES DIRECTOR FOR THAT PET FOOD WEBSITE.
AND THIS JOB--I'M GETTING.

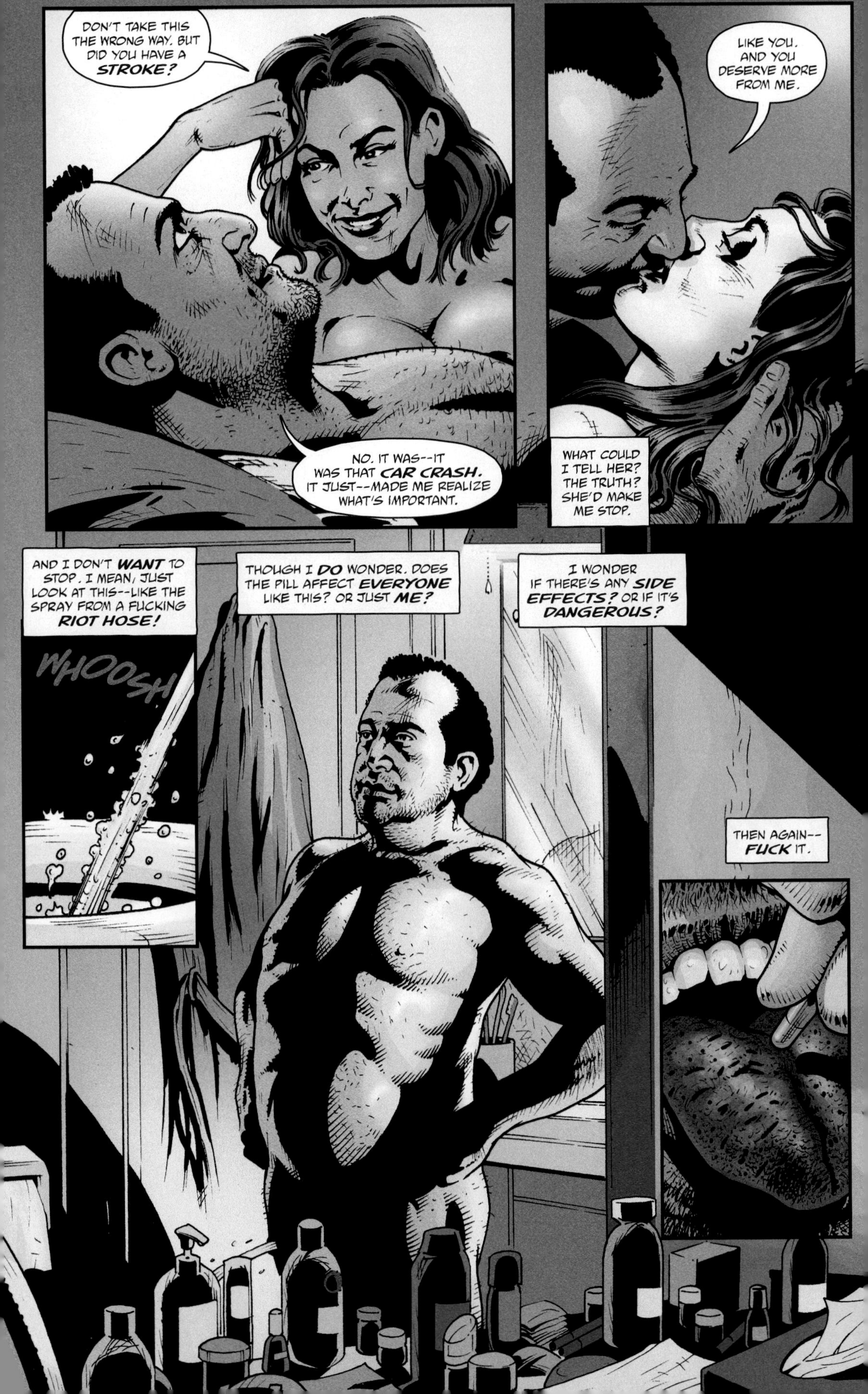
DON'T TAKE THIS THE WRONG WAY. BUT DID YOU HAVE A STROKE?
NO. IT WAS--IT WAS THAT CAR CRASH. IT JUST--MADE ME REALIZE WHAT'S IMPORTANT.
LIKE YOU. AND YOU DESERVE MORE FROM ME.
WHAT COULD I TELL HER? THE TRUTH? SHE'D MAKE ME STOP.
AND I DON'T WANT TO STOP. I MEAN, JUST LOOK AT THIS--LIKE THE SPRAY FROM A FUCKING RIOT HOSE!
WHOOSH
THOUGH I DO WONDER. DOES THE PILL AFFECT EVERYONE LIKE THIS? OR JUST ME?
I WONDER IF THERE'S ANY SIDE EFFECTS? OR IF IT'S DANGEROUS?
THEN AGAIN-- FUCK IT.

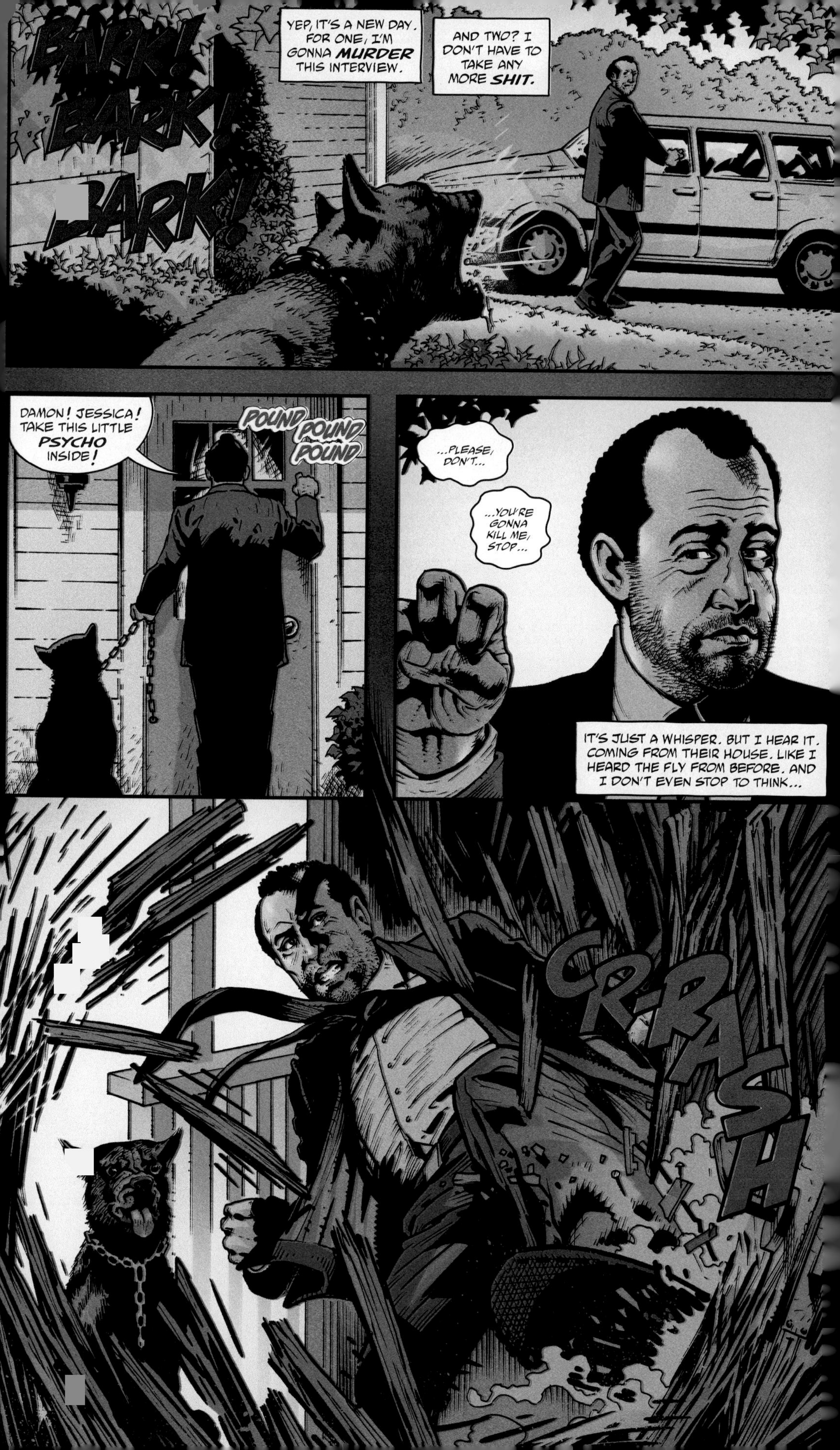
BARK! BARK! BARK!
YEP, IT'S A NEW DAY. FOR ONE, I'M GONNA MURDER THIS INTERVIEW.
AND TWO? I DON'T HAVE TO TAKE ANY MORE SHIT.
DAMON! JESSICA! TAKE THIS LITTLE PSYCHO INSIDE!
POUND POUND POUND
...PLEASE, DON'T...
...YOU'RE GONNA KILL ME, STOP...
IT'S JUST A WHISPER. BUT I HEAR IT. COMING FROM THEIR HOUSE. LIKE I HEARD THE FLY FROM BEFORE. AND I DON'T EVEN STOP TO THINK...
CR-RASH

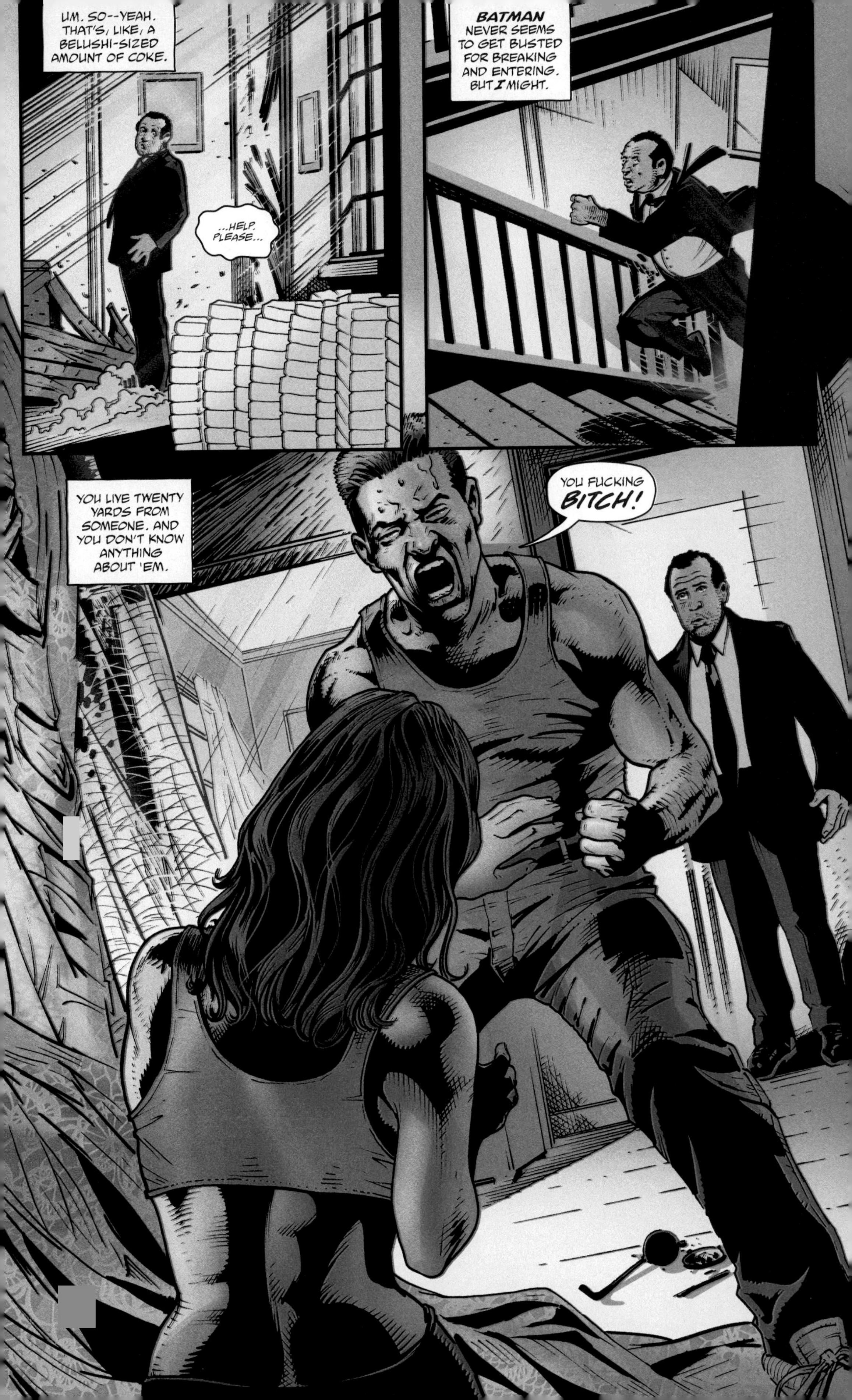
UM. SO--YEAH. THAT'S, LIKE, A BELUSHI-SIZED AMOUNT OF COKE.
...HELP. PLEASE...
BATMAN NEVER SEEMS TO GET BUSTED FOR BREAKING AND ENTERING. BUT I MIGHT.
YOU LIVE TWENTY YARDS FROM SOMEONE. AND YOU DON'T KNOW ANYTHING ABOUT 'EM.
YOU FUCKING BITCH!

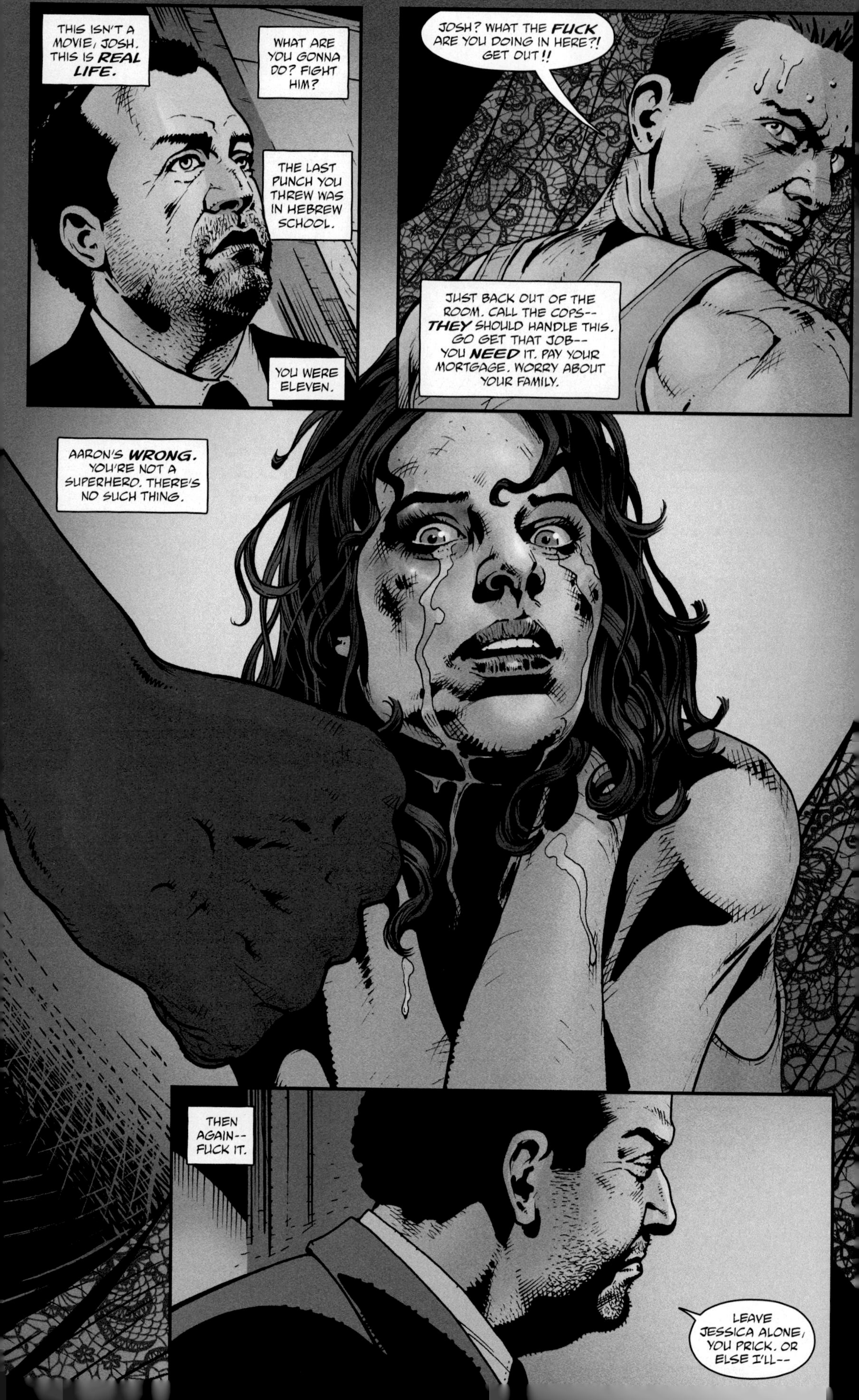
THIS ISN'T A MOVIE, JOSH. THIS IS REAL LIFE.
WHAT ARE YOU GONNA DO? FIGHT HIM?
THE LAST PUNCH YOU THREW WAS IN HEBREW SCHOOL.
YOU WERE ELEVEN.
JOSH? WHAT THE FUCK ARE YOU DOING IN HERE?! GET OUT!!
JUST BACK OUT OF THE ROOM. CALL THE COPS-- THEY SHOULD HANDLE THIS. GO GET THAT JOB-- YOU NEED IT. PAY YOUR MORTGAGE. WORRY ABOUT YOUR FAMILY.
AARON'S WRONG. YOU'RE NOT A SUPERHERO. THERE'S NO SUCH THING.
THEN AGAIN-- FUCK IT.
LEAVE JESSICA ALONE, YOU PRICK. OR ELSE I'LL--

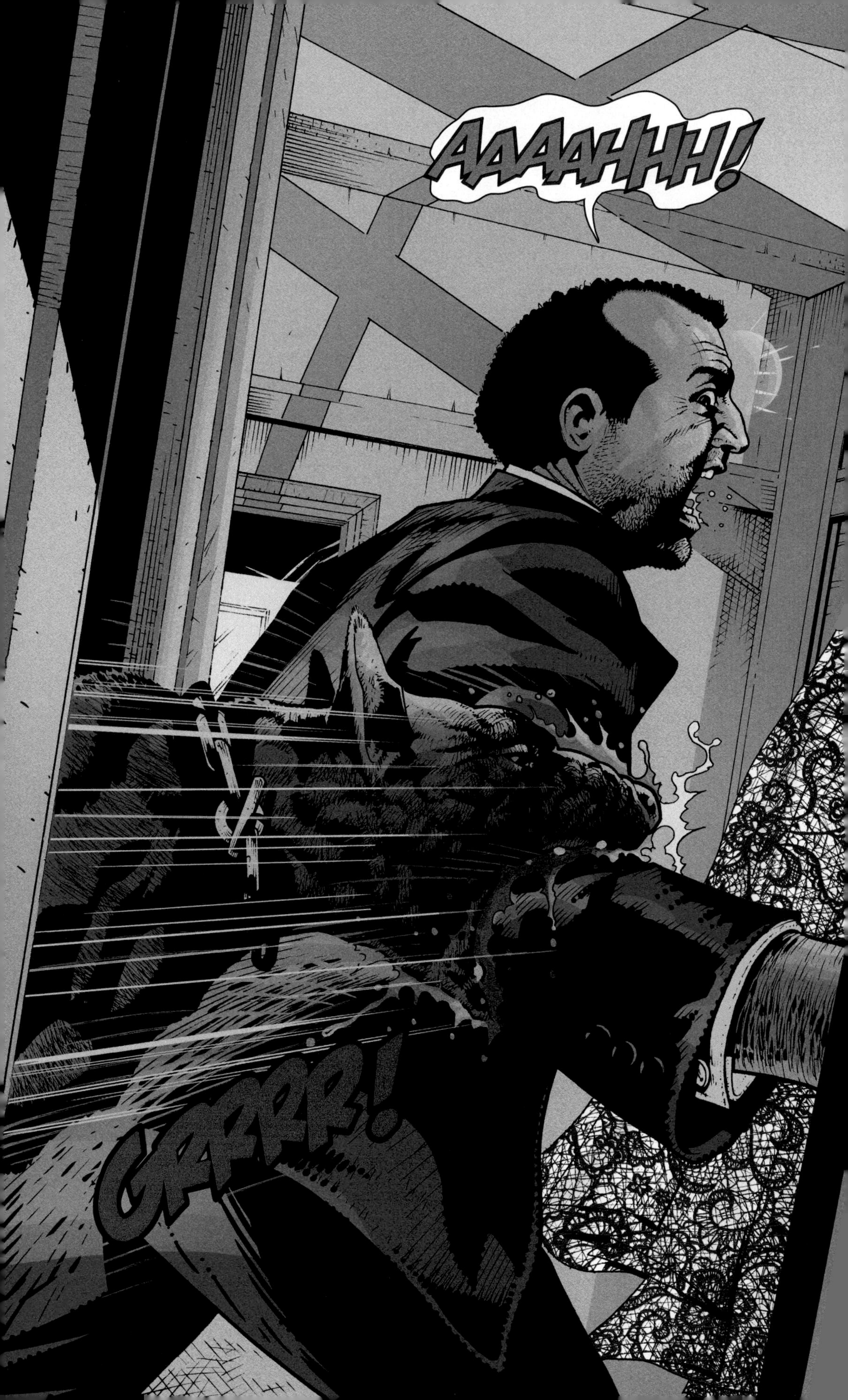
AAAAHHH!
GRRRR!

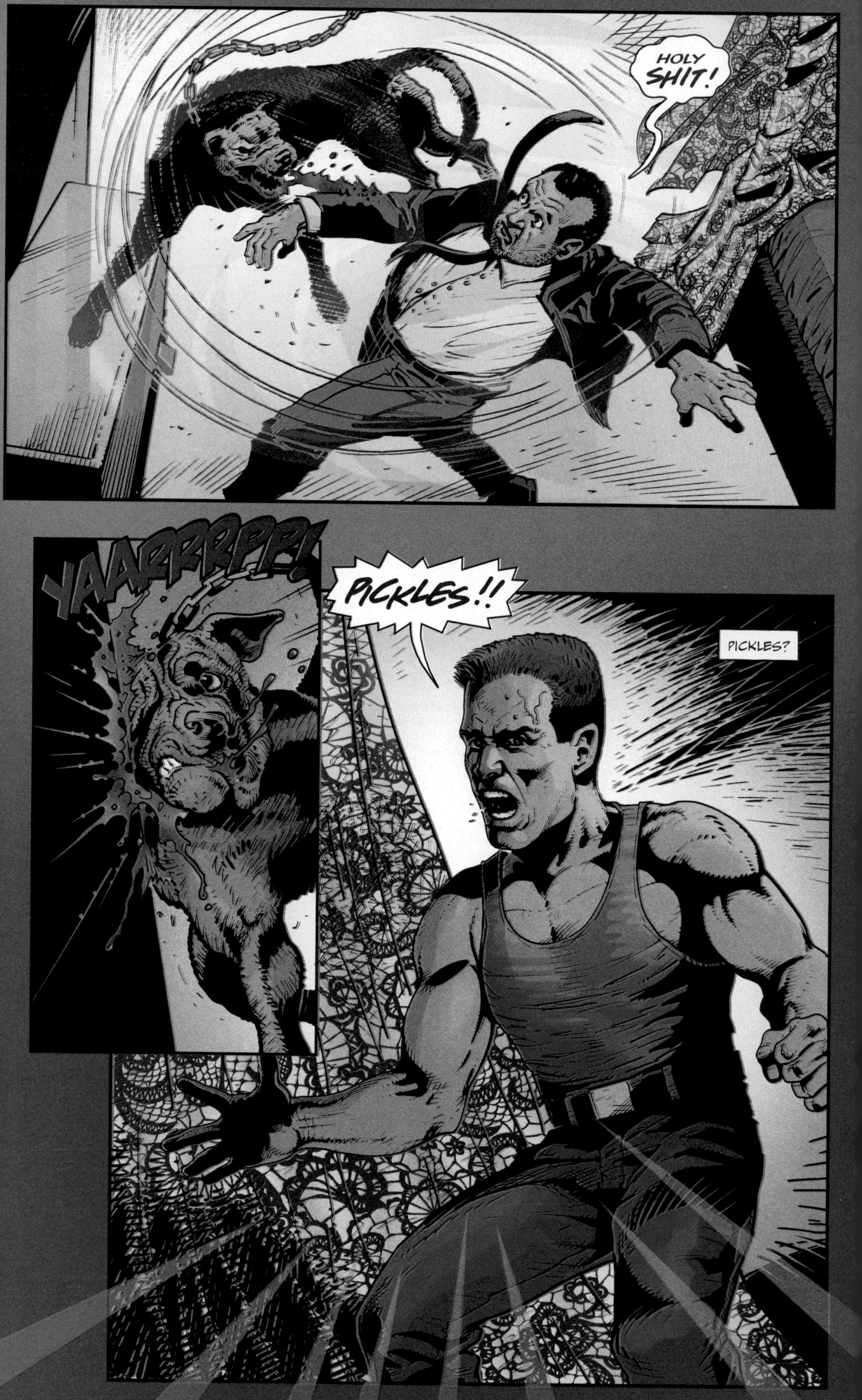
HOLY SHIT!
YAARRRPP!
PICKLES!!
PICKLES?

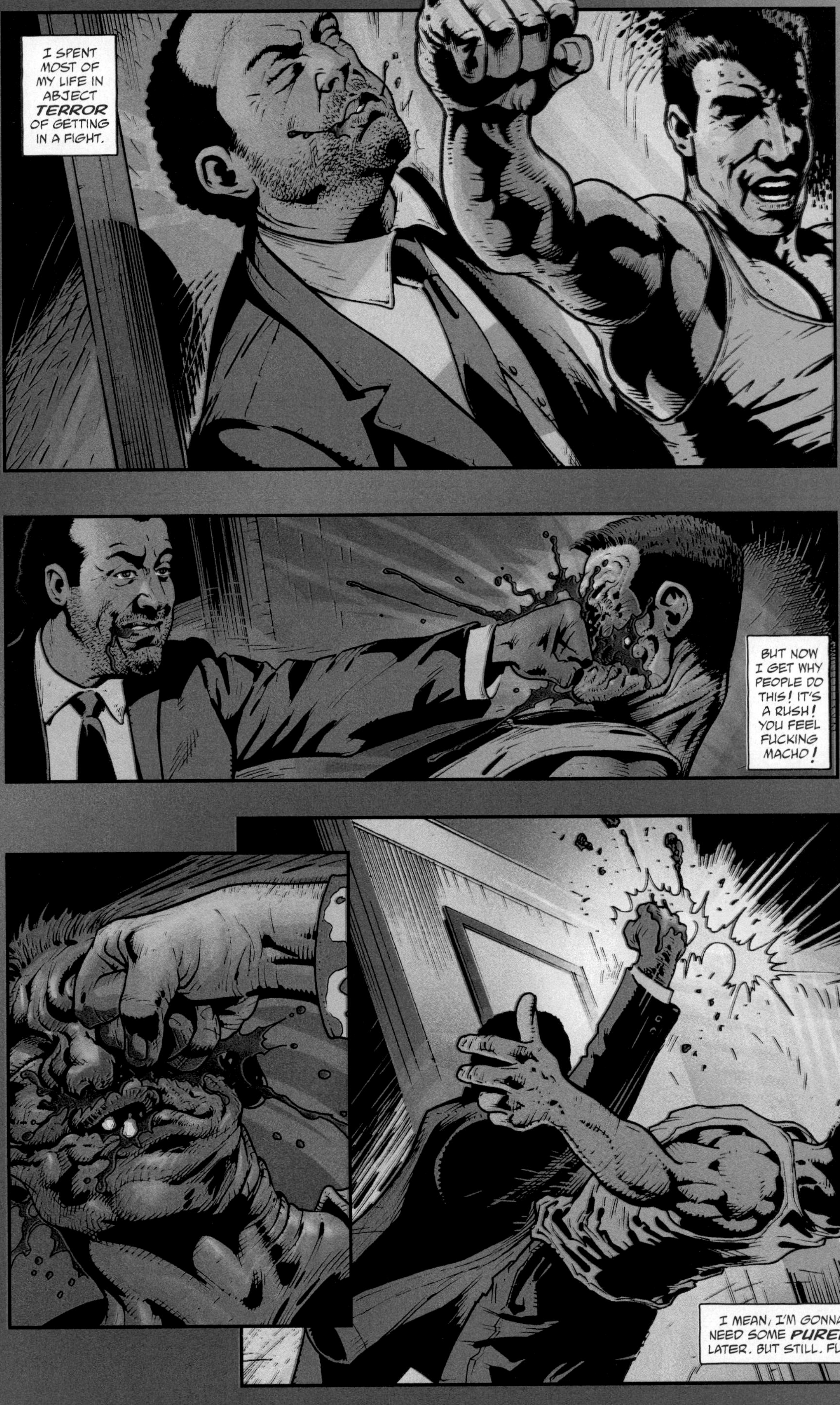
I SPENT MOST OF MY LIFE IN ABJECT TERROR OF GETTING IN A FIGHT.
BUT NOW I GET WHY PEOPLE DO THIS! IT'S A RUSH! YOU FEEL FUCKING MACHO!
I MEAN, I'M GONNA NEED SOME PURELL LATER. BUT STILL. FUN!

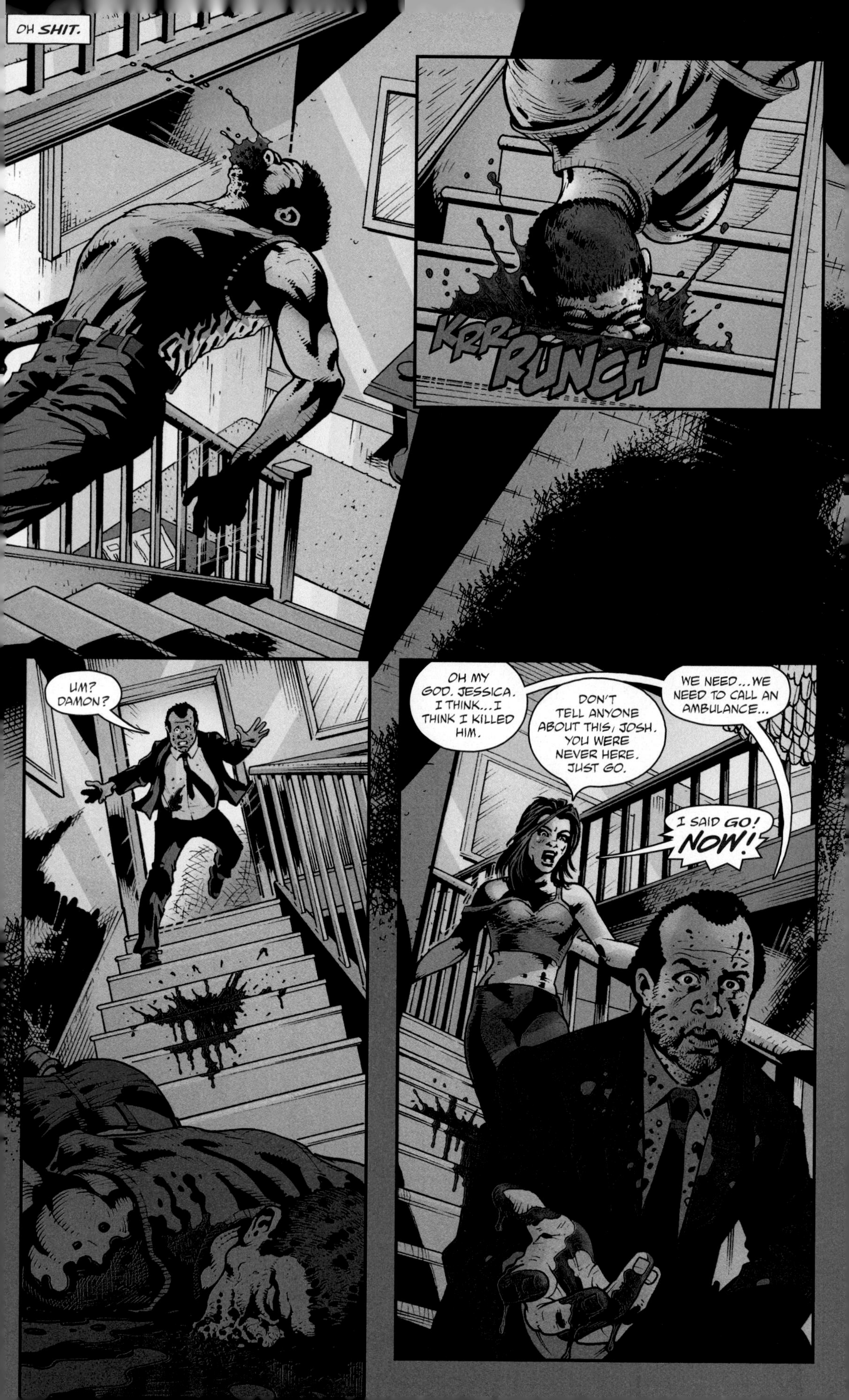
OH SHIT.
KRR-RUNCH
UM? DAMON?
OH MY GOD. JESSICA. I THINK... I THINK I KILLED HIM.
DON'T TELL ANYONE ABOUT THIS, JOSH. YOU WERE NEVER HERE. JUST GO.
WE NEED... WE NEED TO CALL AN AMBULANCE...
I SAID GO! NOW!

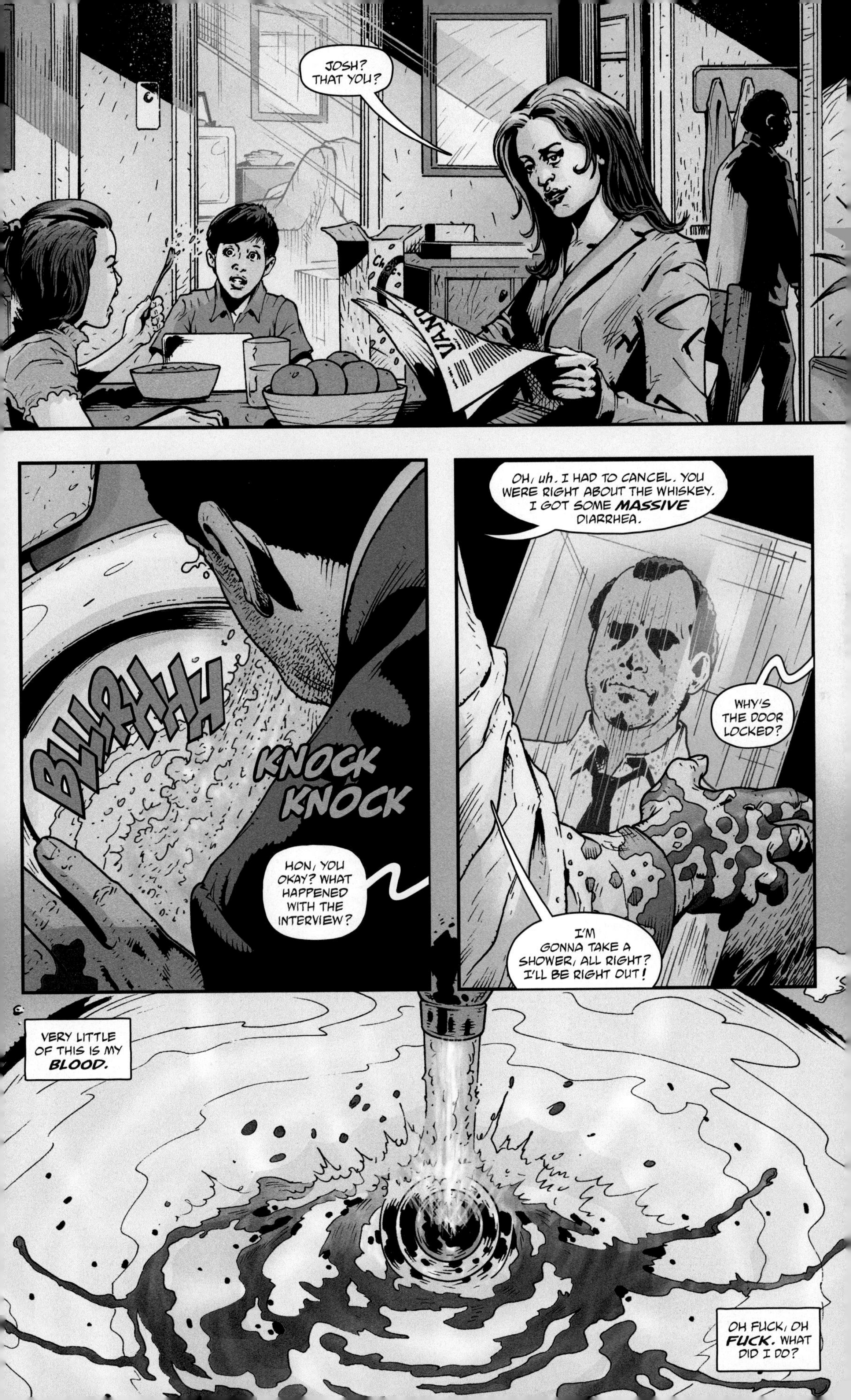
JOSH? THAT YOU?
BLLRHHH
KNOCK KNOCK
HON, YOU OKAY? WHAT HAPPENED WITH THE INTERVIEW?
OH, uh. I HAD TO CANCEL. YOU WERE RIGHT ABOUT THE WHISKEY. I GOT SOME MASSIVE DIARRHEA.
WHY'S THE DOOR LOCKED?
I'M GONNA TAKE A SHOWER, ALL RIGHT? I'LL BE RIGHT OUT!
VERY LITTLE OF THIS IS MY BLOOD.
OH FUCK, OH FUCK. WHAT DID I DO?

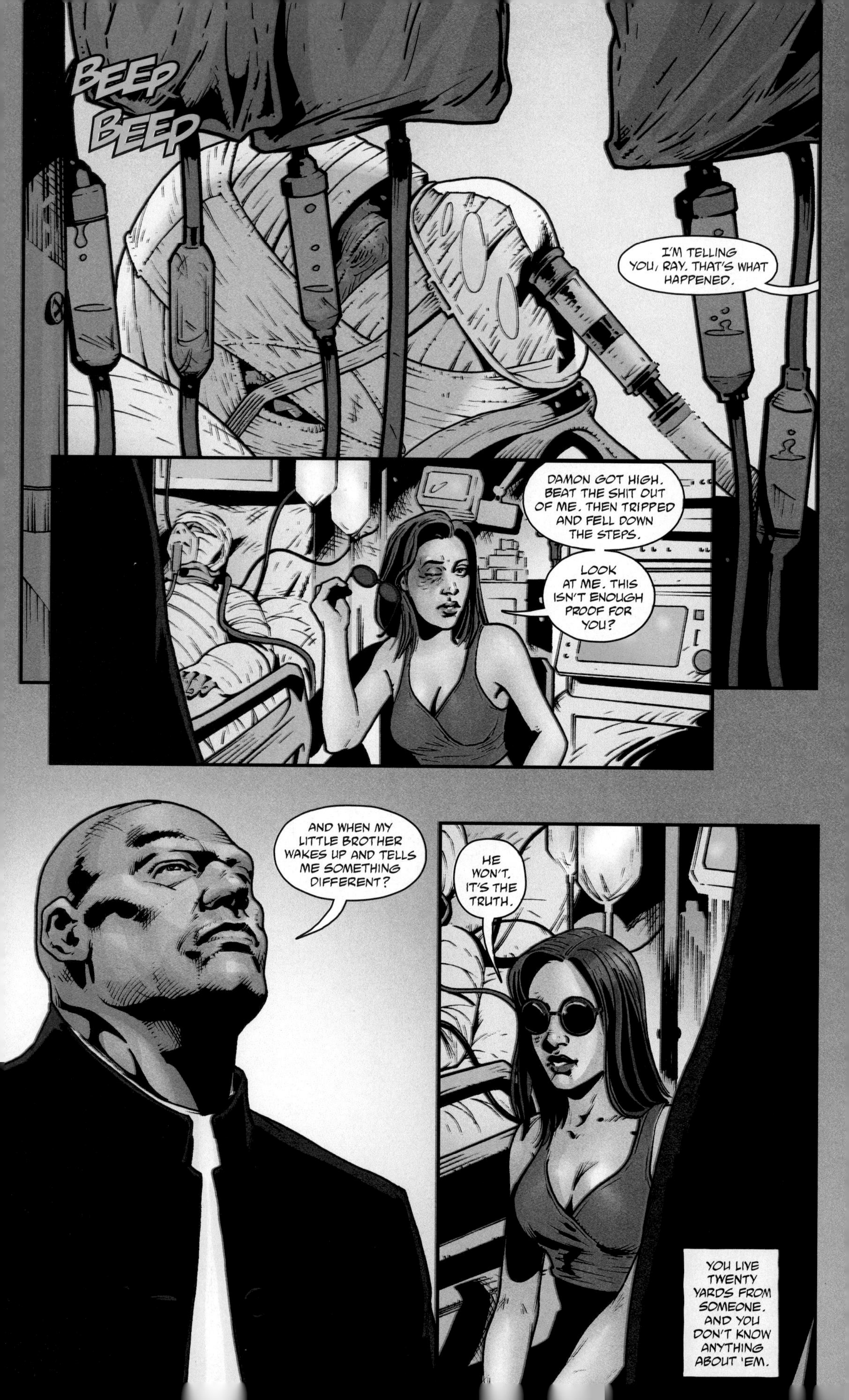
BEEP BEEP
I'M TELLING YOU, RAY. THAT'S WHAT HAPPENED.
DAMON GOT HIGH. BEAT THE SHIT OUT OF ME. THEN TRIPPED AND FELL DOWN THE STEPS.
LOOK AT ME. THIS ISN'T ENOUGH PROOF FOR YOU?
AND WHEN MY LITTLE BROTHER WAKES UP AND TELLS ME SOMETHING DIFFERENT?
HE WON'T. IT'S THE TRUTH.
YOU LIVE TWENTY YARDS FROM SOMEONE. AND YOU DON'T KNOW ANYTHING ABOUT 'EM.

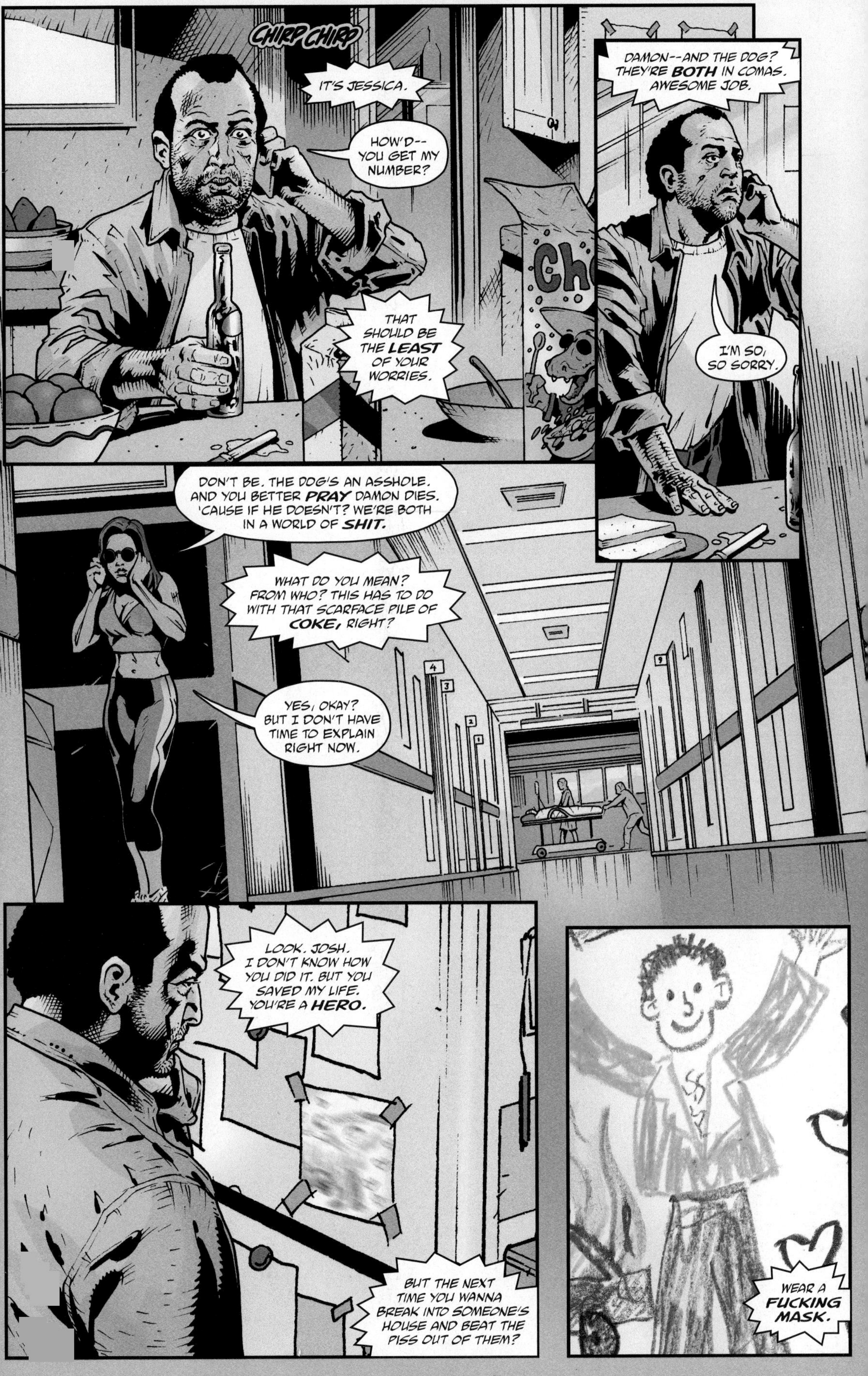
CHIRP CHIRP
IT'S JESSICA.
HOW'D-- YOU GET MY NUMBER?
THAT SHOULD BE THE LEAST OF YOUR WORRIES.
DAMON--AND THE DOG? THEY'RE BOTH IN COMAS. AWESOME JOB.
I'M SO, SO SORRY.
DON'T BE. THE DOG'S AN ASSHOLE. AND YOU BETTER PRAY DAMON DIES. 'CAUSE IF HE DOESN'T? WE'RE BOTH IN A WORLD OF SHIT.
WHAT DO YOU MEAN? FROM WHO? THIS HAS TO DO WITH THAT SCARFACE PILE OF COKE, RIGHT?
YES, OKAY? BUT I DON'T HAVE TIME TO EXPLAIN RIGHT NOW.
LOOK, JOSH. I DON'T KNOW HOW YOU DID IT. BUT YOU SAVED MY LIFE. YOU'RE A HERO.
BUT THE NEXT TIME YOU WANNA BREAK INTO SOMEONE'S HOUSE AND BEAT THE PISS OUT OF THEM?
WEAR A FUCKING MASK.

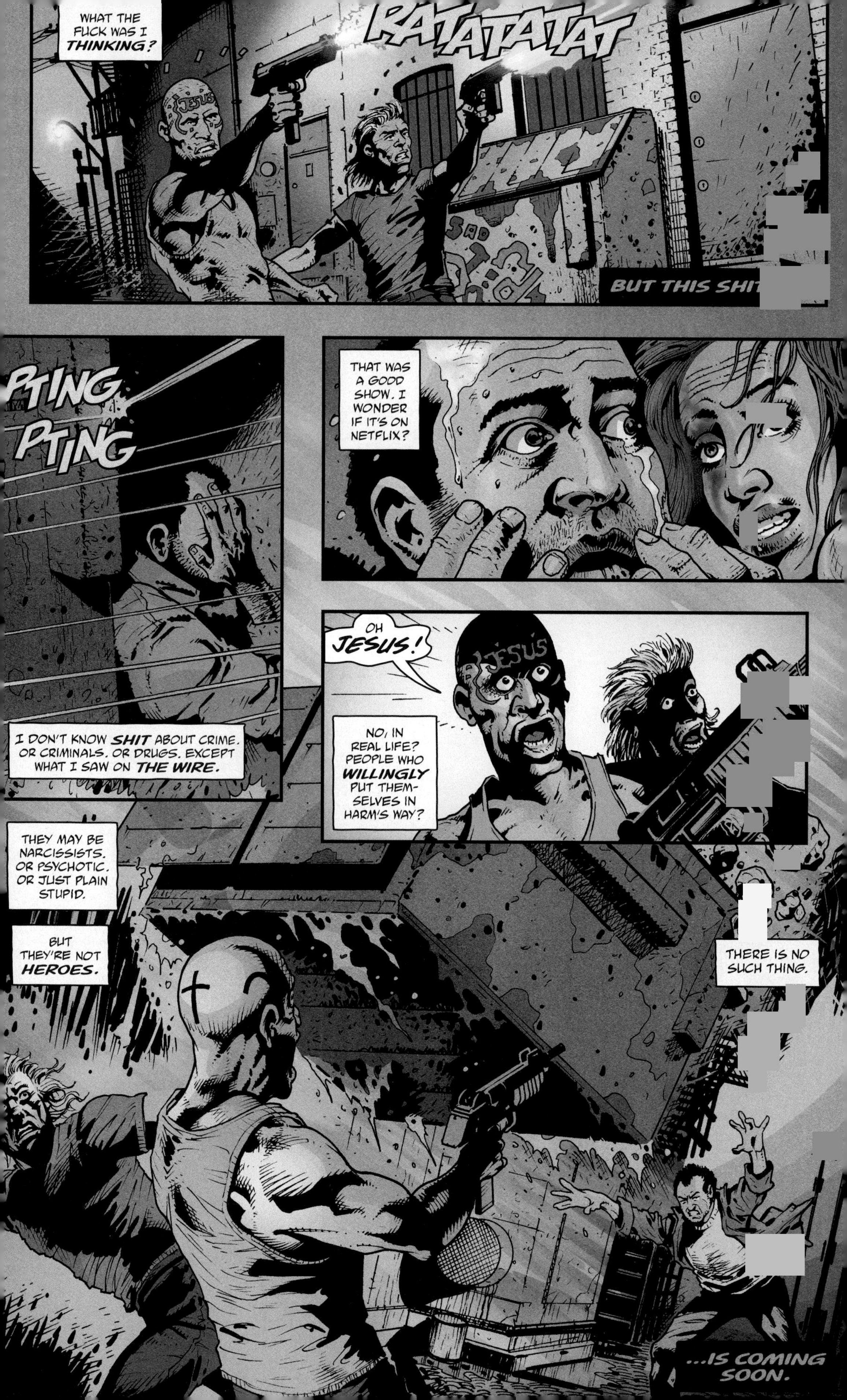
WHAT THE FUCK WAS I THINKING?
RATATATAT
JESUS
BUT THIS SHIT
PTING
PTING
I DON'T KNOW SHIT ABOUT CRIME. OR CRIMINALS. OR DRUGS. EXCEPT WHAT I SAW ON THE WIRE.
THAT WAS A GOOD SHOW. I WONDER IF IT'S ON NETFLIX?
NO, IN REAL LIFE? PEOPLE WHO WILLINGLY PUT THEMSELVES IN HARM'S WAY?
OH JESUS!
JESUS
THEY MAY BE NARCISSISTS. OR PSYCHOTIC. OR JUST PLAIN STUPID.
BUT THEY'RE NOT HEROES.
THERE IS NO SUCH THING.
...IS COMING SOON.

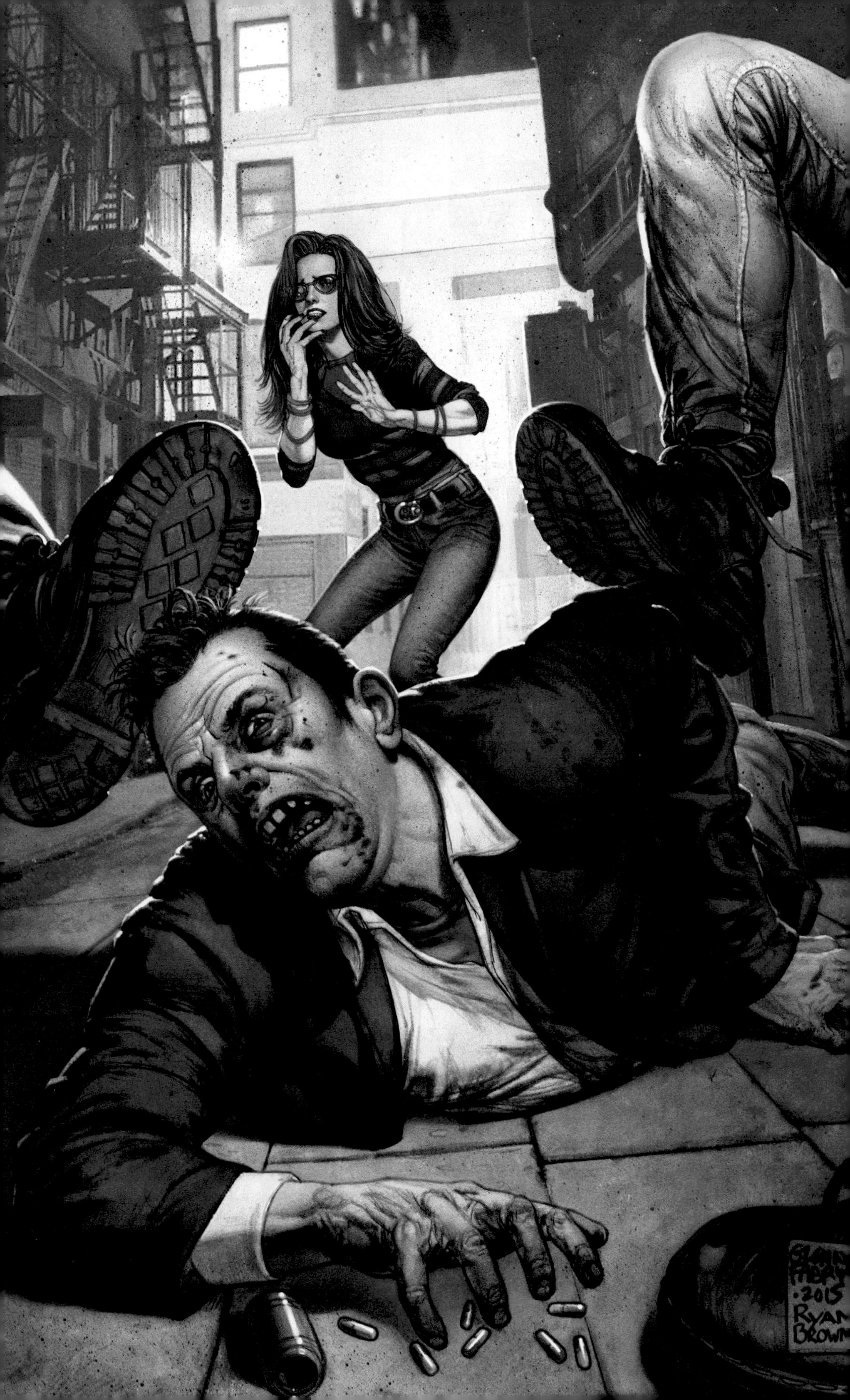

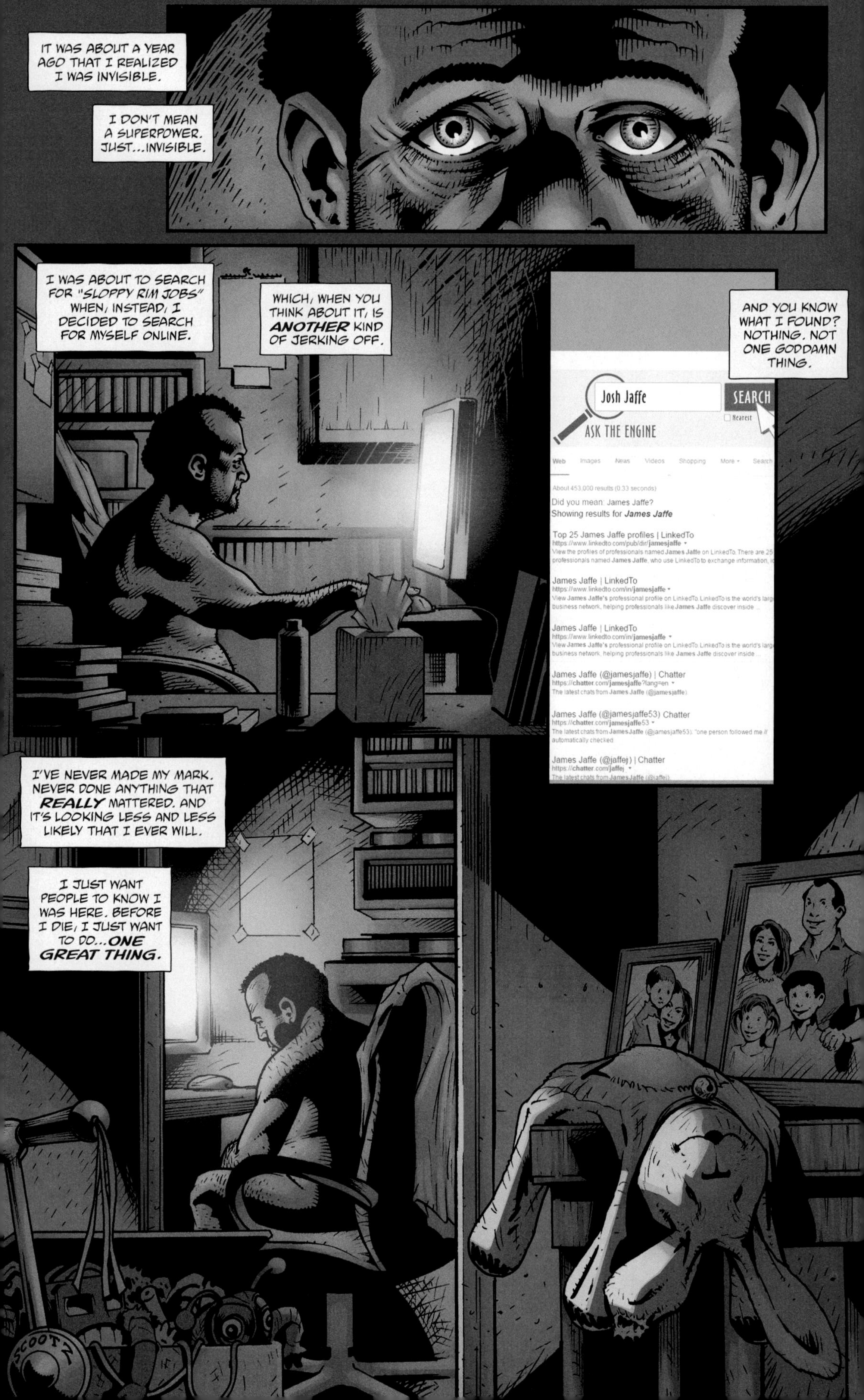
IT WAS ABOUT A YEAR AGO THAT I REALIZED I WAS INVISIBLE.
I DON'T MEAN A SUPERPOWER. JUST...INVISIBLE.
I WAS ABOUT TO SEARCH FOR "SLOPPY RIM JOBS" WHEN, INSTEAD, I DECIDED TO SEARCH FOR MYSELF ONLINE.
WHICH, WHEN YOU THINK ABOUT IT, IS ANOTHER KIND OF JERKING OFF.
Josh Jaffe
SEARCH
Nearest
ASK THE ENGINE
Web Images News Videos Shopping More Search
About 453,000 results (0.33 seconds)
Did you mean: James Jaffe?
Showing results for James Jaffe
Top 25 James Jaffe profiles | LinkedTo
https://www.linkedto.com/pub/dir/jamesjaffe
View the profiles of professionals named James Jaffe on LinkedTo. There are 25 professionals named James Jaffe, who use LinkedTo to exchange information,
James Jaffe | LinkedTo
https://www.linkedto.com/in/jamesjaffe
View James Jaffe's professional profile on LinkedTo. LinkedTo is the world's larg business network, helping professionals like James Jaffe discover inside ...
James Jaffe | LinkedTo
https://www.linkedto.com/in/jamesjaffe
View James Jaffe's professional profile on LinkedTo. LinkedTo is the world's larg business network, helping professionals like James Jaffe discover inside ...
James Jaffe (@jamesjaffe) | Chatter
https://chatter.com/jamesjaffe?lang=en
The latest chats from James Jaffe (@jamesjaffe).
James Jaffe (@jamesjaffe53) Chatter
https://chatter.com/jamesjaffe53
The latest chats from James Jaffe (@jamesjaffe53): "one person followed me // automatically checked
James Jaffe (@jaffej) | Chatter
https://chatter.com/jaffej
AND YOU KNOW WHAT I FOUND? NOTHING. NOT ONE GODDAMN THING.
I'VE NEVER MADE MY MARK. NEVER DONE ANYTHING THAT REALLY MATTERED. AND IT'S LOOKING LESS AND LESS LIKELY THAT I EVER WILL.
I JUST WANT PEOPLE TO KNOW I WAS HERE. BEFORE I DIE, I JUST WANT TO DO...ONE GREAT THING.
SCOOT 2

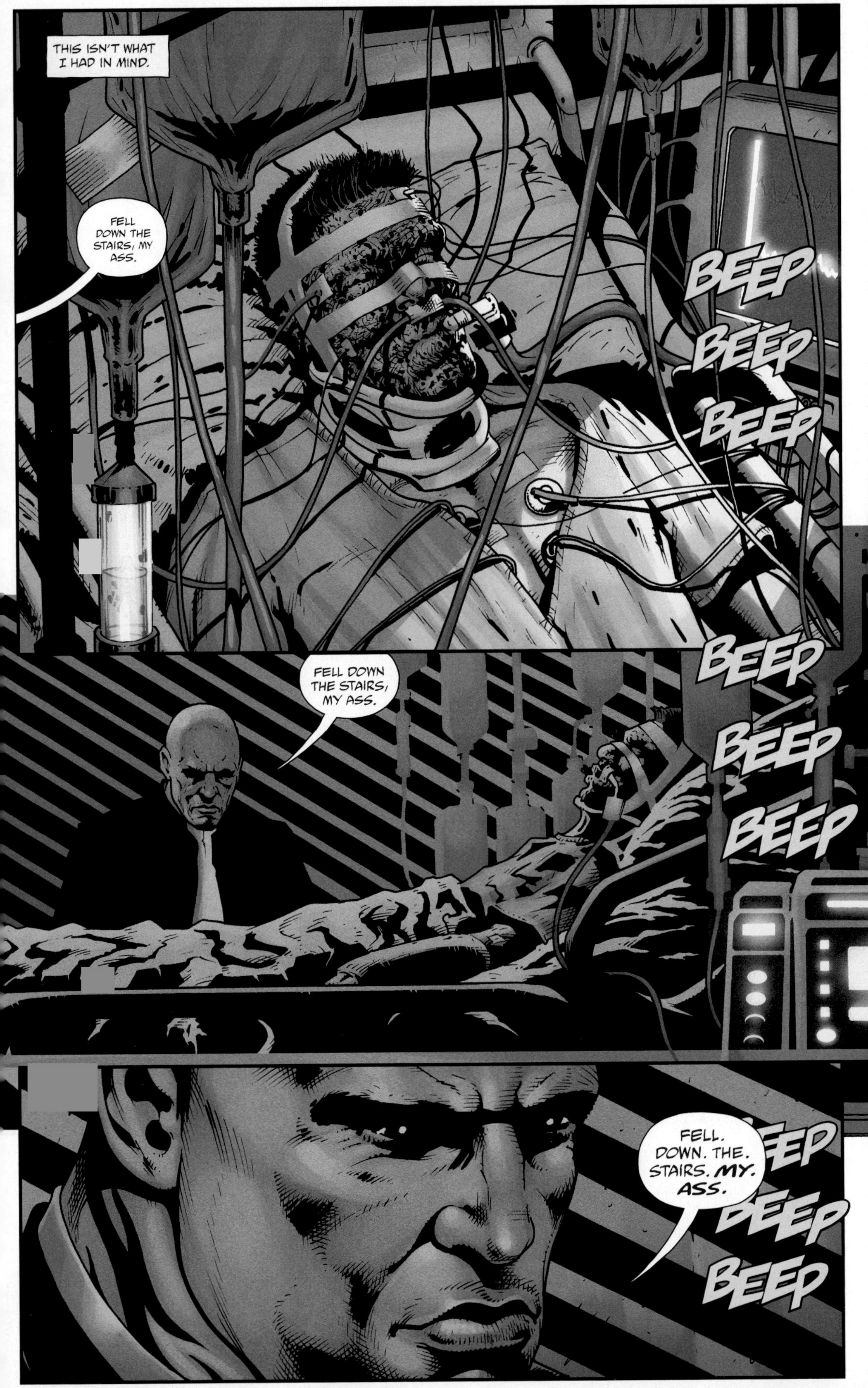
THIS ISN'T WHAT I HAD IN MIND.
FELL DOWN THE STAIRS, MY ASS.
BEEP
BEEP
BEEP
FELL DOWN THE STAIRS, MY ASS.
BEEP
BEEP
BEEP
FELL. DOWN. THE. STAIRS. MY. ASS.
BEEP
BEEP

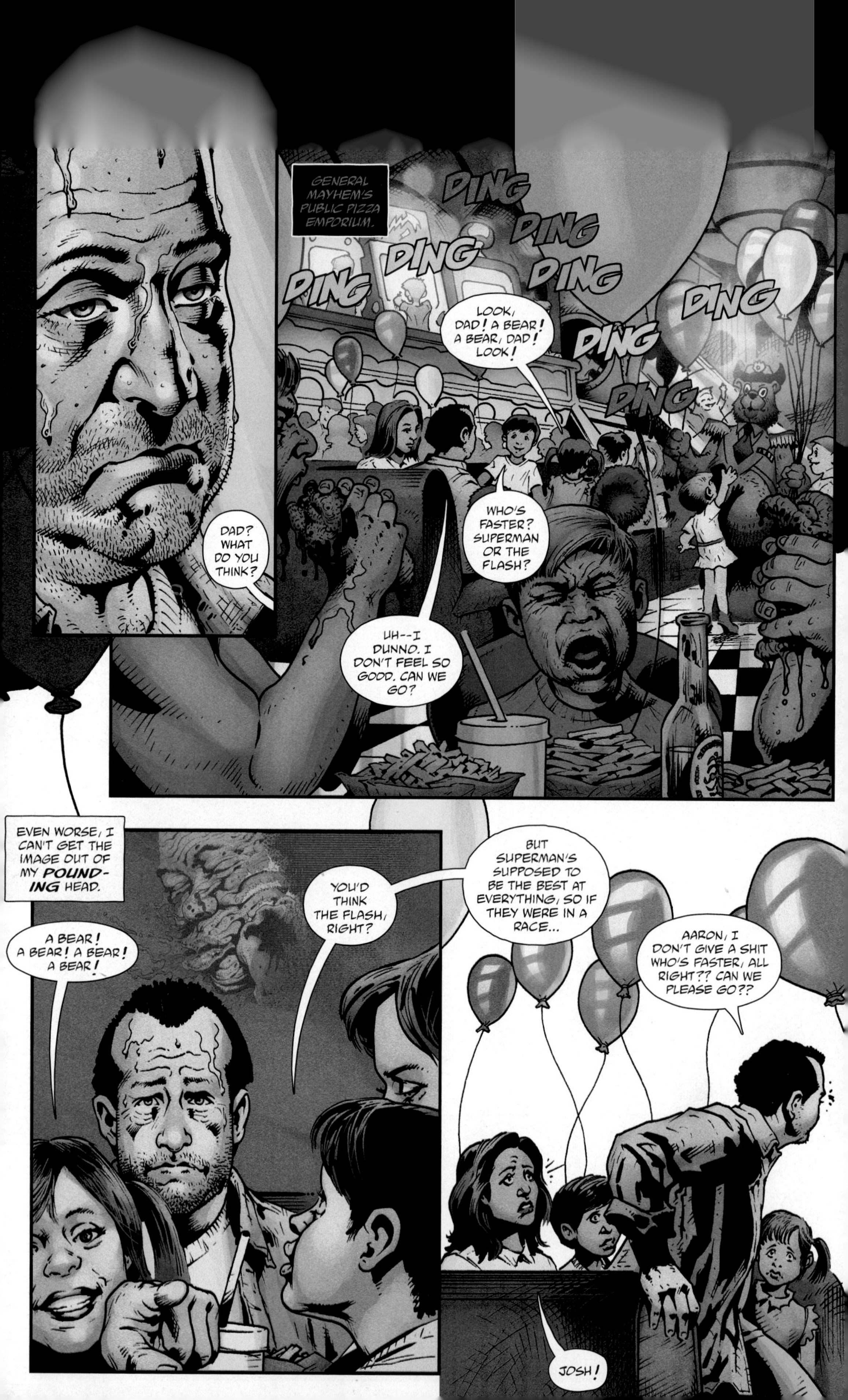
GENERAL MAYHEM'S PUBLIC PIZZA EMPORIUM.
DING
DING
DING
DING
DING
DING
DING
DING
DAD? WHAT DO YOU THINK?
LOOK, DAD! A BEAR! A BEAR, DAD! LOOK!
WHO'S FASTER? SUPERMAN OR THE FLASH?
UH--I DUNNO. I DON'T FEEL SO GOOD. CAN WE GO?
EVEN WORSE, I CAN'T GET THE IMAGE OUT OF MY **POUNDING** HEAD.
A BEAR! A BEAR! A BEAR! A BEAR!
YOU'D THINK THE FLASH, RIGHT?
BUT SUPERMAN'S SUPPOSED TO BE THE BEST AT EVERYTHING, SO IF THEY WERE IN A RACE...
AARON, I DON'T GIVE A SHIT WHO'S FASTER, ALL RIGHT?? CAN WE PLEASE GO??
JOSH!

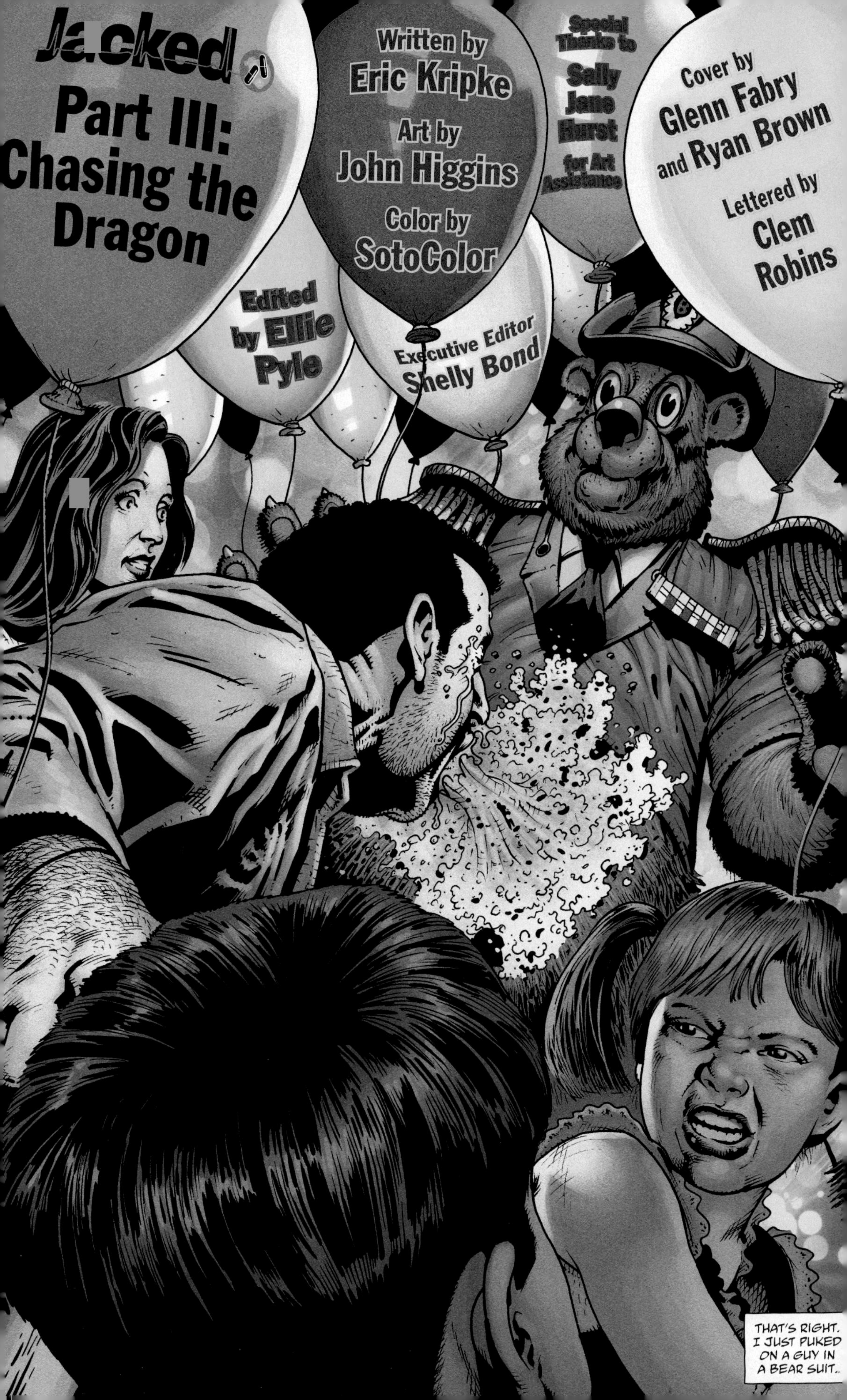
Jacked
Part III: Chasing the Dragon
Written by Eric Kripke
Art by John Higgins
Color by SotoColor
Special Thanks to Sally Jane Hurst for Art Assistance
Cover by Glenn Fabry and Ryan Brown
Lettered by Clem Robins
Edited by Ellie Pyle
Executive Editor Shelly Bond
THAT'S RIGHT. I JUST PUKED ON A GUY IN A BEAR SUIT..

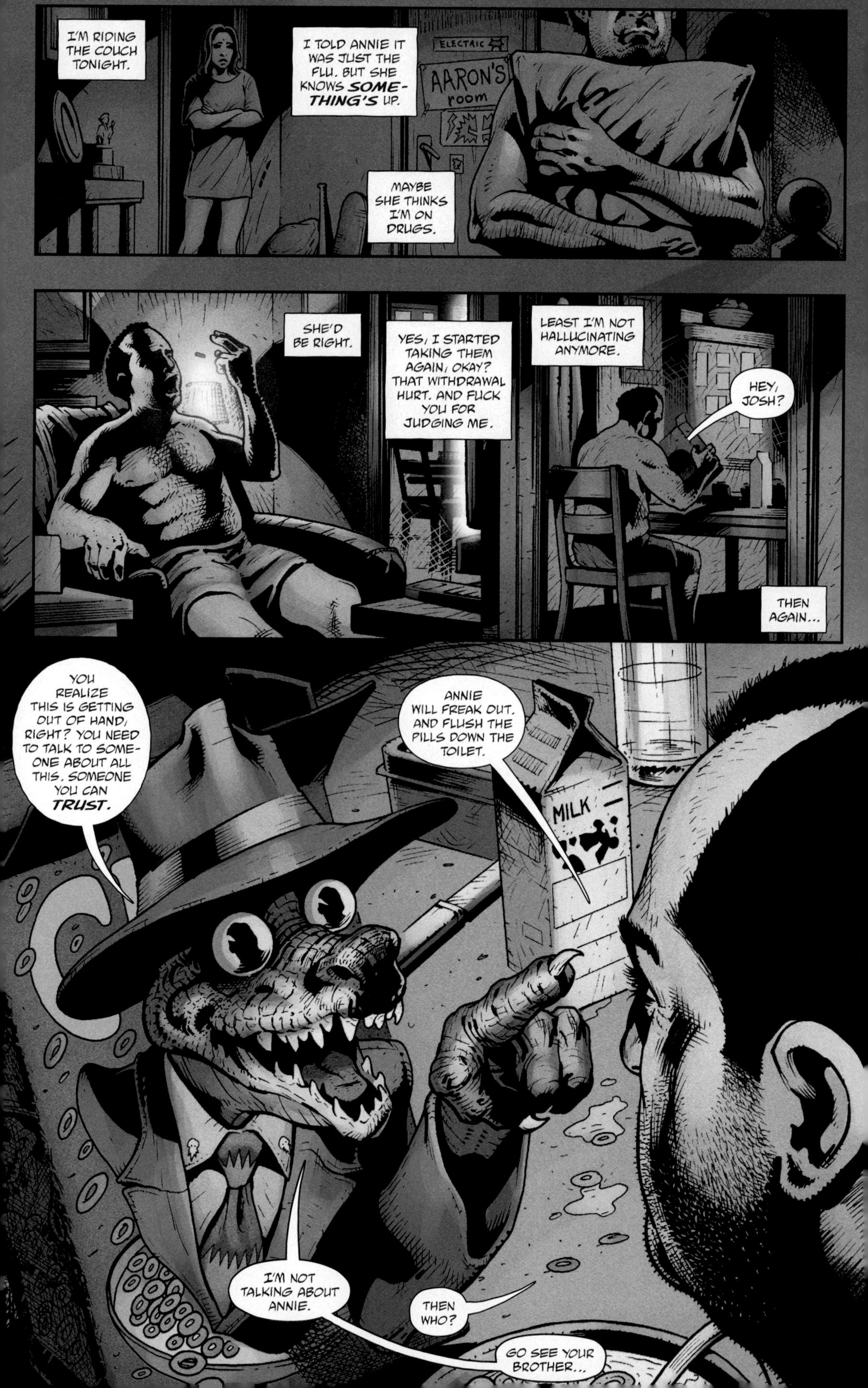
I'M RIDING THE COUCH TONIGHT.
I TOLD ANNIE IT WAS JUST THE FLU. BUT SHE KNOWS SOMETHING'S UP.
ELECTRIC
AARON'S room
MAYBE SHE THINKS I'M ON DRUGS.
SHE'D BE RIGHT.
YES, I STARTED TAKING THEM AGAIN, OKAY? THAT WITHDRAWAL HURT. AND FUCK YOU FOR JUDGING ME.
LEAST I'M NOT HALLUCINATING ANYMORE.
HEY, JOSH?
THEN AGAIN...
YOU REALIZE THIS IS GETTING OUT OF HAND, RIGHT? YOU NEED TO TALK TO SOMEONE ABOUT ALL THIS. SOMEONE YOU CAN TRUST.
ANNIE WILL FREAK OUT. AND FLUSH THE PILLS DOWN THE TOILET.
MILK
I'M NOT TALKING ABOUT ANNIE.
THEN WHO?
GO SEE YOUR BROTHER...

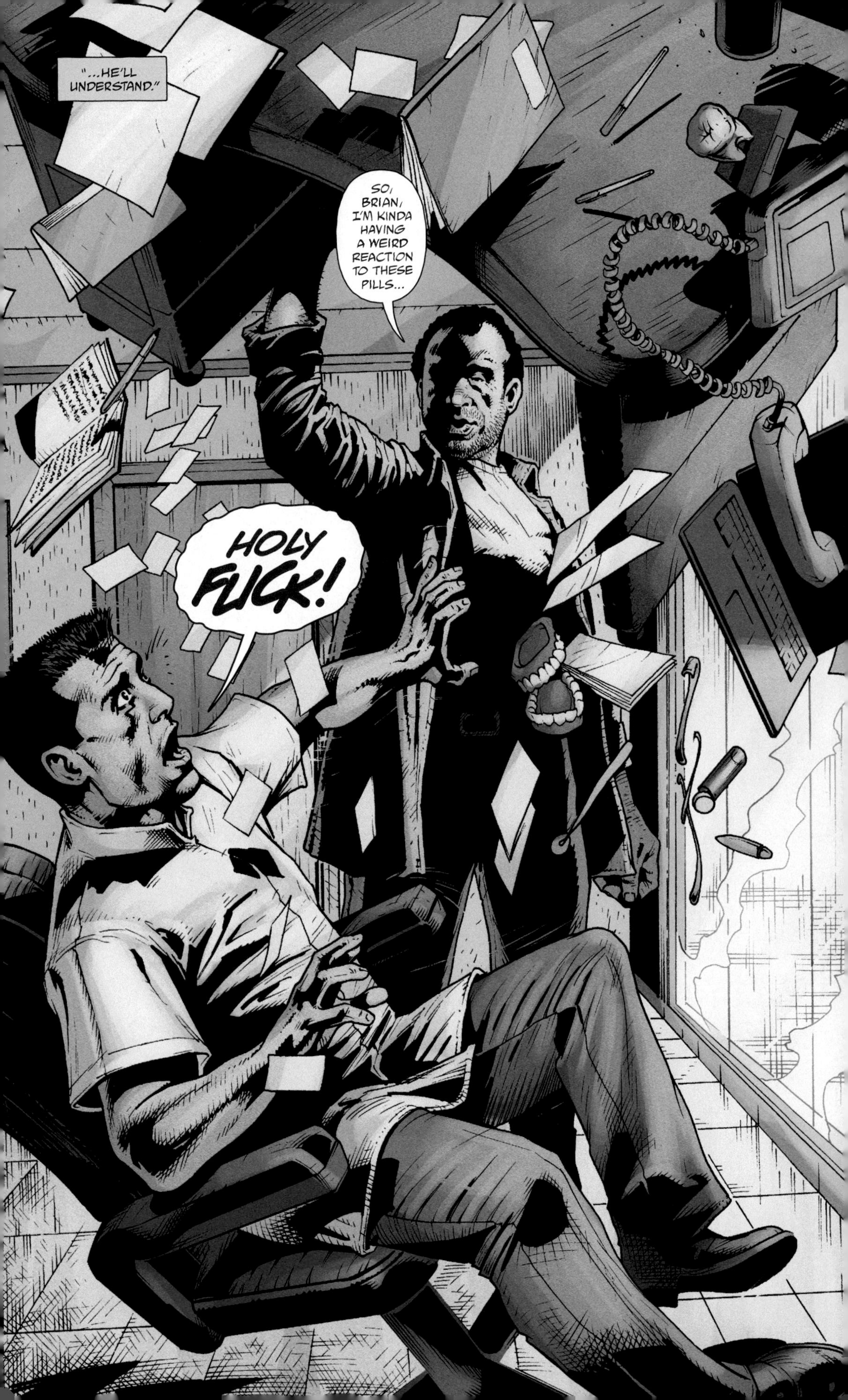
"...HE'LL UNDERSTAND."
SO, BRIAN, I'M KINDA HAVING A WEIRD REACTION TO THESE PILLS...
HOLY FUCK!

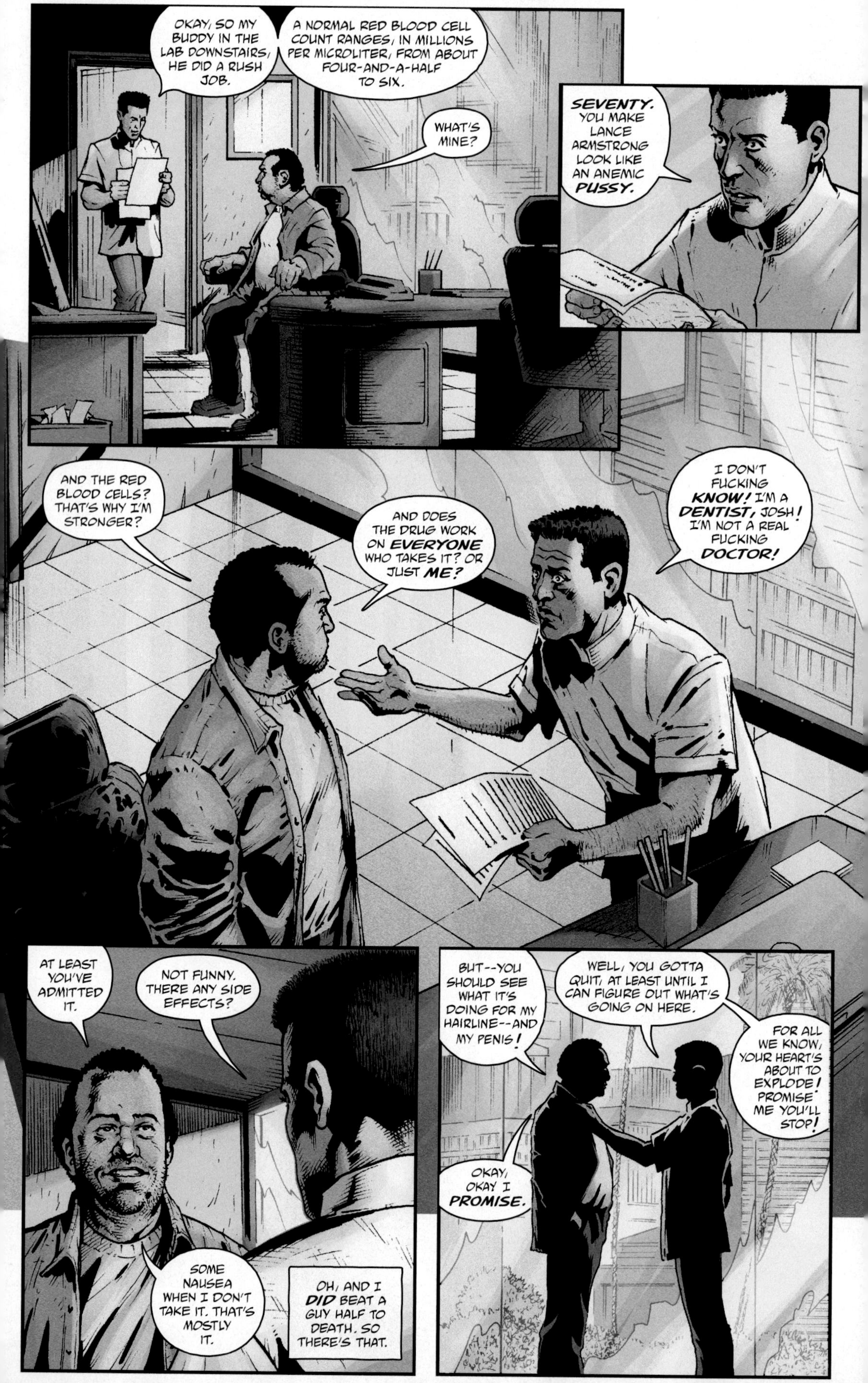
OKAY, SO MY BUDDY IN THE LAB DOWNSTAIRS, HE DID A RUSH JOB.
A NORMAL RED BLOOD CELL COUNT RANGES, IN MILLIONS PER MICROLITER, FROM ABOUT FOUR-AND-A-HALF TO SIX.
WHAT'S MINE?
SEVENTY. YOU MAKE LANCE ARMSTRONG LOOK LIKE AN ANEMIC PUSSY.
AND THE RED BLOOD CELLS? THAT'S WHY I'M STRONGER?
AND DOES THE DRUG WORK ON EVERYONE WHO TAKES IT? OR JUST ME?
I DON'T FUCKING KNOW! I'M A DENTIST, JOSH! I'M NOT A REAL FUCKING DOCTOR!
AT LEAST YOU'VE ADMITTED IT.
NOT FUNNY. THERE ANY SIDE EFFECTS?
SOME NAUSEA WHEN I DON'T TAKE IT. THAT'S MOSTLY IT.
OH, AND I DID BEAT A GUY HALF TO DEATH. SO THERE'S THAT.
BUT--YOU SHOULD SEE WHAT IT'S DOING FOR MY HAIRLINE--AND MY PENIS!
WELL, YOU GOTTA QUIT, AT LEAST UNTIL I CAN FIGURE OUT WHAT'S GOING ON HERE.
FOR ALL WE KNOW, YOUR HEART'S ABOUT TO EXPLODE! PROMISE ME YOU'LL STOP!
OKAY, OKAY I PROMISE.

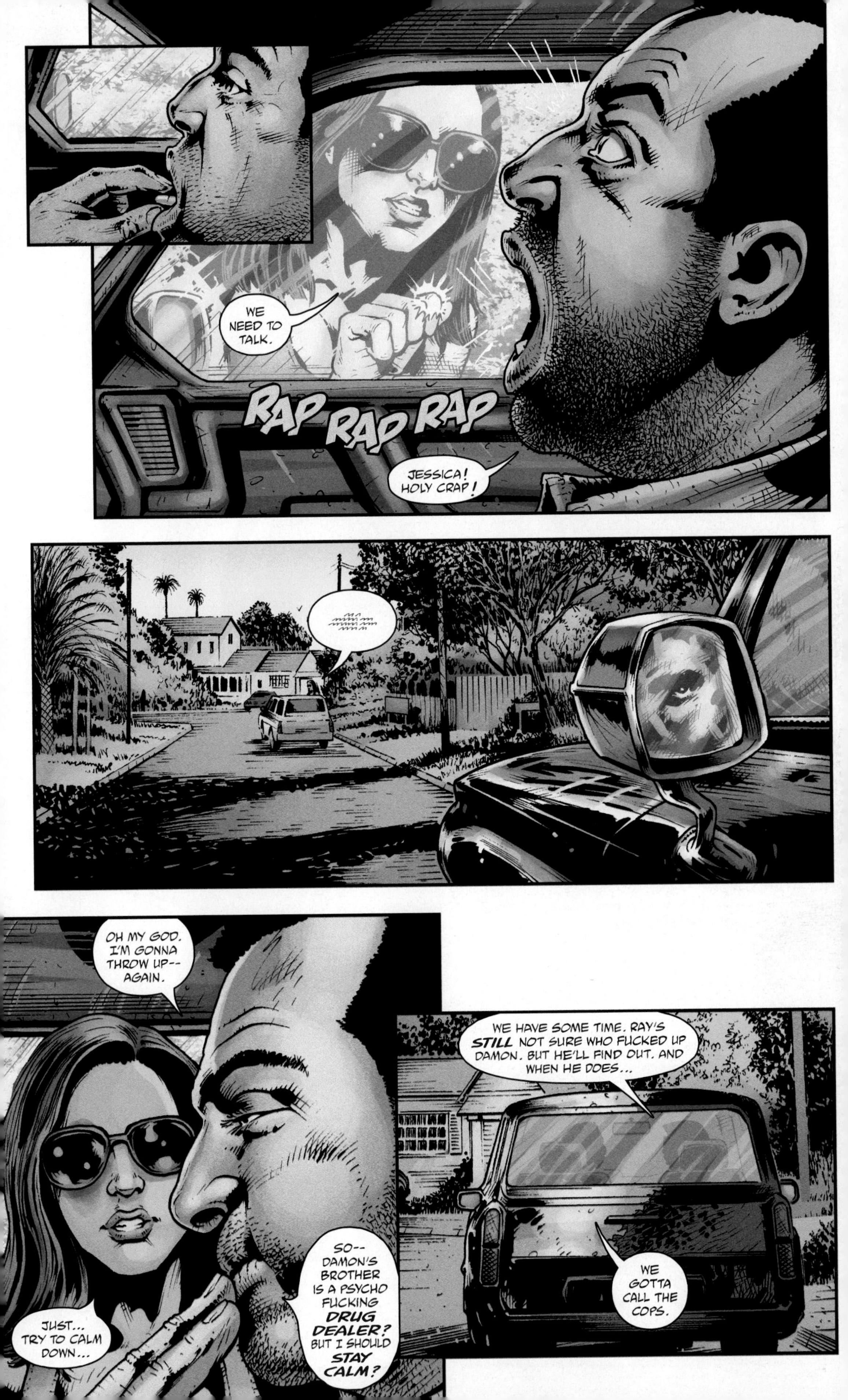
WE NEED TO TALK.
RAP RAP RAP
JESSICA! HOLY CRAP!
OH MY GOD. I'M GONNA THROW UP-- AGAIN.
JUST... TRY TO CALM DOWN...
SO-- DAMON'S BROTHER IS A PSYCHO FUCKING DRUG DEALER? BUT I SHOULD STAY CALM?
WE HAVE SOME TIME. RAY'S STILL NOT SURE WHO FUCKED UP DAMON. BUT HE'LL FIND OUT. AND WHEN HE DOES...
WE GOTTA CALL THE COPS.

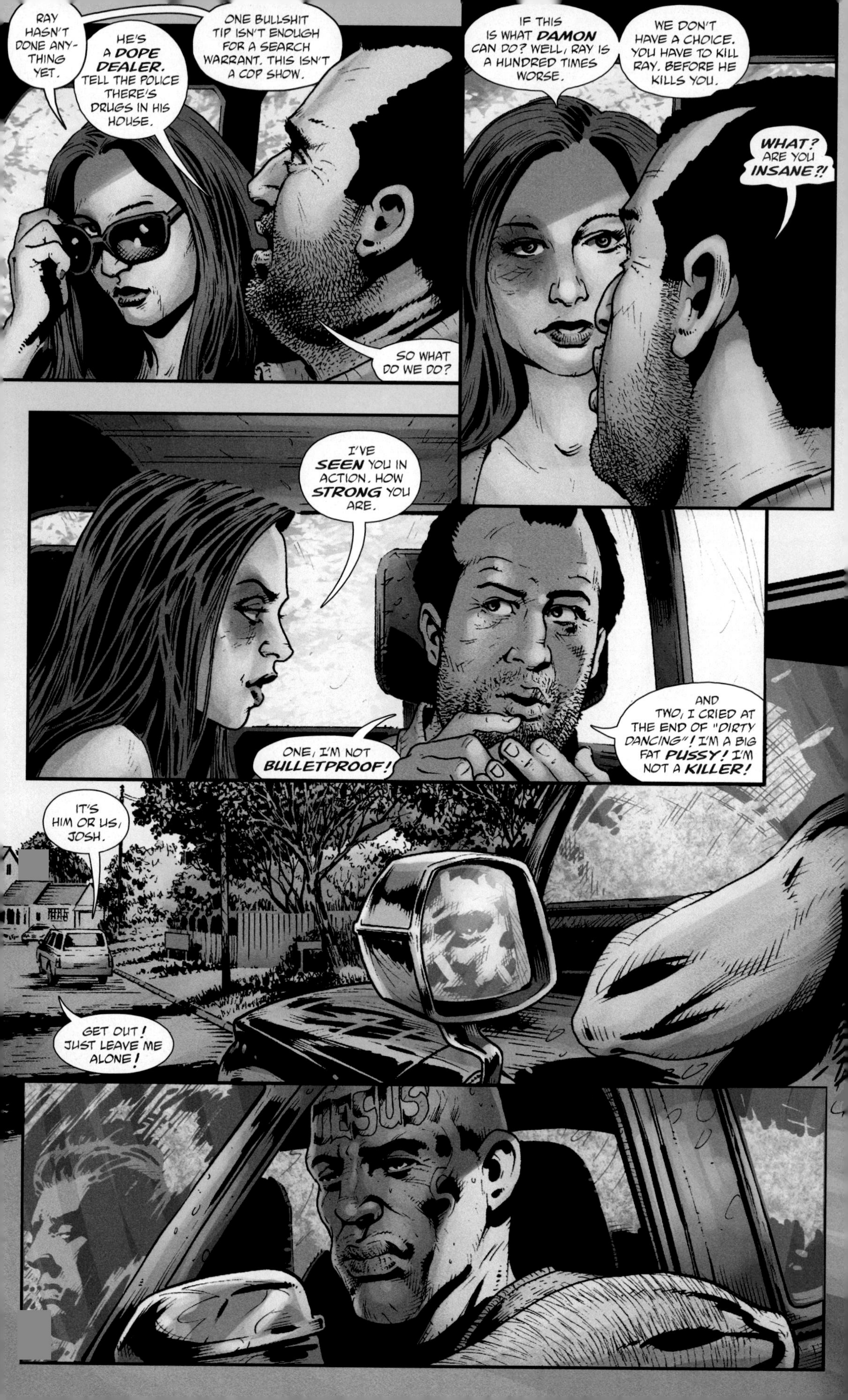
RAY HASN'T DONE ANYTHING YET.
HE'S A DOPE DEALER. TELL THE POLICE THERE'S DRUGS IN HIS HOUSE.
ONE BULLSHIT TIP ISN'T ENOUGH FOR A SEARCH WARRANT. THIS ISN'T A COP SHOW.
SO WHAT DO WE DO?
IF THIS IS WHAT DAMON CAN DO? WELL, RAY IS A HUNDRED TIMES WORSE.
WE DON'T HAVE A CHOICE. YOU HAVE TO KILL RAY. BEFORE HE KILLS YOU.
WHAT? ARE YOU INSANE?!
I'VE SEEN YOU IN ACTION. HOW STRONG YOU ARE.
ONE, I'M NOT BULLETPROOF!
AND TWO, I CRIED AT THE END OF "DIRTY DANCING"! I'M A BIG FAT PUSSY! I'M NOT A KILLER!
IT'S HIM OR US, JOSH.
GET OUT! JUST LEAVE ME ALONE!
JESUS

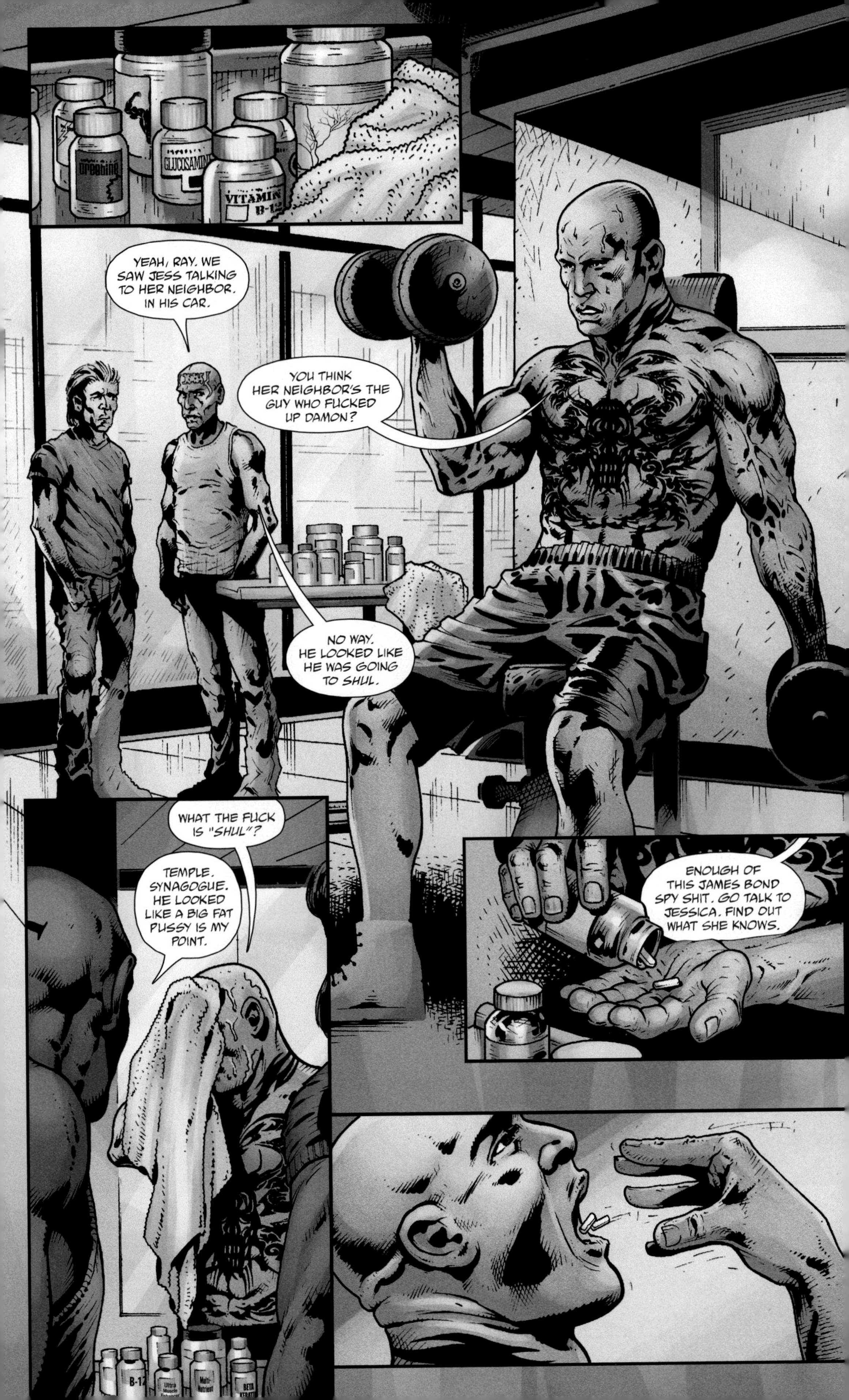
GLUCOSAMINE
VITAMIN B-12
YEAH, RAY. WE SAW JESS TALKING TO HER NEIGHBOR. IN HIS CAR.
YOU THINK HER NEIGHBOR'S THE GUY WHO FUCKED UP DAMON?
NO WAY. HE LOOKED LIKE HE WAS GOING TO SHUL.
WHAT THE FUCK IS "SHUL"?
TEMPLE. SYNAGOGUE. HE LOOKED LIKE A BIG FAT PUSSY IS MY POINT.
ENOUGH OF THIS JAMES BOND SPY SHIT. GO TALK TO JESSICA. FIND OUT WHAT SHE KNOWS.

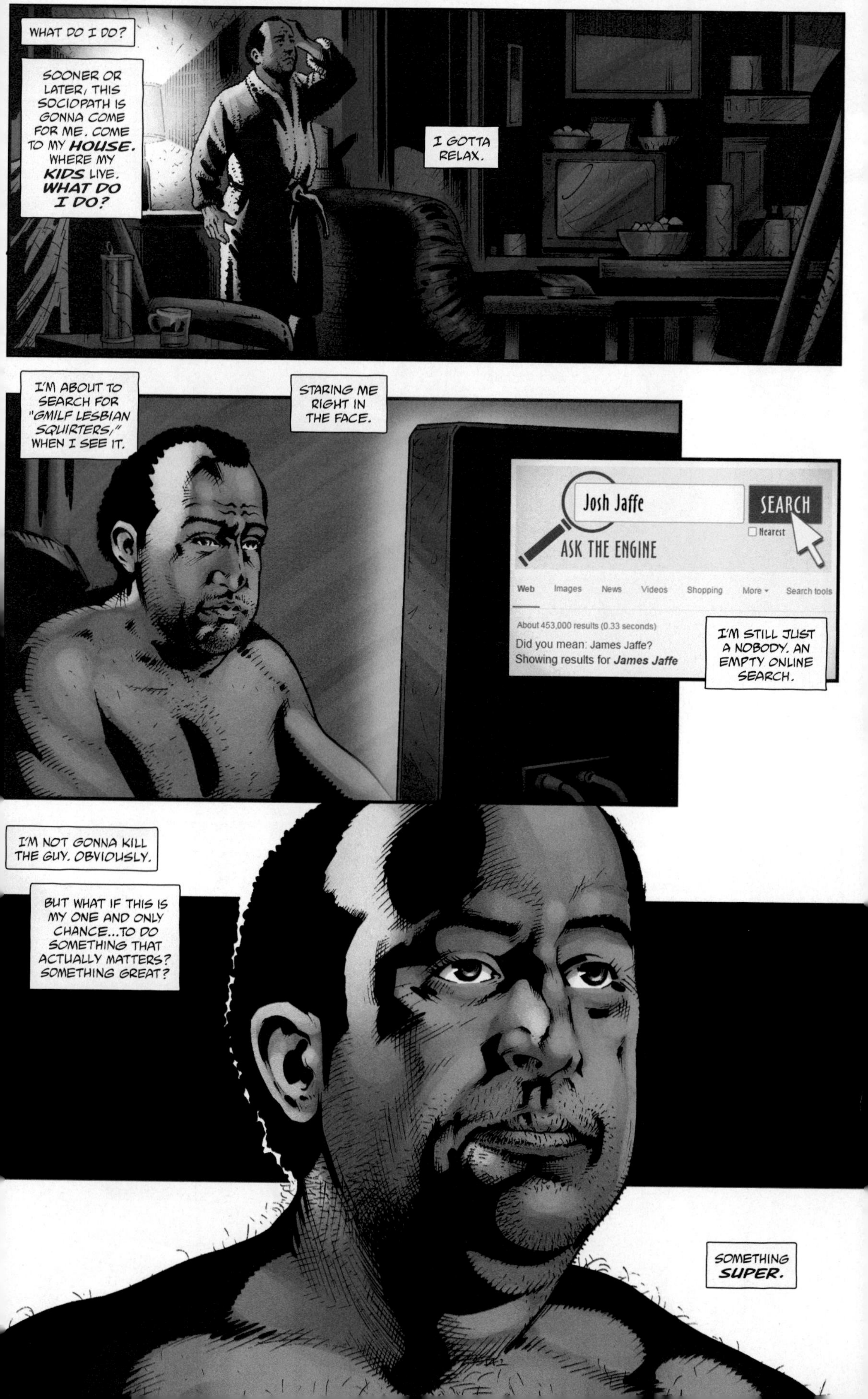
WHAT DO I DO?
SOONER OR LATER, THIS SOCIOPATH IS GONNA COME FOR ME. COME TO MY HOUSE. WHERE MY KIDS LIVE. WHAT DO I DO?
I GOTTA RELAX.
I'M ABOUT TO SEARCH FOR "GMILF LESBIAN SQUIRTERS," WHEN I SEE IT.
STARING ME RIGHT IN THE FACE.
Josh Jaffe
SEARCH
Nearest
ASK THE ENGINE
Web
Images
News
Videos
Shopping
More
Search tools
About 453,000 results (0.33 seconds)
Did you mean: James Jaffe?
Showing results for James Jaffe
I'M STILL JUST A NOBODY. AN EMPTY ONLINE SEARCH.
I'M NOT GONNA KILL THE GUY. OBVIOUSLY.
BUT WHAT IF THIS IS MY ONE AND ONLY CHANCE...TO DO SOMETHING THAT ACTUALLY MATTERS? SOMETHING GREAT?
SOMETHING SUPER.

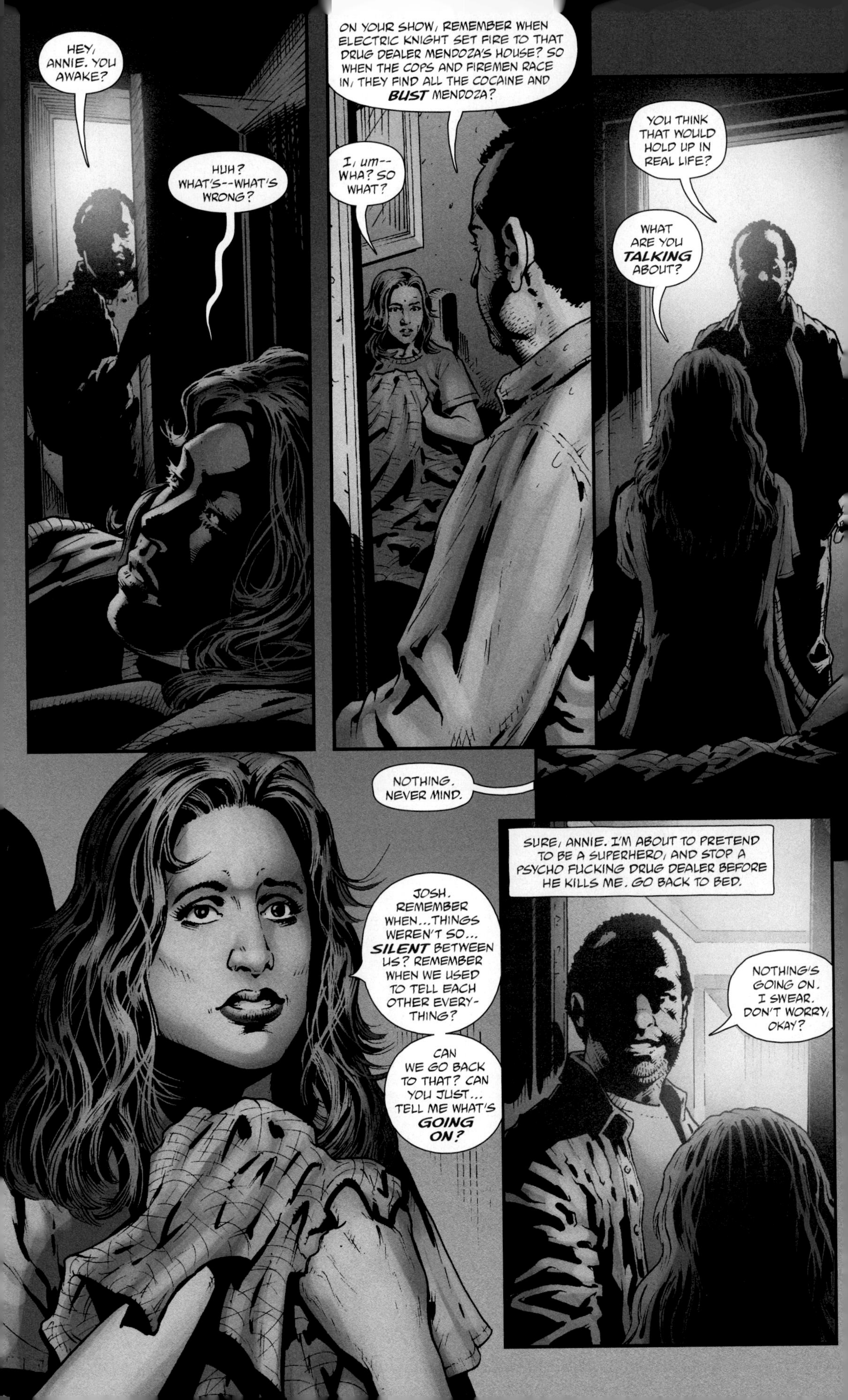
HEY, ANNIE. YOU AWAKE?
HUH? WHAT'S--WHAT'S WRONG?
ON YOUR SHOW, REMEMBER WHEN ELECTRIC KNIGHT SET FIRE TO THAT DRUG DEALER MENDOZA'S HOUSE? SO WHEN THE COPS AND FIREMEN RACE IN, THEY FIND ALL THE COCAINE AND BUST MENDOZA?
I, UM-- WHA? SO WHAT?
YOU THINK THAT WOULD HOLD UP IN REAL LIFE?
WHAT ARE YOU TALKING ABOUT?
NOTHING. NEVER MIND.
SURE, ANNIE. I'M ABOUT TO PRETEND TO BE A SUPERHERO, AND STOP A PSYCHO FUCKING DRUG DEALER BEFORE HE KILLS ME. GO BACK TO BED.
JOSH. REMEMBER WHEN...THINGS WEREN'T SO... SILENT BETWEEN US? REMEMBER WHEN WE USED TO TELL EACH OTHER EVERY-THING?
CAN WE GO BACK TO THAT? CAN YOU JUST... TELL ME WHAT'S GOING ON?
NOTHING'S GOING ON. I SWEAR. DON'T WORRY, OKAY?

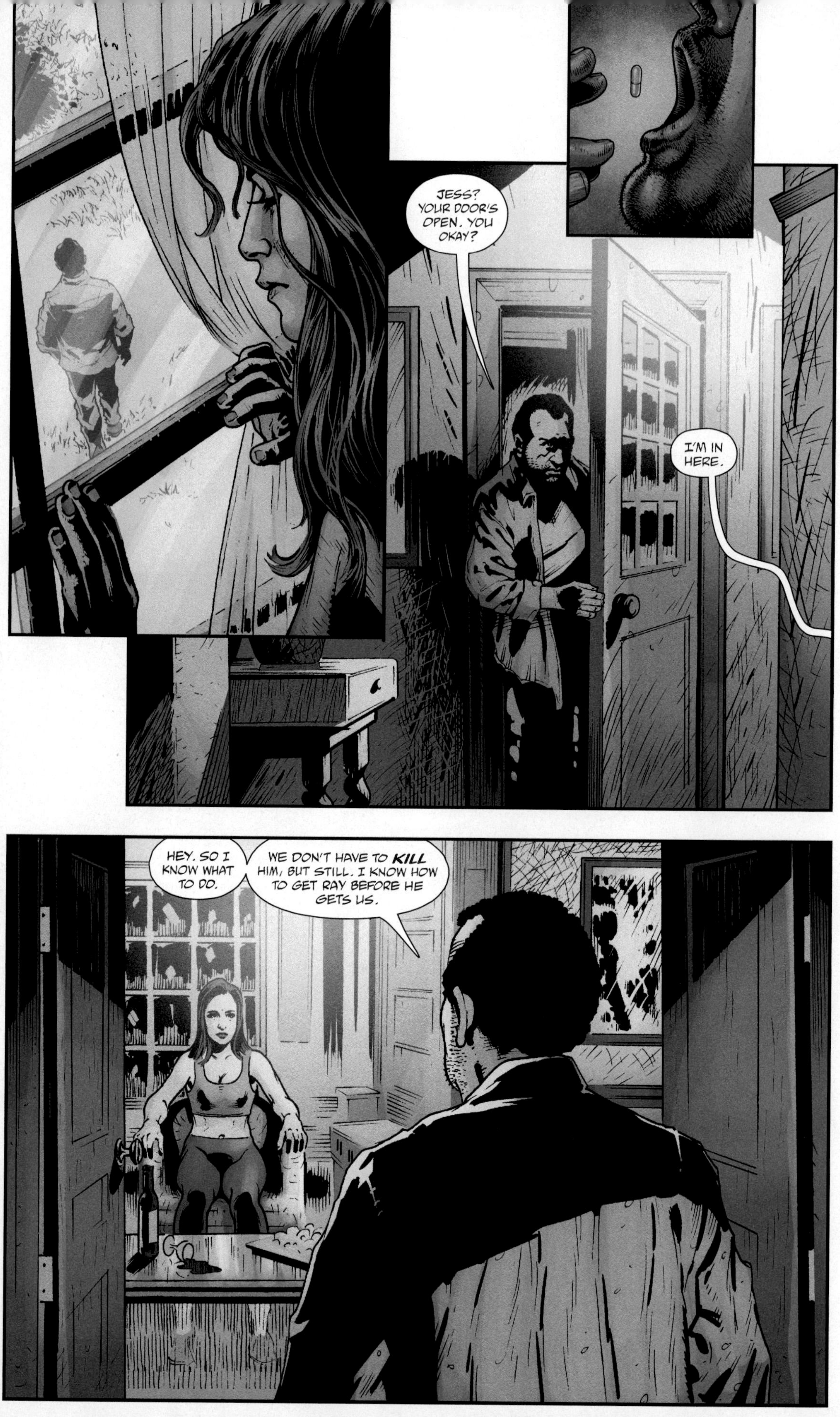

JESS? YOUR DOOR'S OPEN. YOU OKAY?
I'M IN HERE.
HEY. SO I KNOW WHAT TO DO.
WE DON'T HAVE TO **KILL** HIM, BUT STILL. I KNOW HOW TO GET RAY BEFORE HE GETS US.

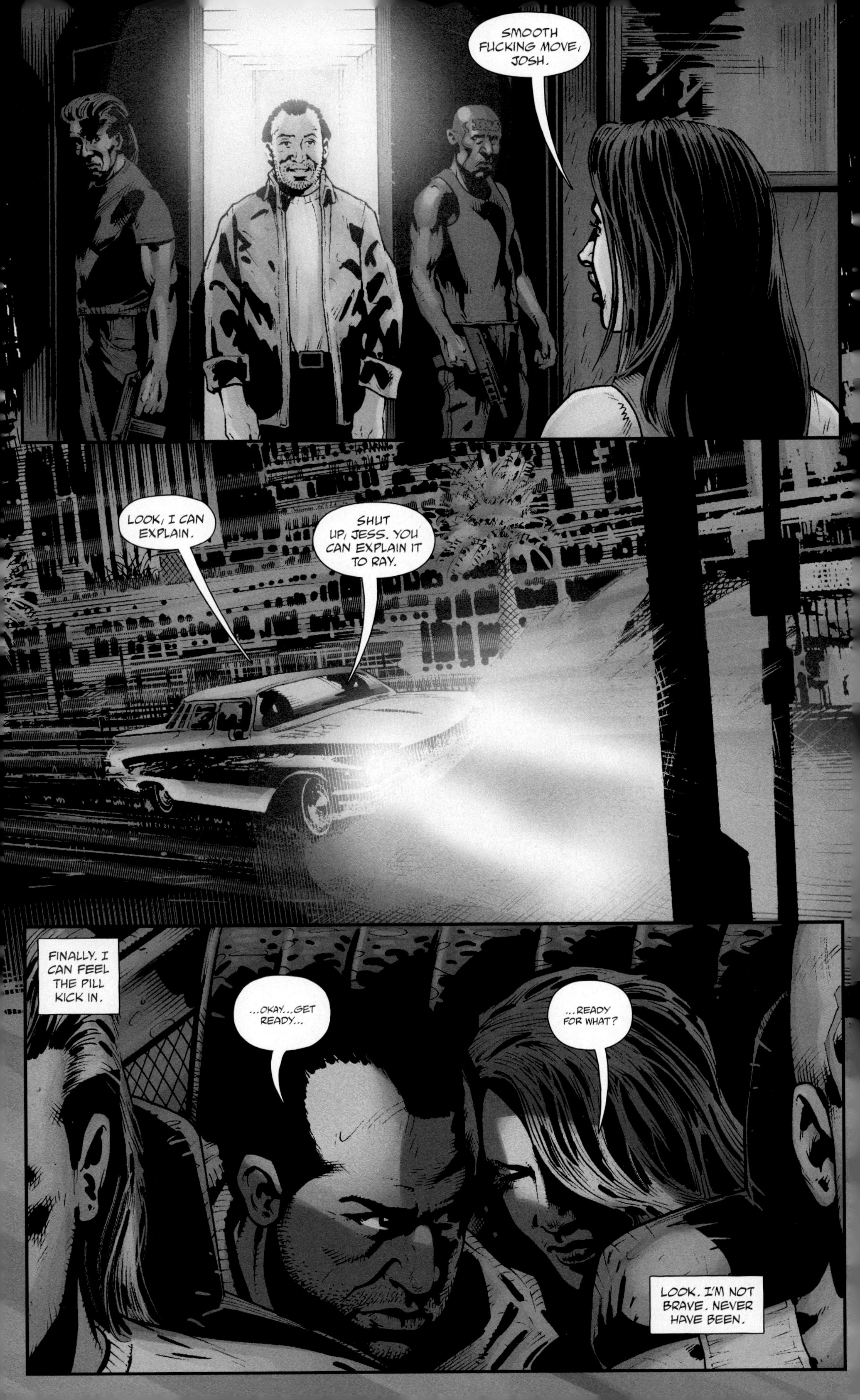
SMOOTH FUCKING MOVE, JOSH.
LOOK, I CAN EXPLAIN.
SHUT UP, JESS. YOU CAN EXPLAIN IT TO RAY.
FINALLY. I CAN FEEL THE PILL KICK IN.
...OKAY...GET READY...
...READY FOR WHAT?
LOOK. I'M NOT BRAVE. NEVER HAVE BEEN.

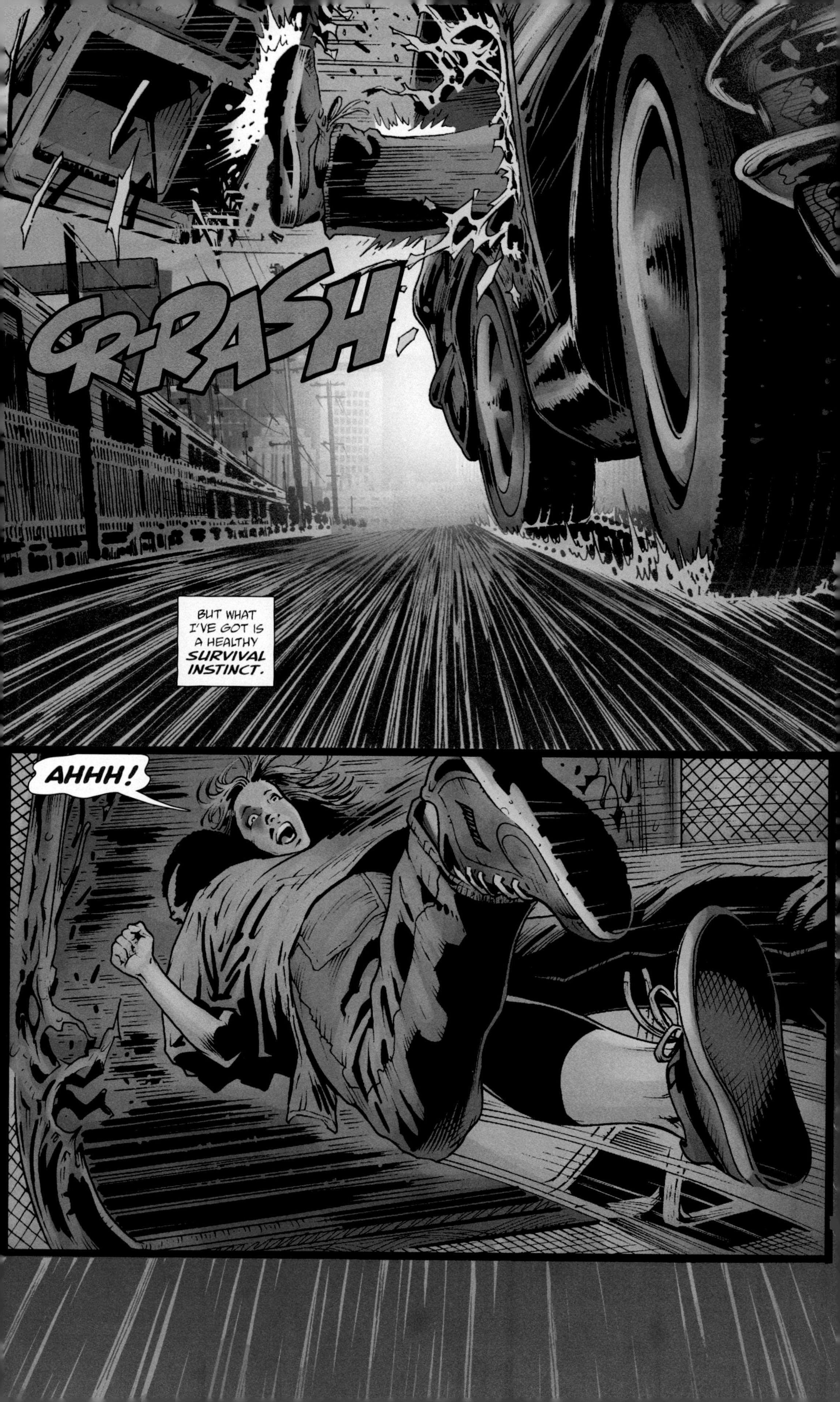
CR-RASH
BUT WHAT I'VE GOT IS A HEALTHY SURVIVAL INSTINCT.
AHHH!

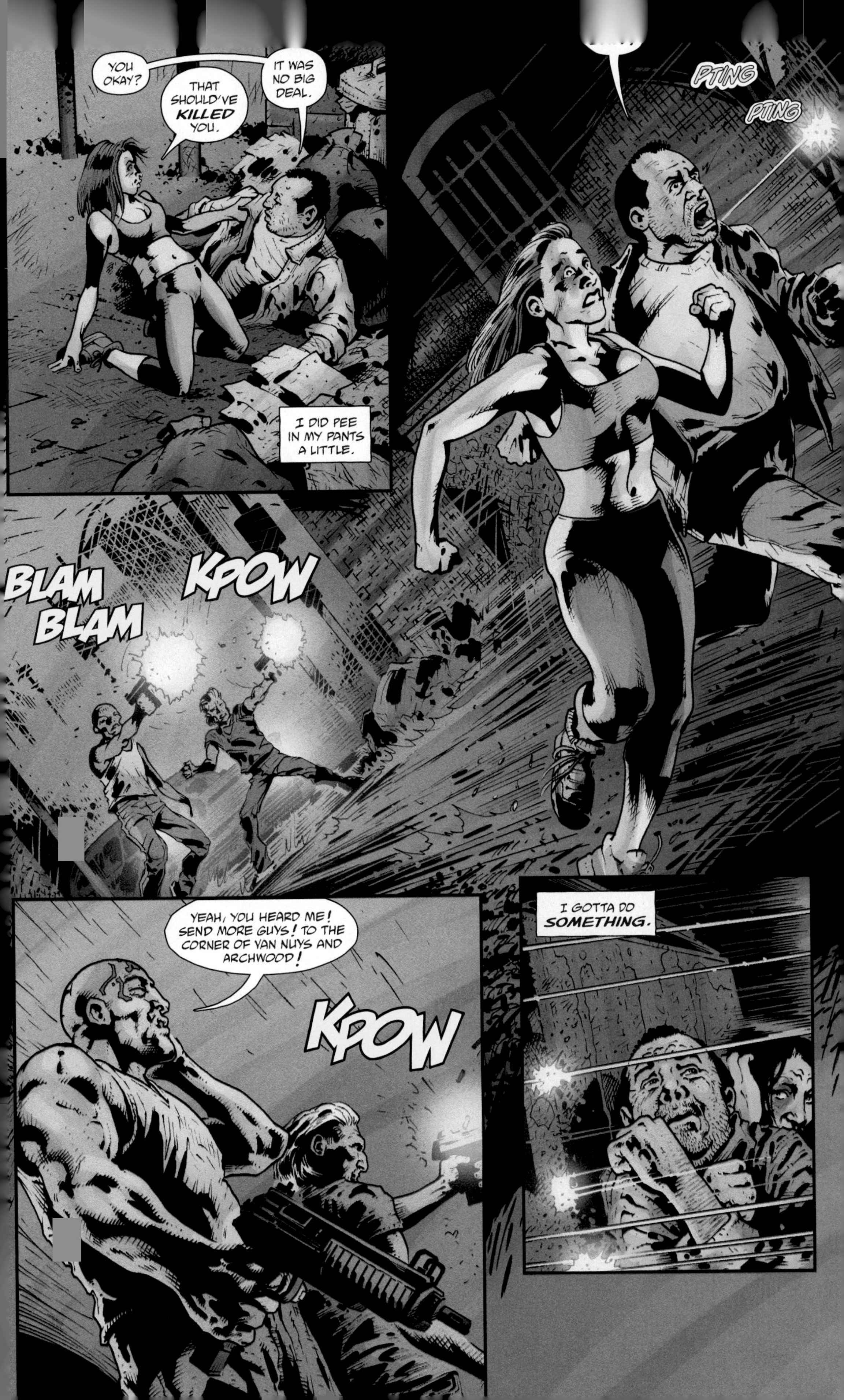

YOU OKAY?
THAT SHOULD'VE KILLED YOU.
IT WAS NO BIG DEAL.
I DID PEE IN MY PANTS A LITTLE.
PTING
PTING
BLAM BLAM
KPOW
YEAH, YOU HEARD ME! SEND MORE GUYS! TO THE CORNER OF VAN NUYS AND ARCHWOOD!
KPOW
I GOTTA DO SOMETHING.

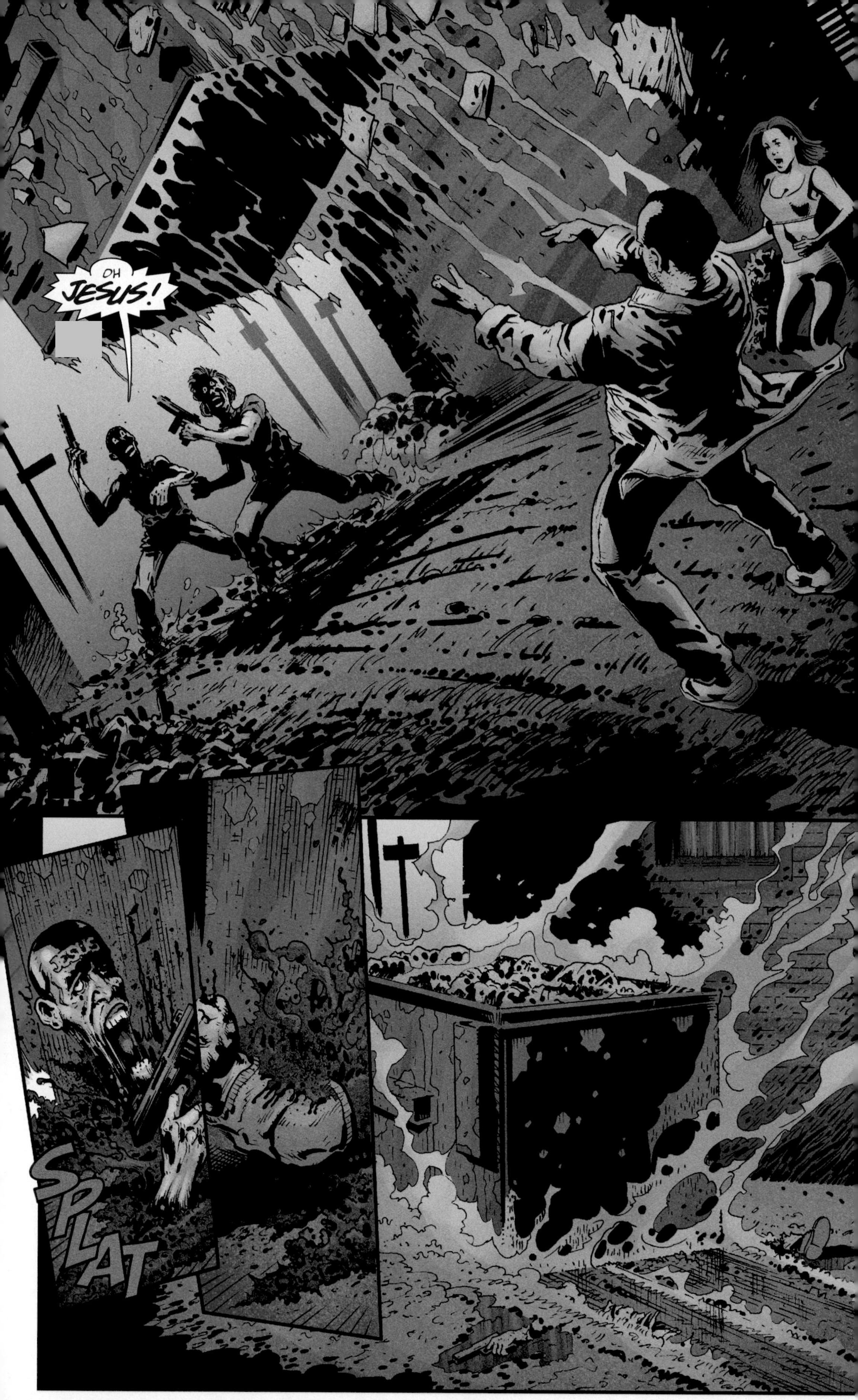
OH JESUS!
SPLAT

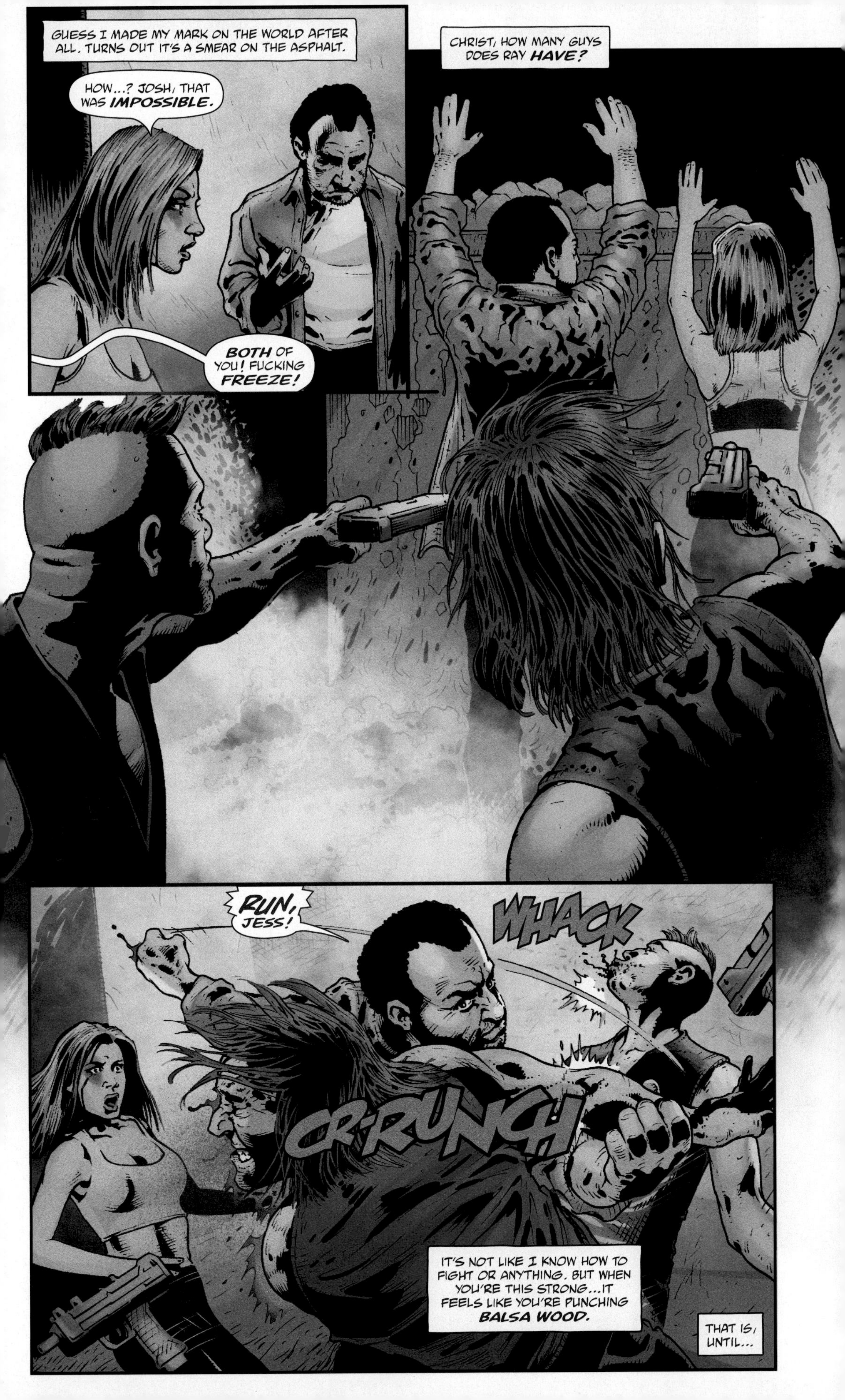
GUESS I MADE MY MARK ON THE WORLD AFTER ALL. TURNS OUT IT'S A SMEAR ON THE ASPHALT.
HOW...? JOSH, THAT WAS IMPOSSIBLE.
BOTH OF YOU! FUCKING FREEZE!
CHRIST, HOW MANY GUYS DOES RAY HAVE?
RUN, JESS!
WHACK
CR-RUNCH
IT'S NOT LIKE I KNOW HOW TO FIGHT OR ANYTHING. BUT WHEN YOU'RE THIS STRONG...IT FEELS LIKE YOU'RE PUNCHING BALSA WOOD.
THAT IS, UNTIL...

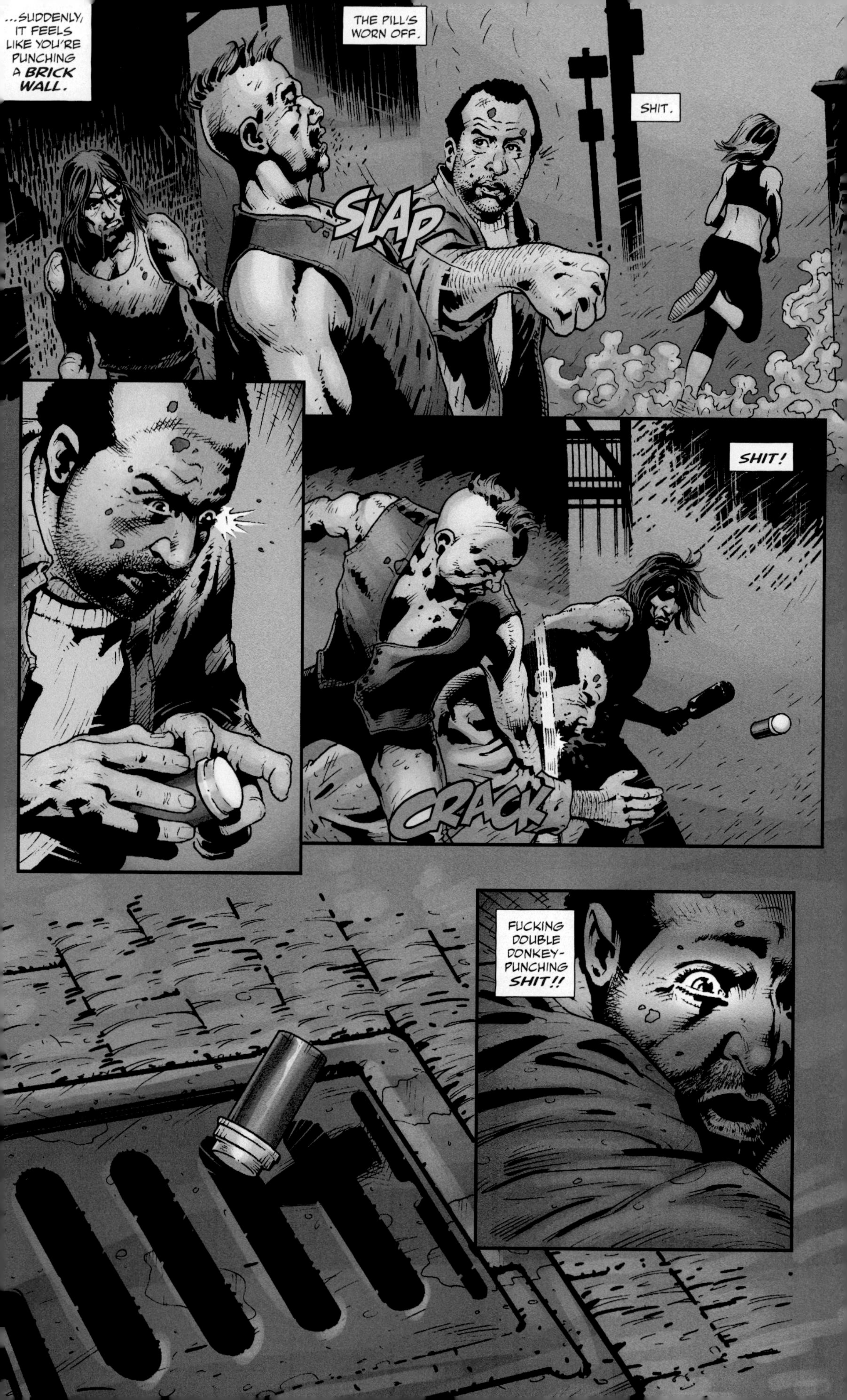
...SUDDENLY, IT FEELS LIKE YOU'RE PUNCHING A BRICK WALL.
THE PILL'S WORN OFF.
SLAP
SHIT.
SHIT!
CRACK
FUCKING DOUBLE DONKEY-PUNCHING SHIT!!

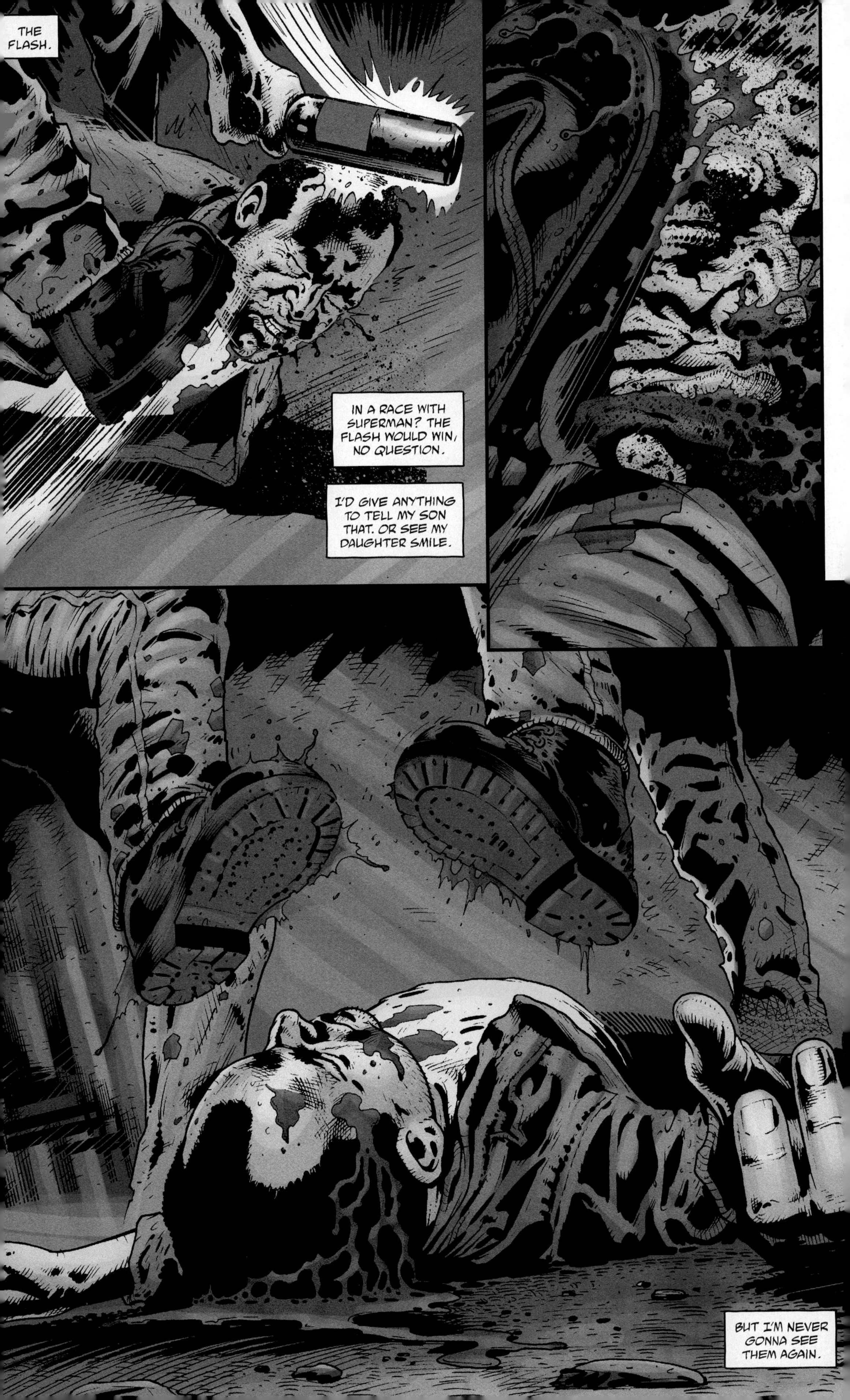
THE FLASH.
IN A RACE WITH SUPERMAN? THE FLASH WOULD WIN, NO QUESTION.
I'D GIVE ANYTHING TO TELL MY SON THAT. OR SEE MY DAUGHTER SMILE.
BUT I'M NEVER GONNA SEE THEM AGAIN.

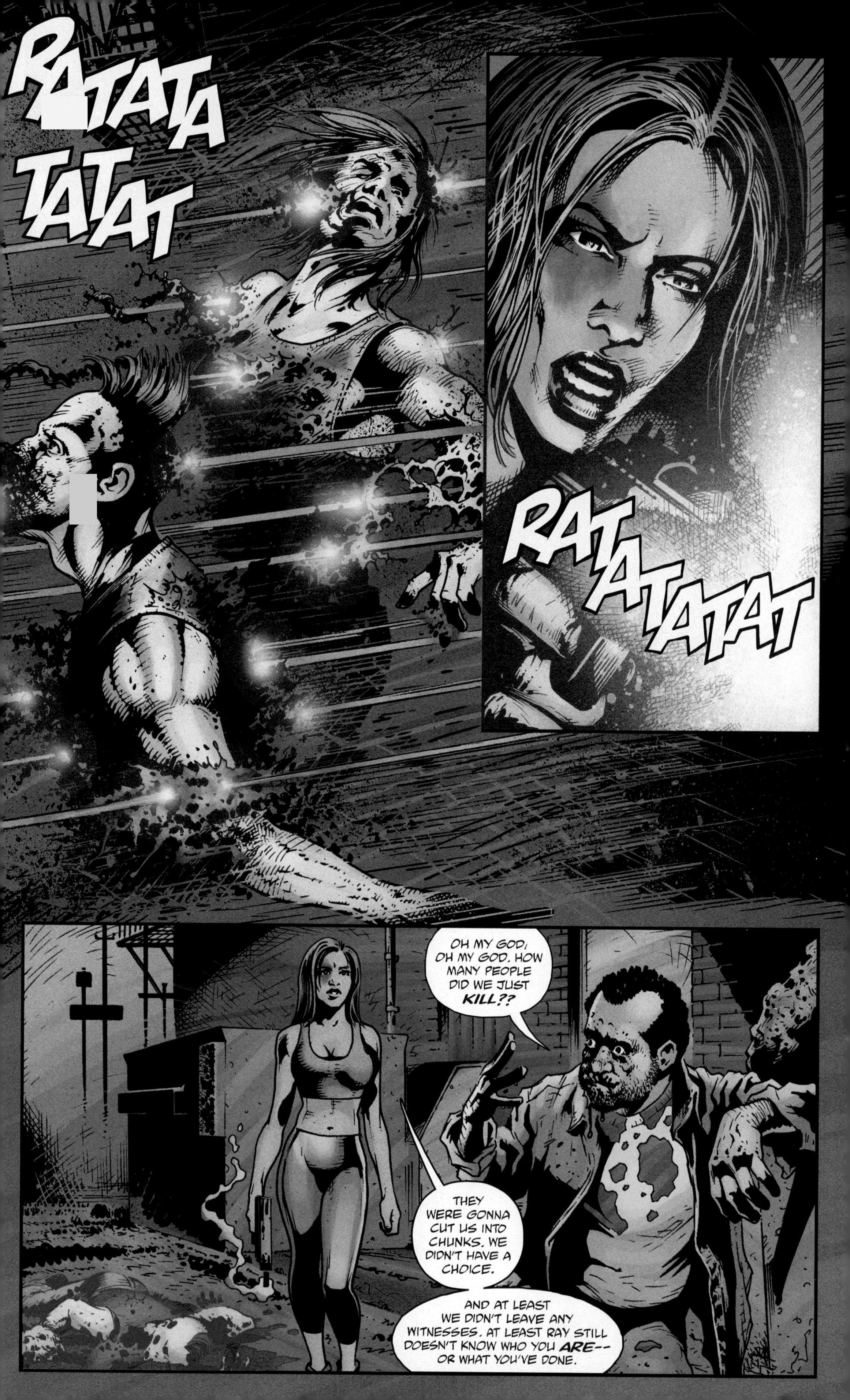
RATATATA
TATAT
RATATATATAT
OH MY GOD, OH MY GOD. HOW MANY PEOPLE DID WE JUST KILL??
THEY WERE GONNA CUT US INTO CHUNKS. WE DIDN'T HAVE A CHOICE.
AND AT LEAST WE DIDN'T LEAVE ANY WITNESSES. AT LEAST RAY STILL DOESN'T KNOW WHO YOU ARE-- OR WHAT YOU'VE DONE.

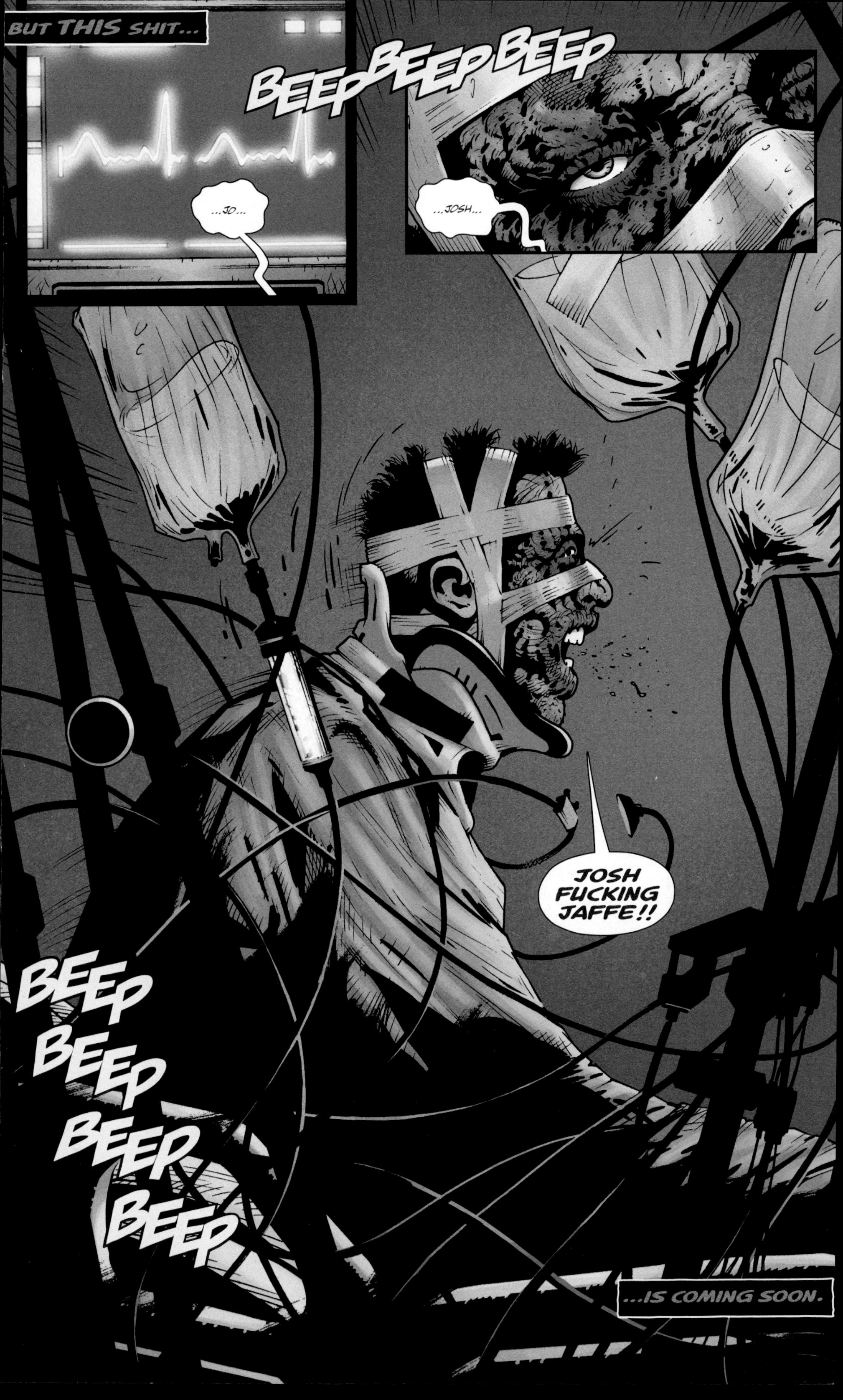
BUT THIS SHIT...
...JO...
BEEP BEEP BEEP
...JOSH...
JOSH FUCKING JAFFE!!
BEEP BEEP BEEP BEEP
...IS COMING SOON.

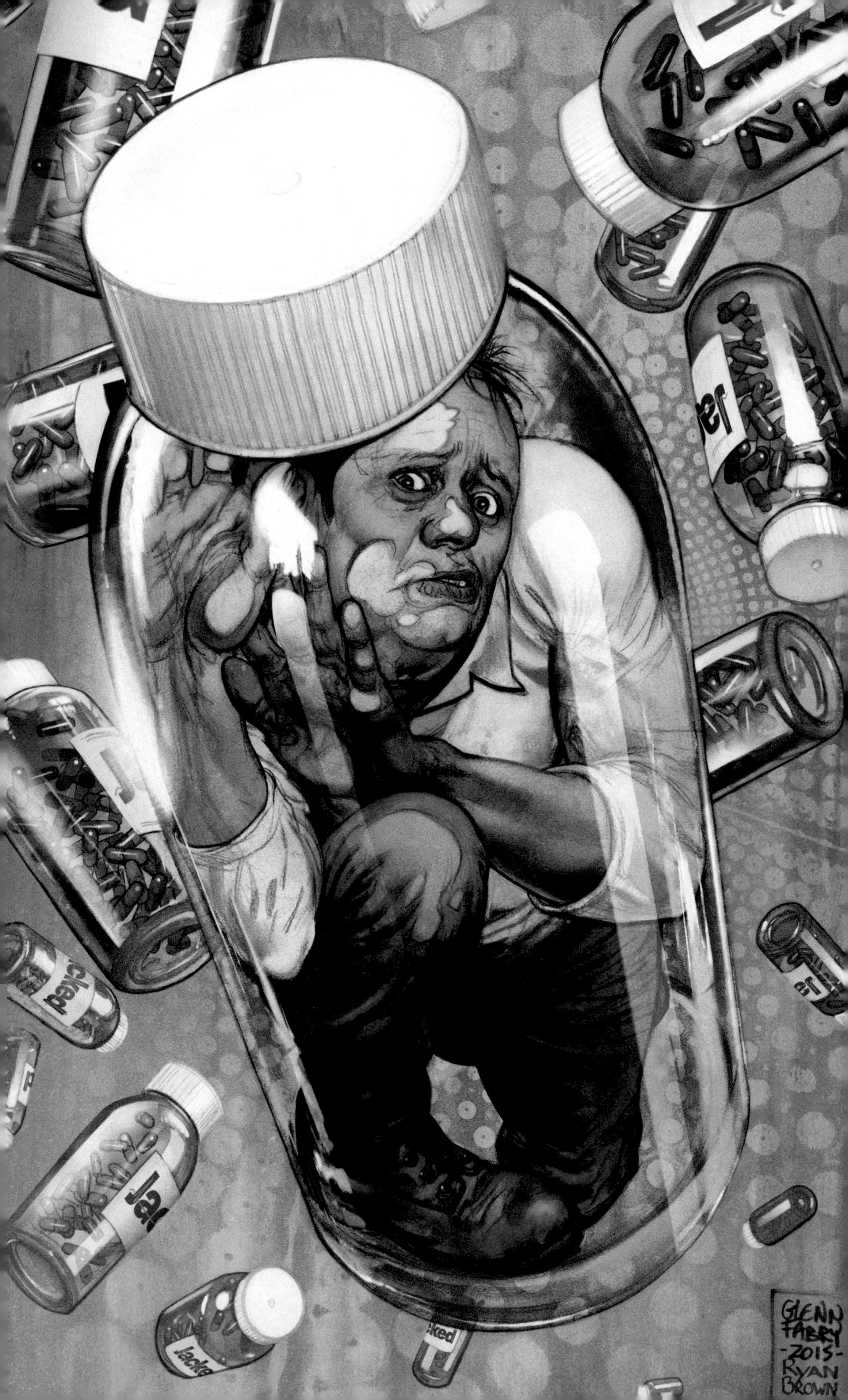
GLENN FABRY
-2015-
RYAN BROWN

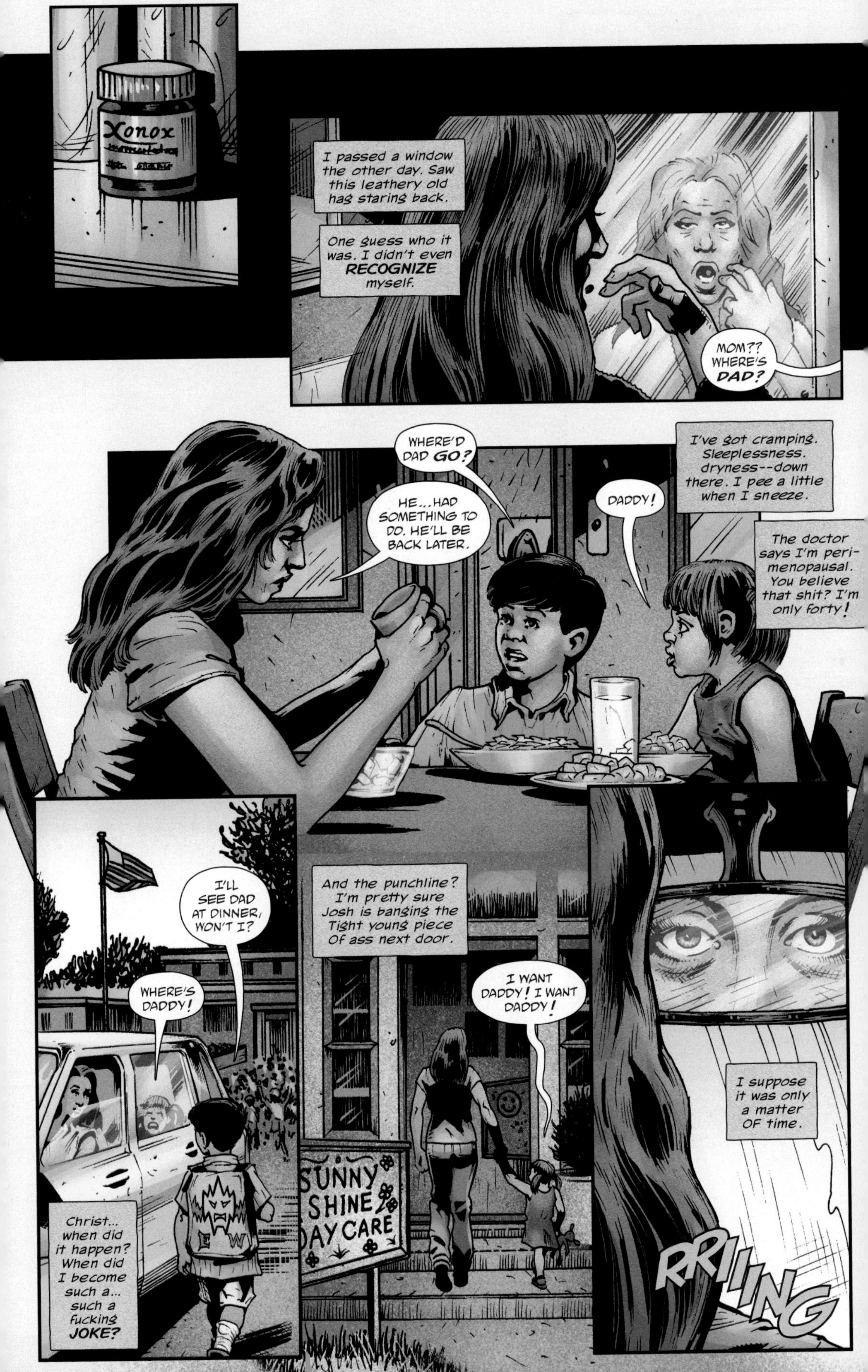
Xonox
I passed a window the other day. Saw this leathery old hag staring back.
One guess who it was. I didn't even RECOGNIZE myself.
MOM?? WHERE'S DAD?
WHERE'D DAD GO?
HE...HAD SOMETHING TO DO. HE'LL BE BACK LATER.
DADDY!
I've got cramping. Sleeplessness. dryness--down there. I pee a little when I sneeze.
The doctor says I'm peri-menopausal. You believe that shit? I'm only forty!
I'LL SEE DAD AT DINNER, WON'T I?
WHERE'S DADDY!
Christ... when did it happen? When did I become such a... such a fucking JOKE?
And the punchline? I'm pretty sure Josh is banging the tight young piece of ass next door.
I WANT DADDY! I WANT DADDY!
SUNNY SHINE DAY CARE
I suppose it was only a matter of time.
RRIIING

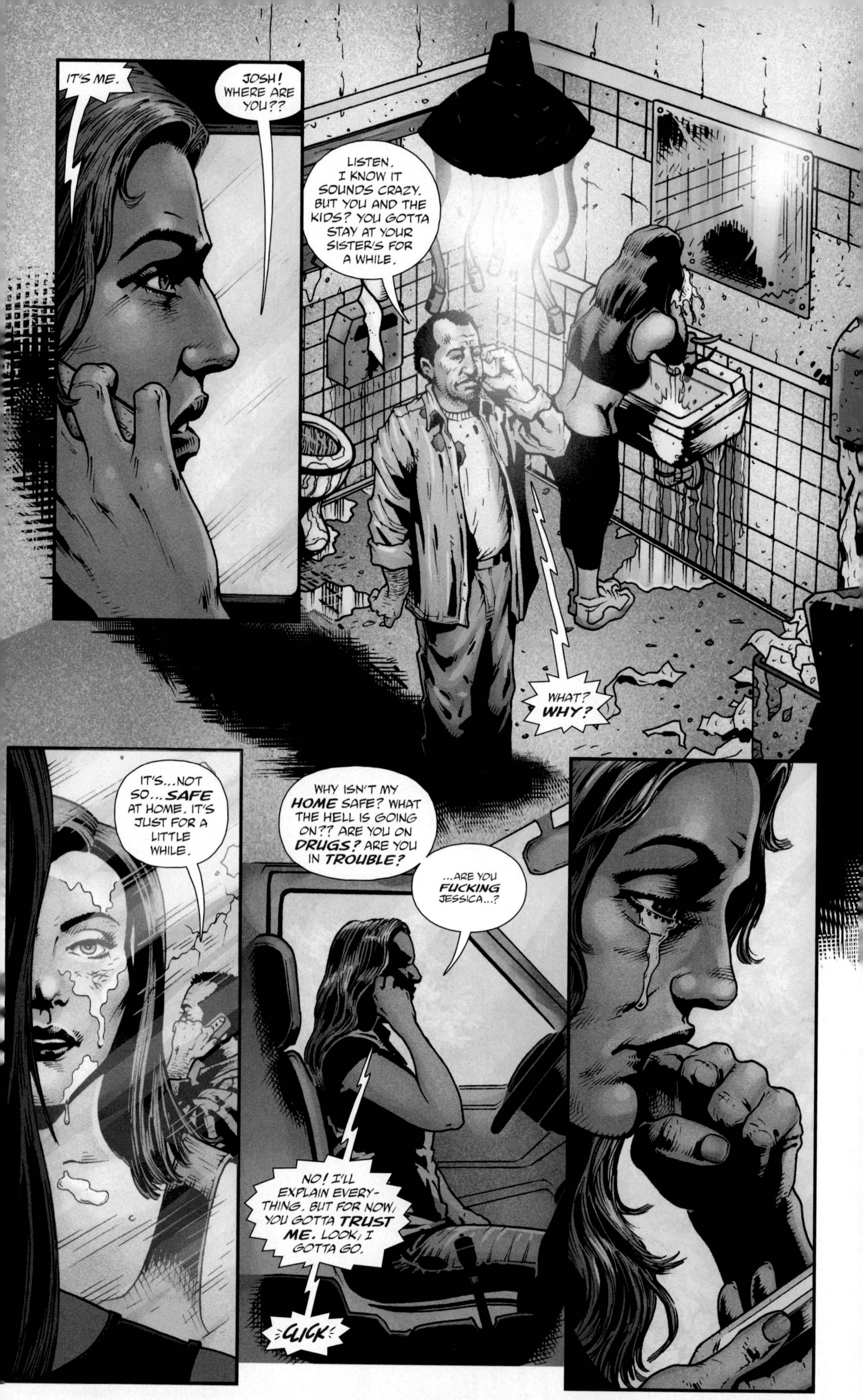
IT'S ME.
JOSH! WHERE ARE YOU??
LISTEN. I KNOW IT SOUNDS CRAZY. BUT YOU AND THE KIDS? YOU GOTTA STAY AT YOUR SISTER'S FOR A WHILE.
WHAT? WHY?
IT'S...NOT SO...SAFE AT HOME. IT'S JUST FOR A LITTLE WHILE.
WHY ISN'T MY HOME SAFE? WHAT THE HELL IS GOING ON?? ARE YOU ON DRUGS? ARE YOU IN TROUBLE?
...ARE YOU FUCKING JESSICA...?
NO! I'LL EXPLAIN EVERY-THING. BUT FOR NOW, YOU GOTTA TRUST ME. LOOK, I GOTTA GO.
CLICK

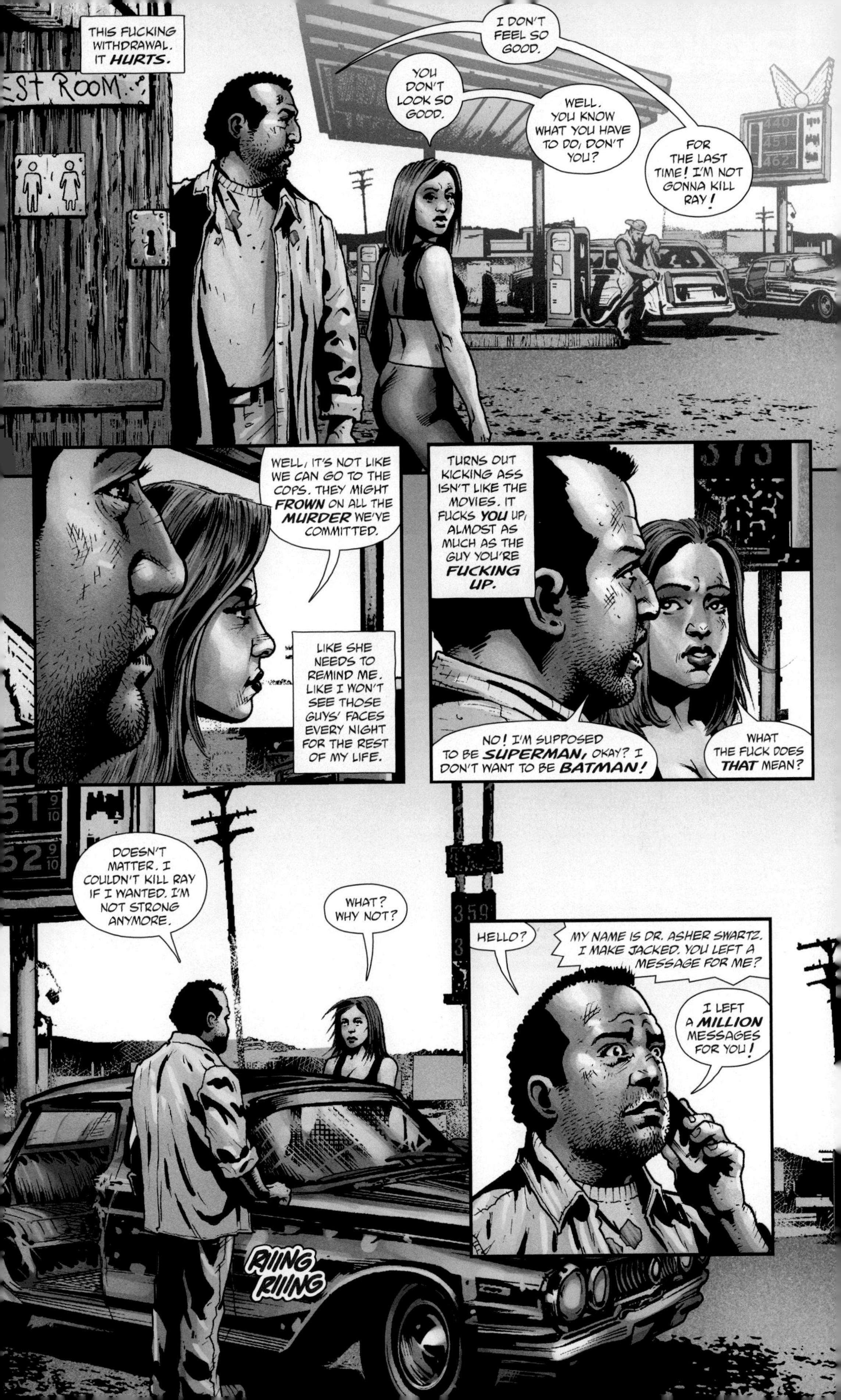

THIS FUCKING WITHDRAWAL. IT HURTS.
EST ROOM
I DON'T FEEL SO GOOD.
YOU DON'T LOOK SO GOOD.
WELL. YOU KNOW WHAT YOU HAVE TO DO, DON'T YOU?
FOR THE LAST TIME! I'M NOT GONNA KILL RAY!
WELL, IT'S NOT LIKE WE CAN GO TO THE COPS. THEY MIGHT FROWN ON ALL THE MURDER WE'VE COMMITTED.
LIKE SHE NEEDS TO REMIND ME. LIKE I WON'T SEE THOSE GUYS' FACES EVERY NIGHT FOR THE REST OF MY LIFE.
TURNS OUT KICKING ASS ISN'T LIKE THE MOVIES. IT FUCKS YOU UP, ALMOST AS MUCH AS THE GUY YOU'RE FUCKING UP.
NO! I'M SUPPOSED TO BE SUPERMAN, OKAY? I DON'T WANT TO BE BATMAN!
WHAT THE FUCK DOES THAT MEAN?
DOESN'T MATTER. I COULDN'T KILL RAY IF I WANTED. I'M NOT STRONG ANYMORE.
WHAT? WHY NOT?
RIIING RIIING
HELLO?
MY NAME IS DR. ASHER SWARTZ. I MAKE JACKED. YOU LEFT A MESSAGE FOR ME?
I LEFT A MILLION MESSAGES FOR YOU!

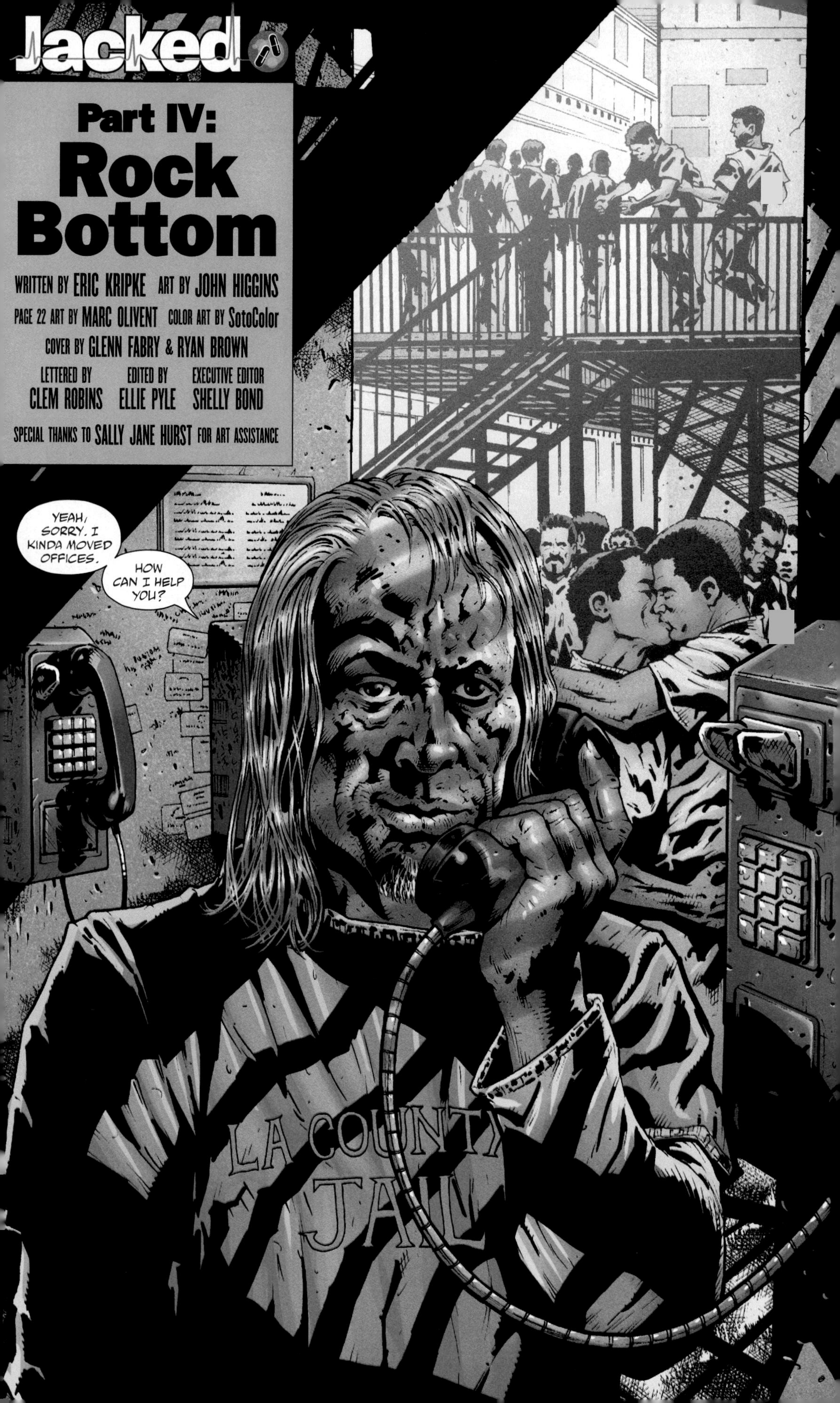
Jacked
Part IV:
Rock Bottom
WRITTEN BY ERIC KRIPKE ART BY JOHN HIGGINS
PAGE 22 ART BY MARC OLIVENT COLOR ART BY SotoColor
COVER BY GLENN FABRY & RYAN BROWN
LETTERED BY CLEM ROBINS
EDITED BY ELLIE PYLE
EXECUTIVE EDITOR SHELLY BOND
SPECIAL THANKS TO SALLY JANE HURST FOR ART ASSISTANCE
YEAH, SORRY. I KINDA MOVED OFFICES.
HOW CAN I HELP YOU?
LA COUNTY JAIL

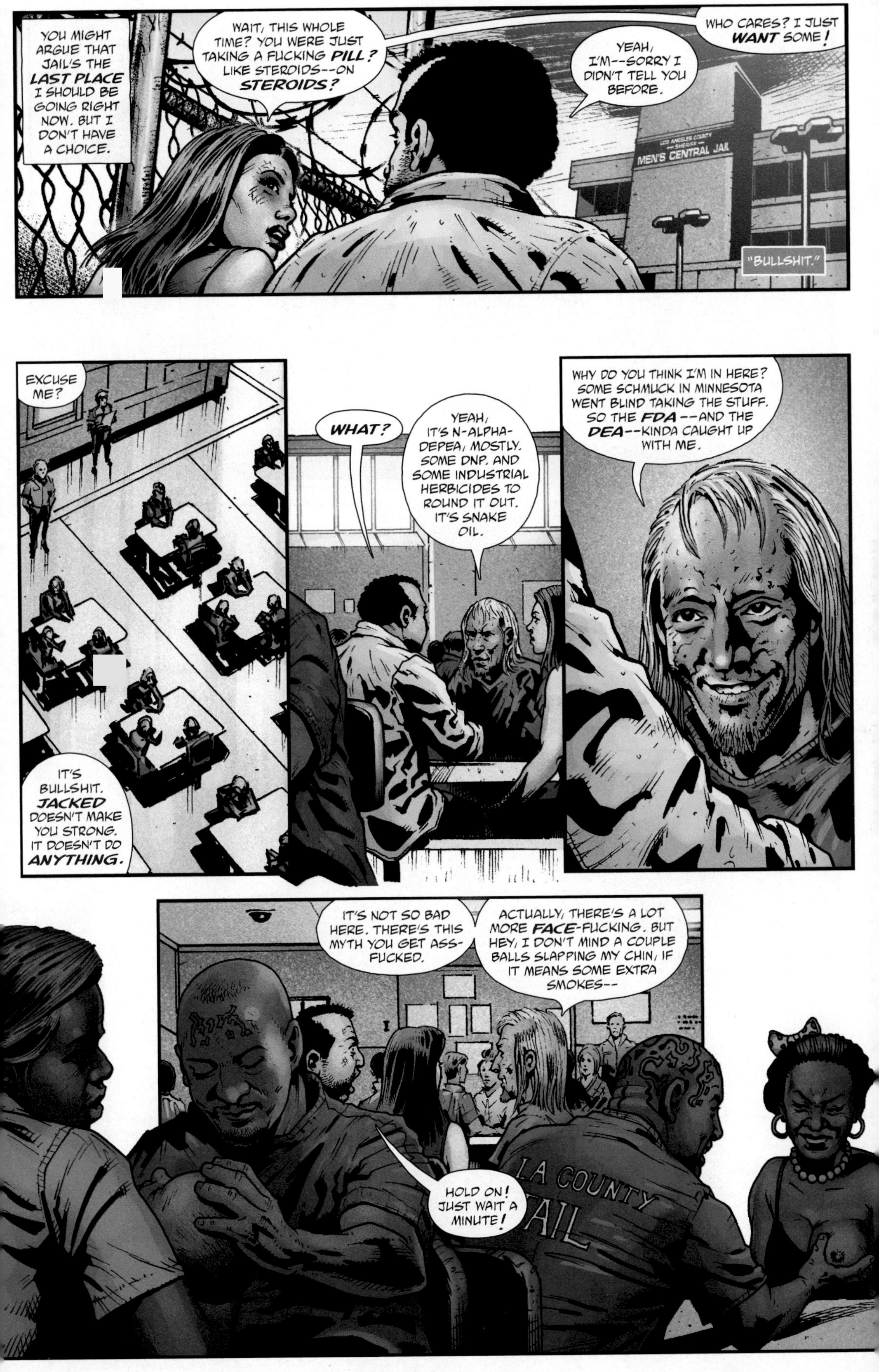
YOU MIGHT ARGUE THAT JAIL'S THE LAST PLACE I SHOULD BE GOING RIGHT NOW. BUT I DON'T HAVE A CHOICE.
WAIT, THIS WHOLE TIME? YOU WERE JUST TAKING A FUCKING PILL? LIKE STEROIDS--ON STEROIDS?
YEAH, I'M--SORRY I DIDN'T TELL YOU BEFORE.
WHO CARES? I JUST WANT SOME!
LOS ANGELES COUNTY SHERIFF MEN'S CENTRAL JAIL
"BULLSHIT."
EXCUSE ME?
IT'S BULLSHIT. JACKED DOESN'T MAKE YOU STRONG. IT DOESN'T DO ANYTHING.
WHAT?
YEAH, IT'S N-ALPHA-DEPEA, MOSTLY. SOME DNP. AND SOME INDUSTRIAL HERBICIDES TO ROUND IT OUT. IT'S SNAKE OIL.
WHY DO YOU THINK I'M IN HERE? SOME SCHMUCK IN MINNESOTA WENT BLIND TAKING THE STUFF. SO THE FDA--AND THE DEA--KINDA CAUGHT UP WITH ME.
IT'S NOT SO BAD HERE. THERE'S THIS MYTH YOU GET ASS-FUCKED.
ACTUALLY, THERE'S A LOT MORE FACE-FUCKING. BUT HEY, I DON'T MIND A COUPLE BALLS SLAPPING MY CHIN, IF IT MEANS SOME EXTRA SMOKES--
HOLD ON! JUST WAIT A MINUTE!
LA COUNTY JAIL

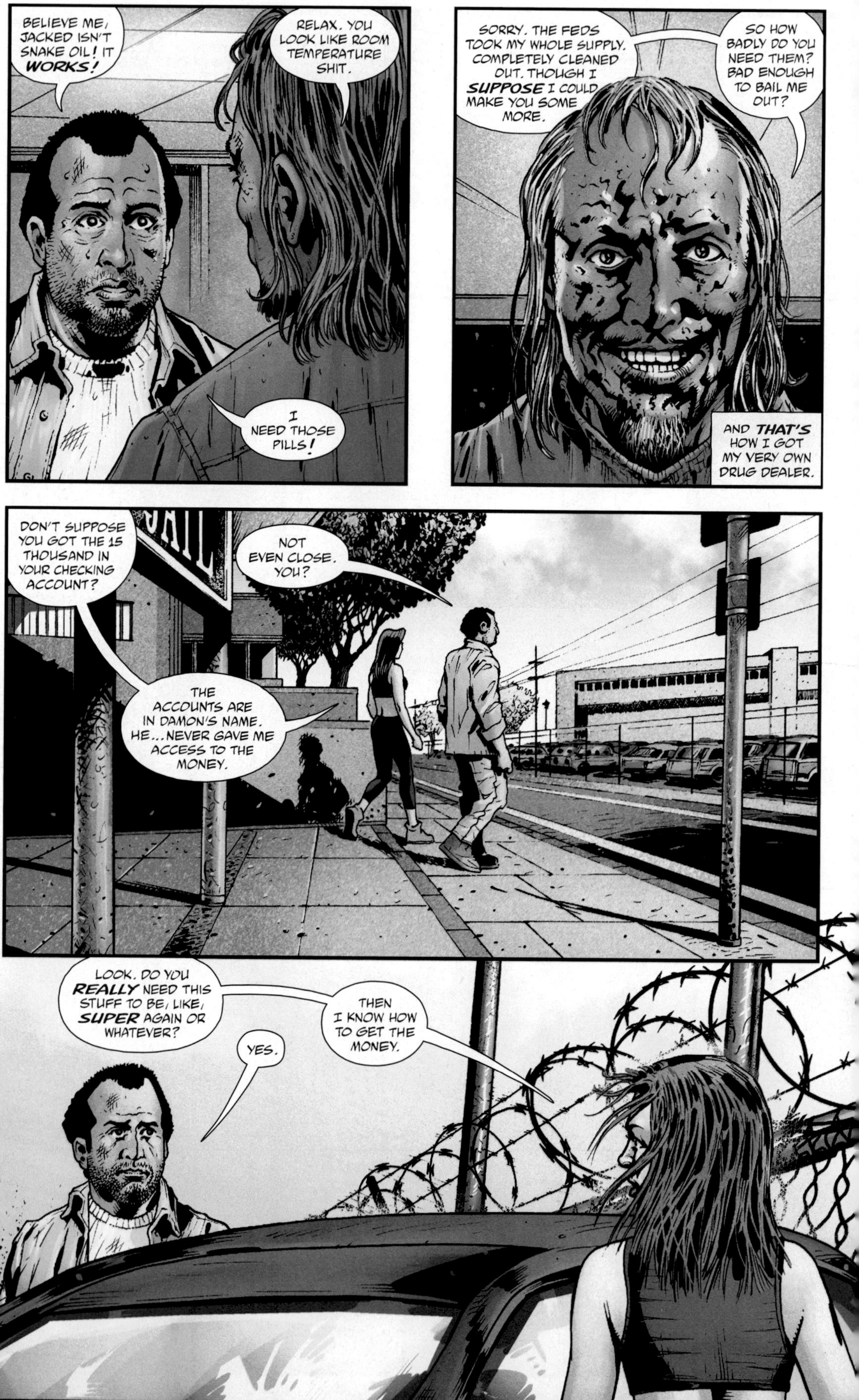
BELIEVE ME, JACKED ISN'T SNAKE OIL! IT WORKS!
RELAX. YOU LOOK LIKE ROOM TEMPERATURE SHIT.
I NEED THOSE PILLS!
SORRY. THE FEDS TOOK MY WHOLE SUPPLY. COMPLETELY CLEANED OUT. THOUGH I SUPPOSE I COULD MAKE YOU SOME MORE.
SO HOW BADLY DO YOU NEED THEM? BAD ENOUGH TO BAIL ME OUT?
AND THAT'S HOW I GOT MY VERY OWN DRUG DEALER.
DON'T SUPPOSE YOU GOT THE 15 THOUSAND IN YOUR CHECKING ACCOUNT?
NOT EVEN CLOSE. YOU?
THE ACCOUNTS ARE IN DAMON'S NAME. HE...NEVER GAVE ME ACCESS TO THE MONEY.
LOOK. DO YOU REALLY NEED THIS STUFF TO BE, LIKE, SUPER AGAIN OR WHATEVER?
YES.
THEN I KNOW HOW TO GET THE MONEY.

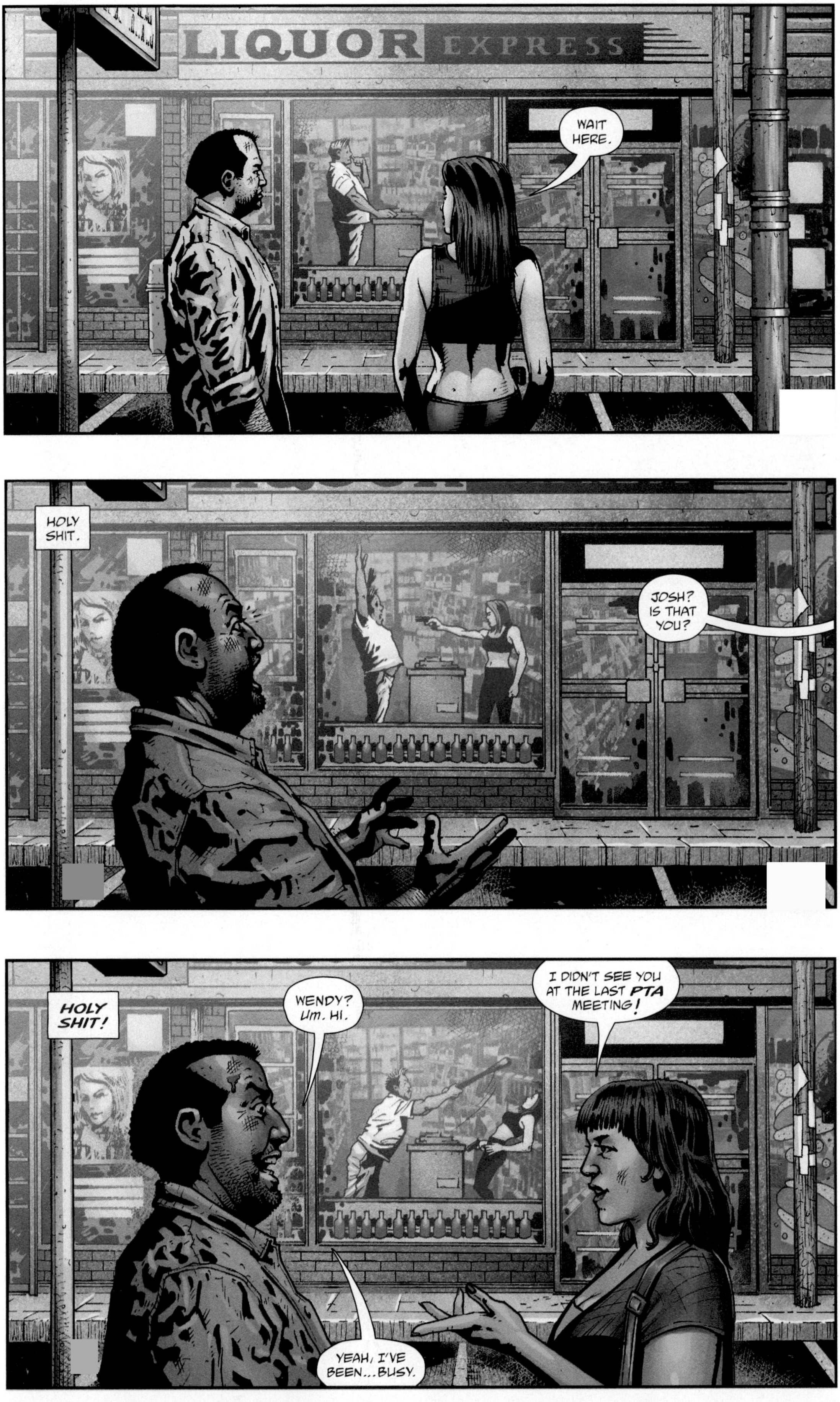
LIQUOR EXPRESS
WAIT HERE.
HOLY SHIT.
JOSH? IS THAT YOU?
HOLY SHIT!
WENDY? UM. HI.
I DIDN'T SEE YOU AT THE LAST PTA MEETING!
YEAH, I'VE BEEN...BUSY.

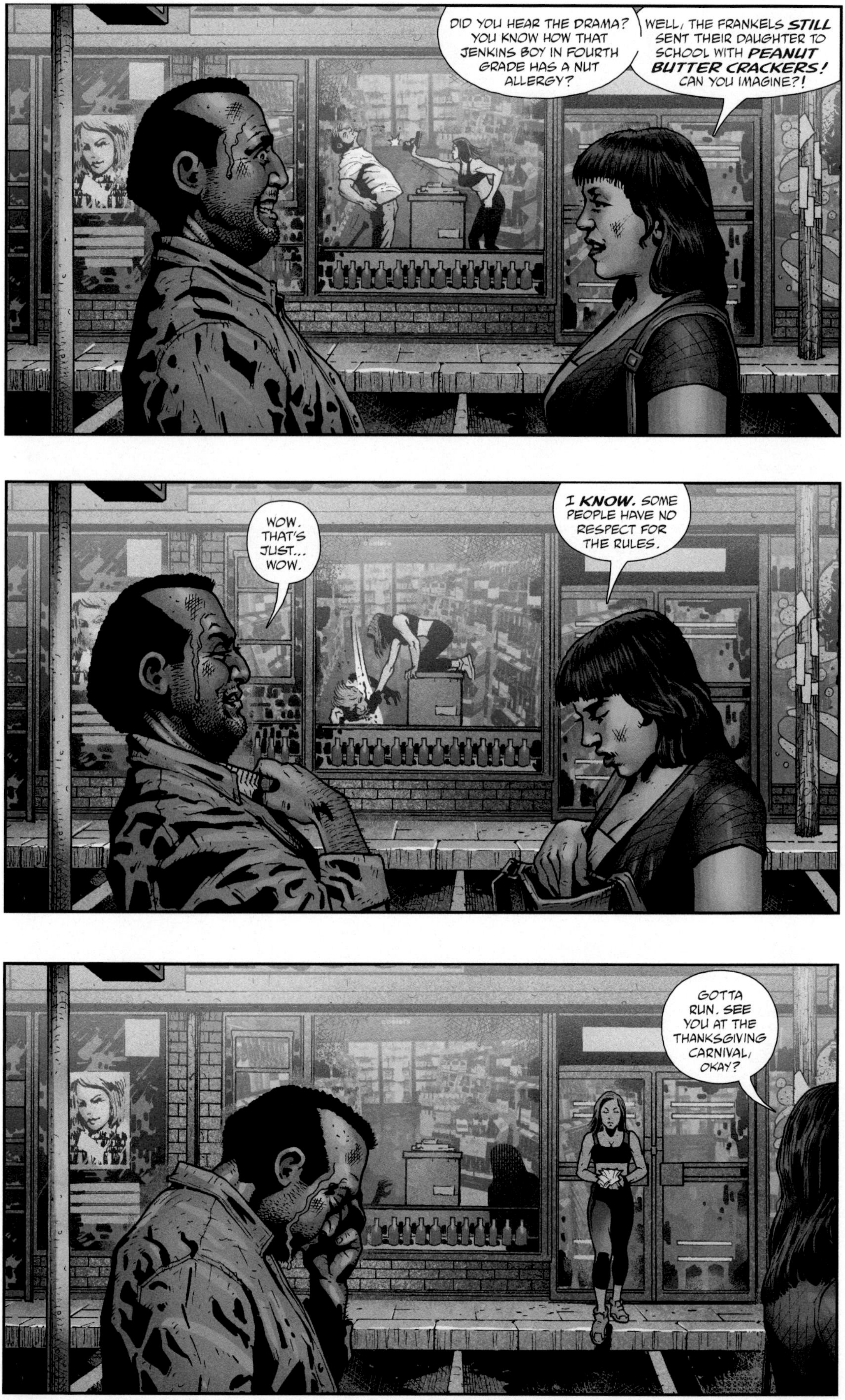
DID YOU HEAR THE DRAMA? YOU KNOW HOW THAT JENKINS BOY IN FOURTH GRADE HAS A NUT ALLERGY?
WELL, THE FRANKELS **STILL** SENT THEIR DAUGHTER TO SCHOOL WITH **PEANUT BUTTER CRACKERS!** CAN YOU IMAGINE?!
WOW. THAT'S JUST... WOW.
I **KNOW.** SOME PEOPLE HAVE NO RESPECT FOR THE RULES.
GOTTA RUN. SEE YOU AT THE THANKSGIVING CARNIVAL, OKAY?

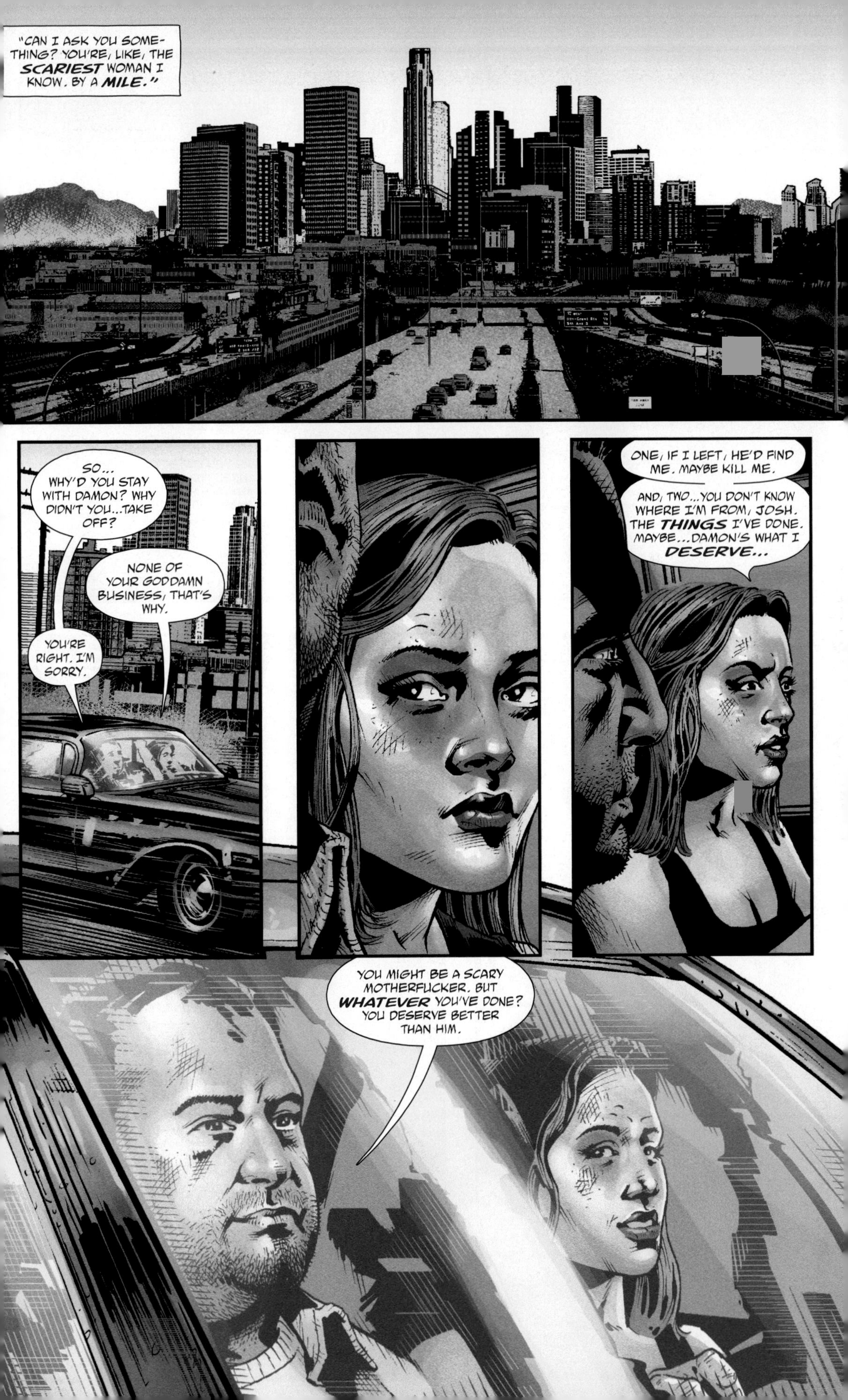
"CAN I ASK YOU SOMETHING? YOU'RE, LIKE, THE SCARIEST WOMAN I KNOW. BY A MILE."
SO... WHY'D YOU STAY WITH DAMON? WHY DIDN'T YOU...TAKE OFF?
NONE OF YOUR GODDAMN BUSINESS, THAT'S WHY.
YOU'RE RIGHT. I'M SORRY.
ONE, IF I LEFT, HE'D FIND ME. MAYBE KILL ME.
AND, TWO...YOU DON'T KNOW WHERE I'M FROM, JOSH. THE THINGS I'VE DONE. MAYBE...DAMON'S WHAT I DESERVE...
YOU MIGHT BE A SCARY MOTHERFUCKER. BUT WHATEVER YOU'VE DONE? YOU DESERVE BETTER THAN HIM.

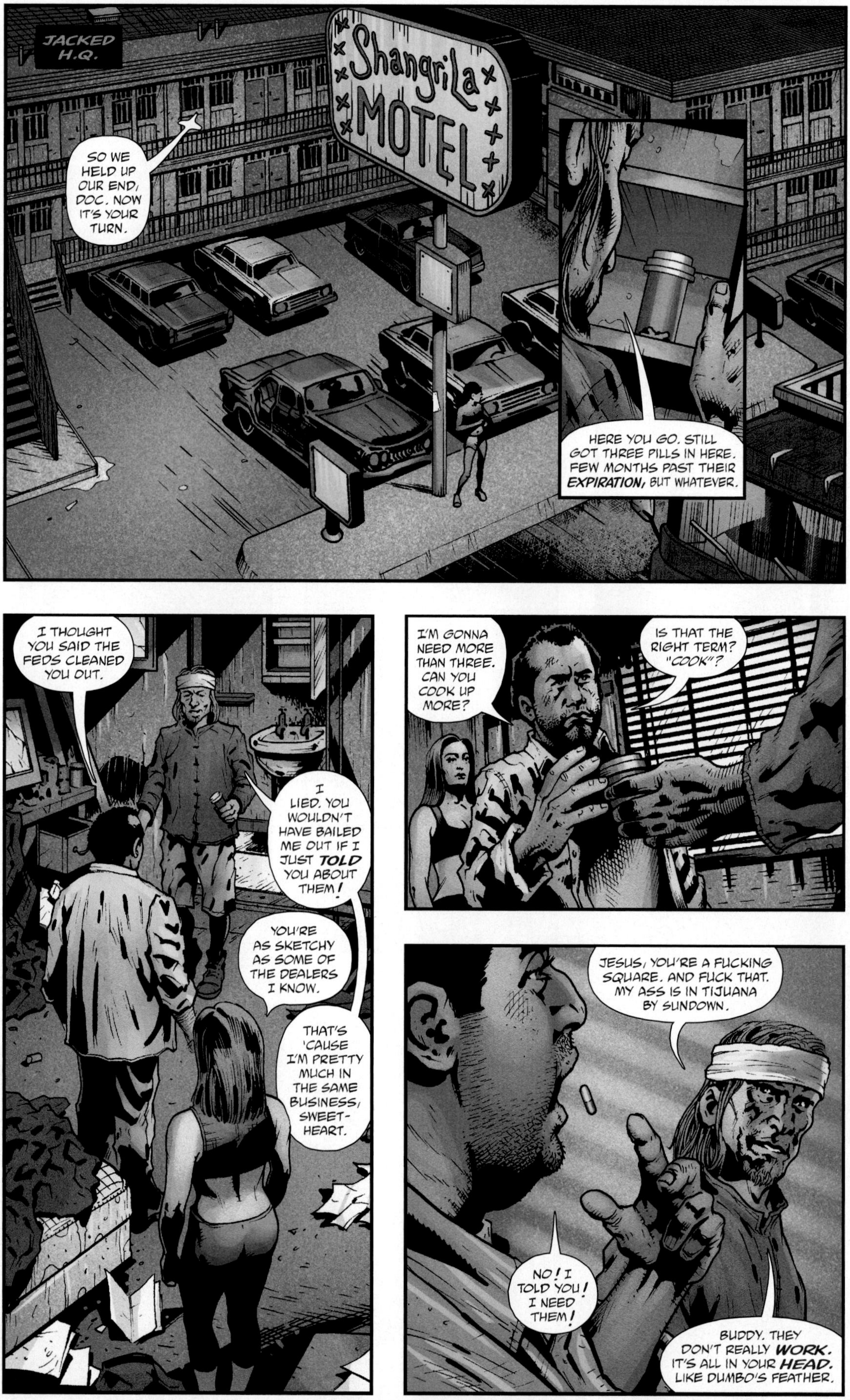
JACKED H.Q.
Shangri La MOTEL
SO WE HELD UP OUR END, DOC. NOW IT'S YOUR TURN.
HERE YOU GO. STILL GOT THREE PILLS IN HERE. FEW MONTHS PAST THEIR EXPIRATION, BUT WHATEVER.
I THOUGHT YOU SAID THE FEDS CLEANED YOU OUT.
I LIED. YOU WOULDN'T HAVE BAILED ME OUT IF I JUST TOLD YOU ABOUT THEM!
YOU'RE AS SKETCHY AS SOME OF THE DEALERS I KNOW.
THAT'S 'CAUSE I'M PRETTY MUCH IN THE SAME BUSINESS, SWEET-HEART.
I'M GONNA NEED MORE THAN THREE. CAN YOU COOK UP MORE?
IS THAT THE RIGHT TERM? "COOK"?
JESUS, YOU'RE A FUCKING SQUARE. AND FUCK THAT. MY ASS IS IN TIJUANA BY SUNDOWN.
NO! I TOLD YOU! I NEED THEM!
BUDDY. THEY DON'T REALLY WORK. IT'S ALL IN YOUR HEAD. LIKE DUMBO'S FEATHER.

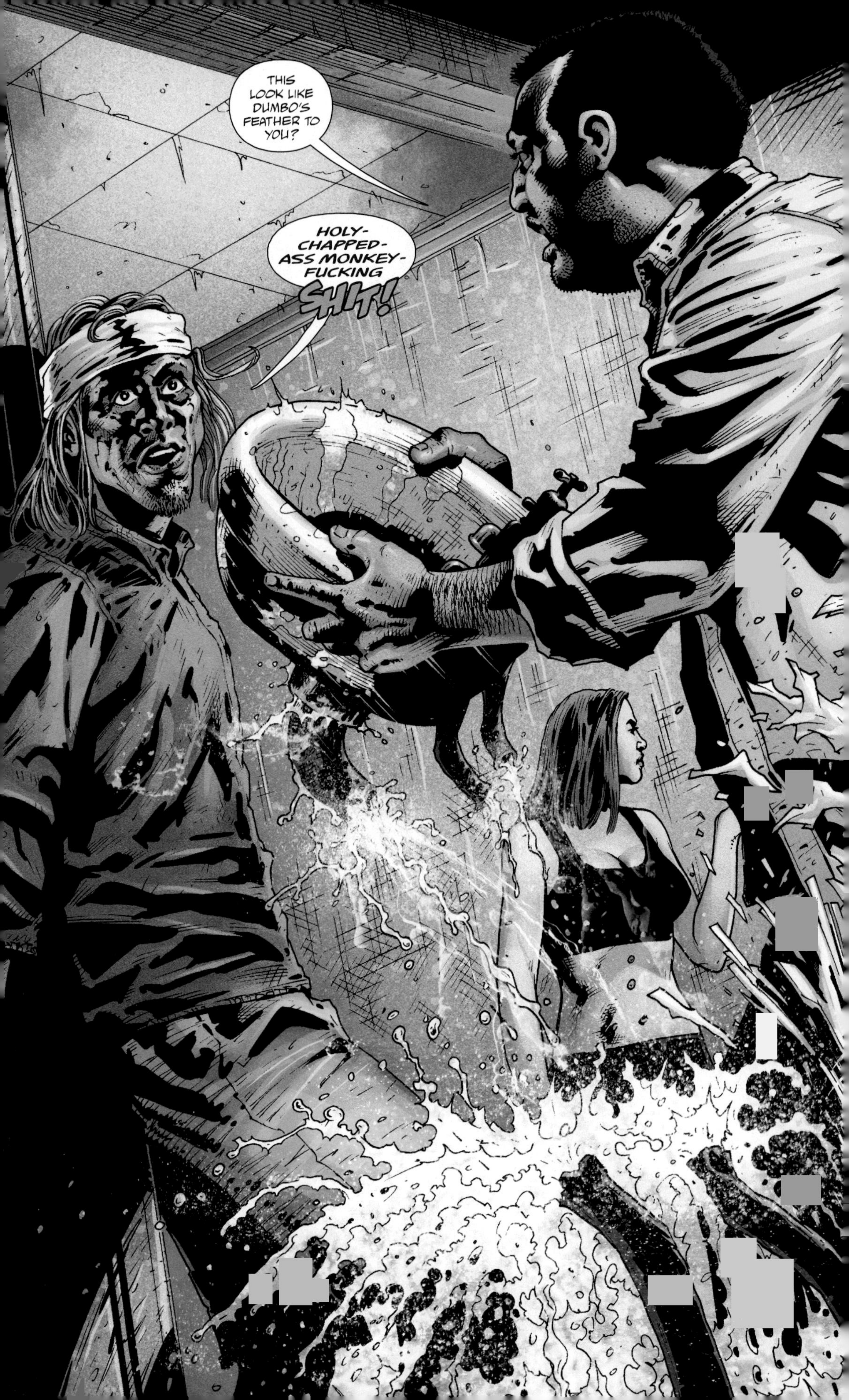
THIS LOOK LIKE DUMBO'S FEATHER TO YOU?
HOLY-CHAPPED-ASS MONKEY-FUCKING SHIT!

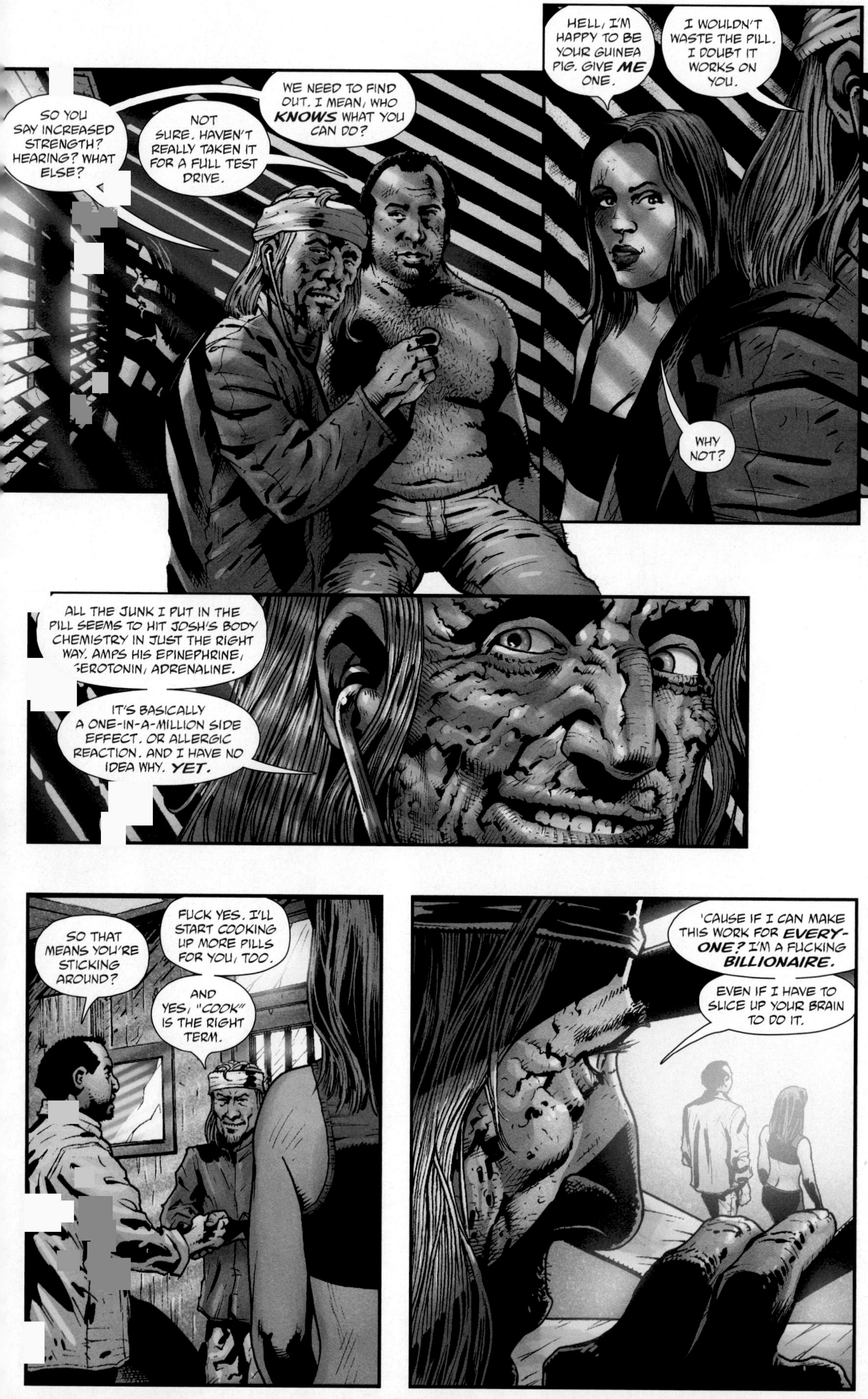
SO YOU SAY INCREASED STRENGTH? HEARING? WHAT ELSE?
NOT SURE. HAVEN'T REALLY TAKEN IT FOR A FULL TEST DRIVE.
WE NEED TO FIND OUT. I MEAN, WHO KNOWS WHAT YOU CAN DO?
HELL, I'M HAPPY TO BE YOUR GUINEA PIG. GIVE ME ONE.
I WOULDN'T WASTE THE PILL. I DOUBT IT WORKS ON YOU.
WHY NOT?
ALL THE JUNK I PUT IN THE PILL SEEMS TO HIT JOSH'S BODY CHEMISTRY IN JUST THE RIGHT WAY. AMPS HIS EPINEPHRINE, SEROTONIN, ADRENALINE.
IT'S BASICALLY A ONE-IN-A-MILLION SIDE EFFECT. OR ALLERGIC REACTION. AND I HAVE NO IDEA WHY. YET.
SO THAT MEANS YOU'RE STICKING AROUND?
FUCK YES. I'LL START COOKING UP MORE PILLS FOR YOU, TOO.
AND YES, "COOK" IS THE RIGHT TERM.
'CAUSE IF I CAN MAKE THIS WORK FOR EVERY-ONE? I'M A FUCKING BILLIONAIRE.
EVEN IF I HAVE TO SLICE UP YOUR BRAIN TO DO IT.

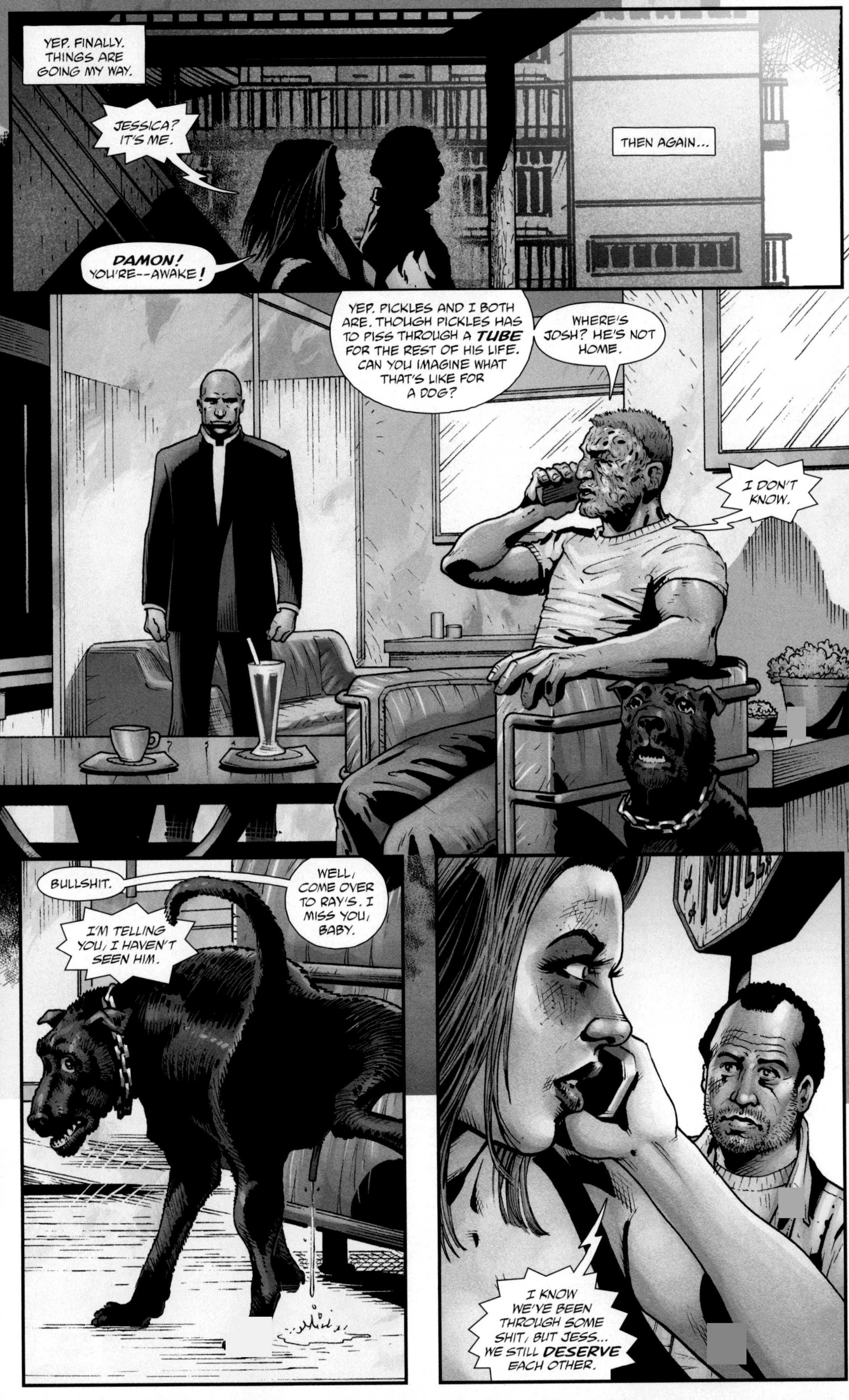
YEP. FINALLY. THINGS ARE GOING MY WAY.
JESSICA? IT'S ME.
DAMON! YOU'RE--AWAKE!
THEN AGAIN...
YEP. PICKLES AND I BOTH ARE. THOUGH PICKLES HAS TO PISS THROUGH A TUBE FOR THE REST OF HIS LIFE. CAN YOU IMAGINE WHAT THAT'S LIKE FOR A DOG?
WHERE'S JOSH? HE'S NOT HOME.
I DON'T KNOW.
BULLSHIT.
I'M TELLING YOU, I HAVEN'T SEEN HIM.
WELL, COME OVER TO RAY'S. I MISS YOU, BABY.
I KNOW WE'VE BEEN THROUGH SOME SHIT, BUT JESS... WE STILL DESERVE EACH OTHER.

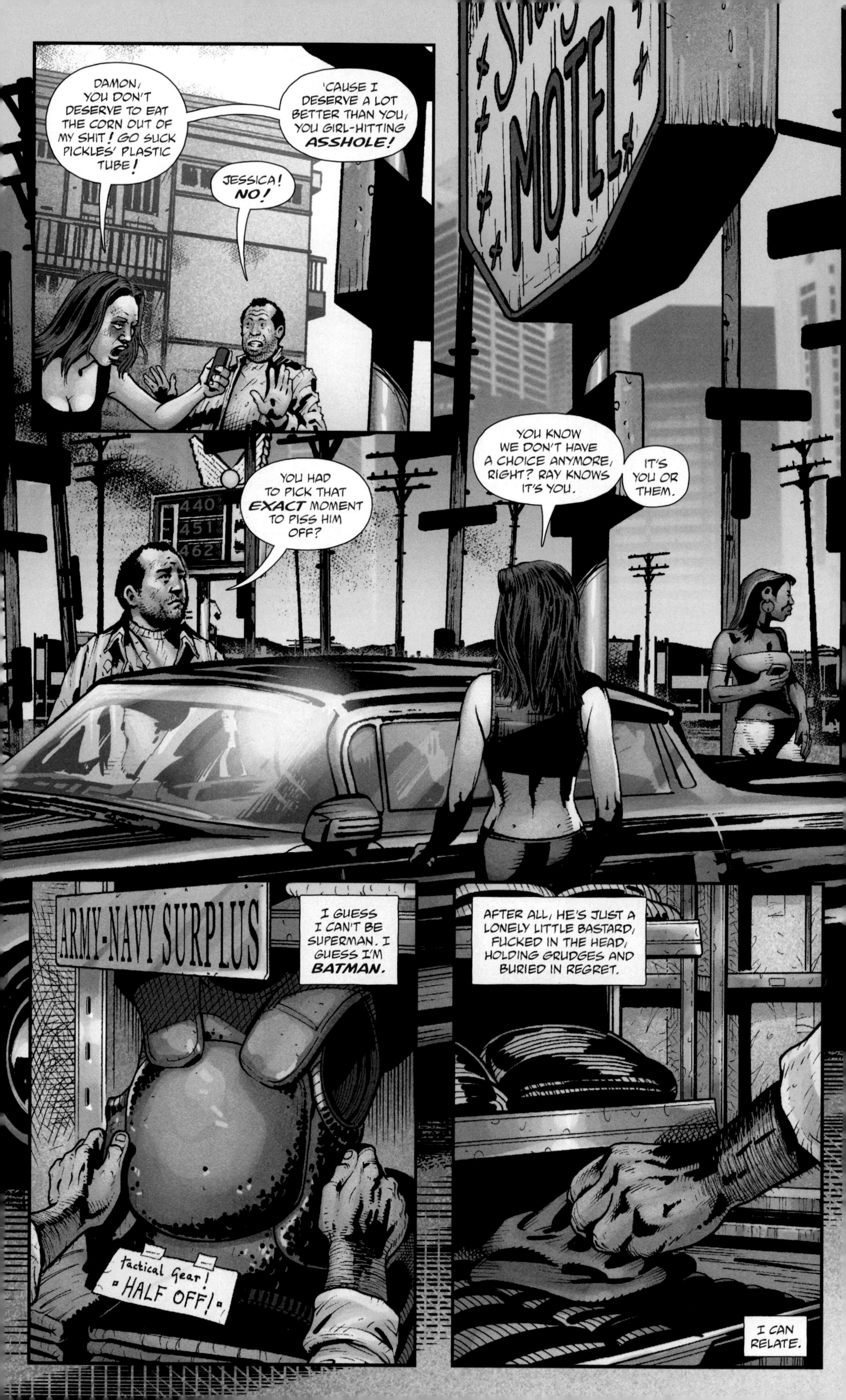

MOTEL
DAMON, YOU DON'T DESERVE TO EAT THE CORN OUT OF MY SHIT! GO SUCK PICKLES' PLASTIC TUBE!
'CAUSE I DESERVE A LOT BETTER THAN YOU, YOU GIRL-HITTING ASSHOLE!
JESSICA! NO!
YOU HAD TO PICK THAT EXACT MOMENT TO PISS HIM OFF?
YOU KNOW WE DON'T HAVE A CHOICE ANYMORE, RIGHT? RAY KNOWS IT'S YOU.
IT'S YOU OR THEM.
ARMY-NAVY SURPLUS
I GUESS I CAN'T BE SUPERMAN. I GUESS I'M BATMAN.
Tactical Gear! HALF OFF!
AFTER ALL, HE'S JUST A LONELY LITTLE BASTARD, FUCKED IN THE HEAD, HOLDING GRUDGES AND BURIED IN REGRET.
I CAN RELATE.

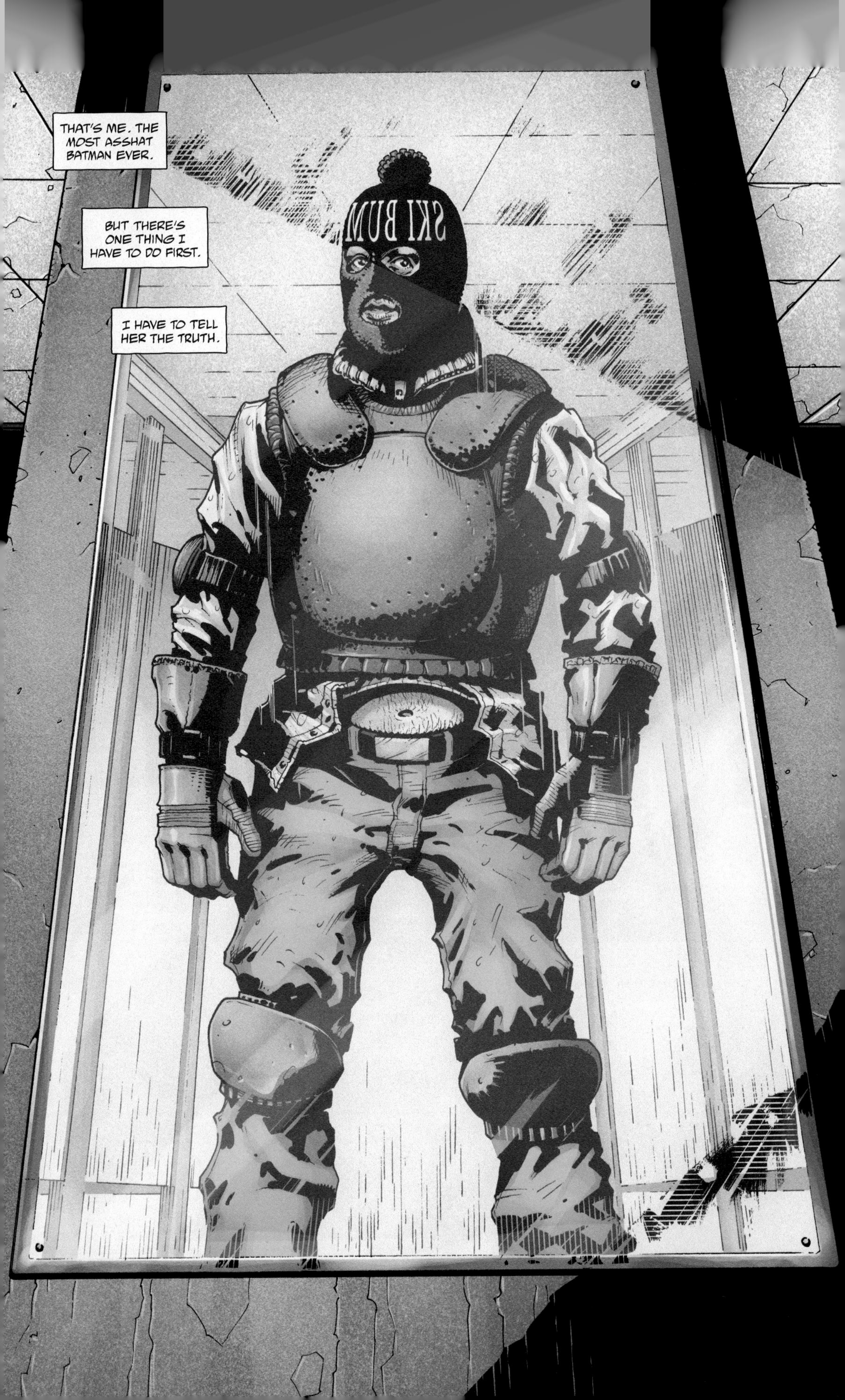
THAT'S ME. THE MOST ASSHAT BATMAN EVER.
BUT THERE'S ONE THING I HAVE TO DO FIRST.
I HAVE TO TELL HER THE TRUTH.

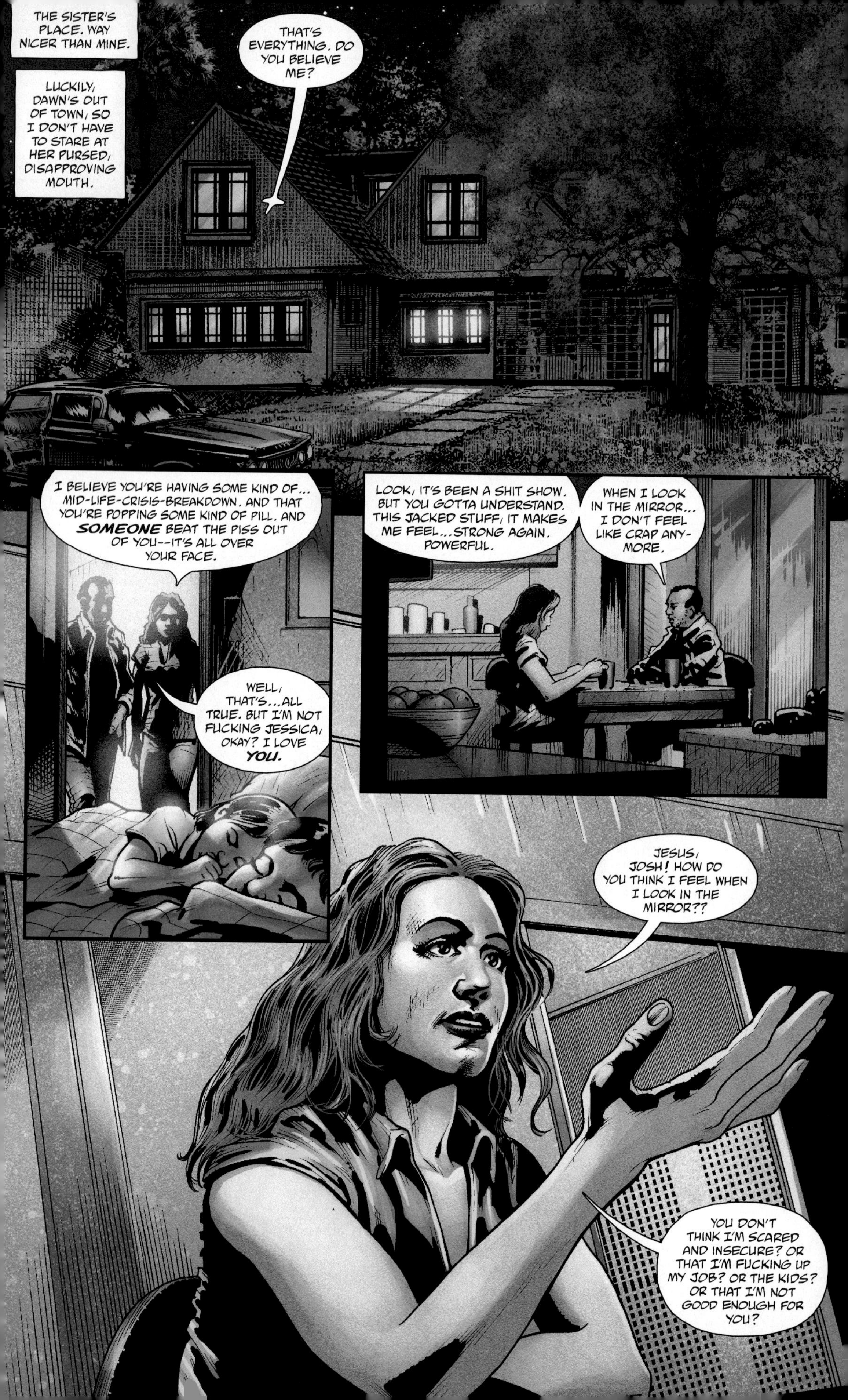
THE SISTER'S PLACE. WAY NICER THAN MINE.
LUCKILY, DAWN'S OUT OF TOWN, SO I DON'T HAVE TO STARE AT HER PURSED, DISAPPROVING MOUTH.
THAT'S EVERYTHING. DO YOU BELIEVE ME?
I BELIEVE YOU'RE HAVING SOME KIND OF... MID-LIFE-CRISIS-BREAKDOWN. AND THAT YOU'RE POPPING SOME KIND OF PILL. AND SOMEONE BEAT THE PISS OUT OF YOU--IT'S ALL OVER YOUR FACE.
WELL, THAT'S...ALL TRUE. BUT I'M NOT FUCKING JESSICA, OKAY? I LOVE YOU.
LOOK, IT'S BEEN A SHIT SHOW. BUT YOU GOTTA UNDERSTAND. THIS JACKED STUFF, IT MAKES ME FEEL...STRONG AGAIN. POWERFUL.
WHEN I LOOK IN THE MIRROR... I DON'T FEEL LIKE CRAP ANY-MORE.
JESUS, JOSH! HOW DO YOU THINK I FEEL WHEN I LOOK IN THE MIRROR??
YOU DON'T THINK I'M SCARED AND INSECURE? OR THAT I'M FUCKING UP MY JOB? OR THE KIDS? OR THAT I'M NOT GOOD ENOUGH FOR YOU?

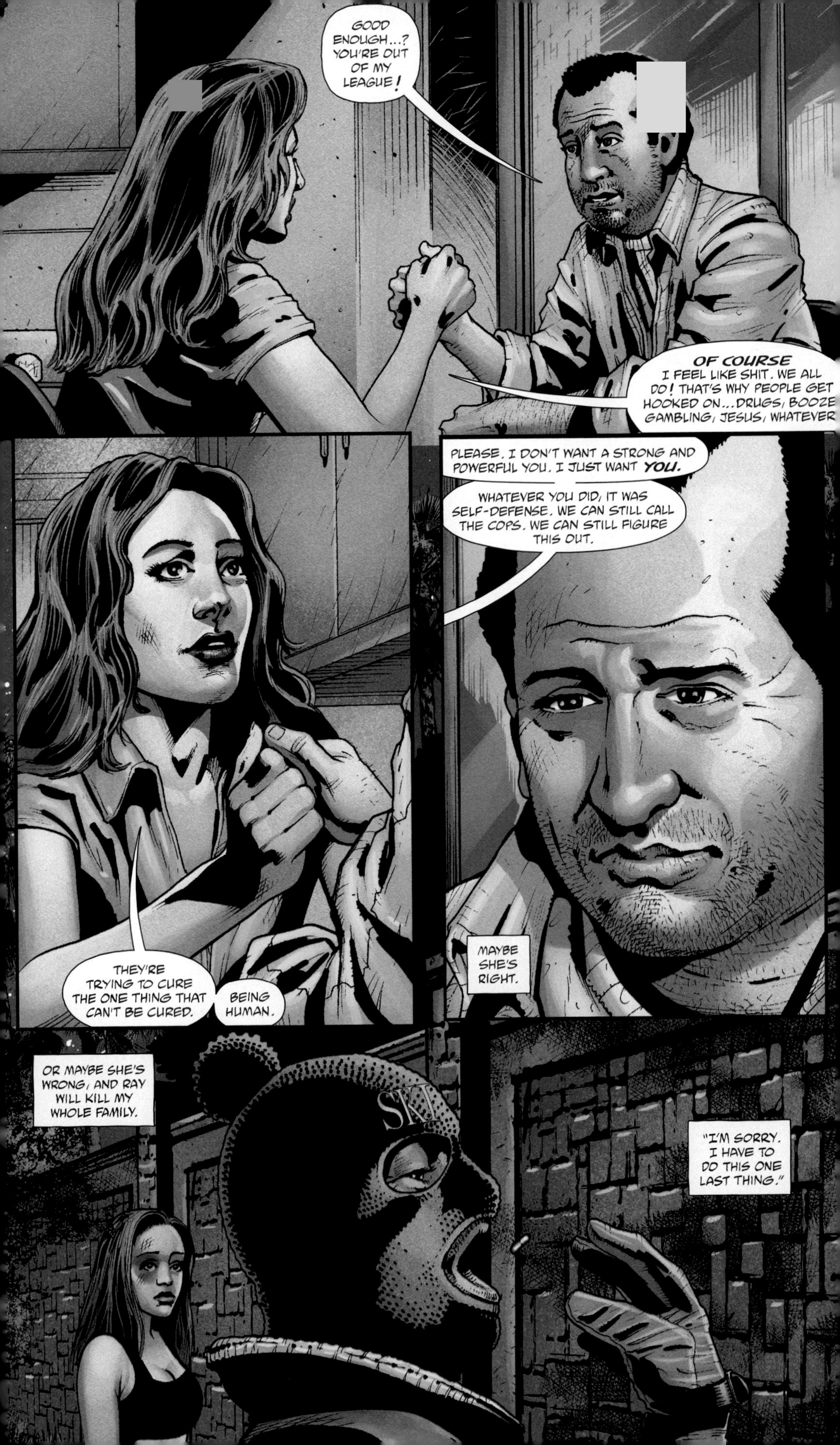
GOOD ENOUGH...? YOU'RE OUT OF MY LEAGUE!
OF COURSE I FEEL LIKE SHIT. WE ALL DO! THAT'S WHY PEOPLE GET HOOKED ON...DRUGS, BOOZE GAMBLING, JESUS, WHATEVER
PLEASE. I DON'T WANT A STRONG AND POWERFUL YOU. I JUST WANT YOU.
WHATEVER YOU DID, IT WAS SELF-DEFENSE. WE CAN STILL CALL THE COPS. WE CAN STILL FIGURE THIS OUT.
THEY'RE TRYING TO CURE THE ONE THING THAT CAN'T BE CURED.
BEING HUMAN.
MAYBE SHE'S RIGHT.
OR MAYBE SHE'S WRONG, AND RAY WILL KILL MY WHOLE FAMILY.
SKI
"I'M SORRY. I HAVE TO DO THIS ONE LAST THING."

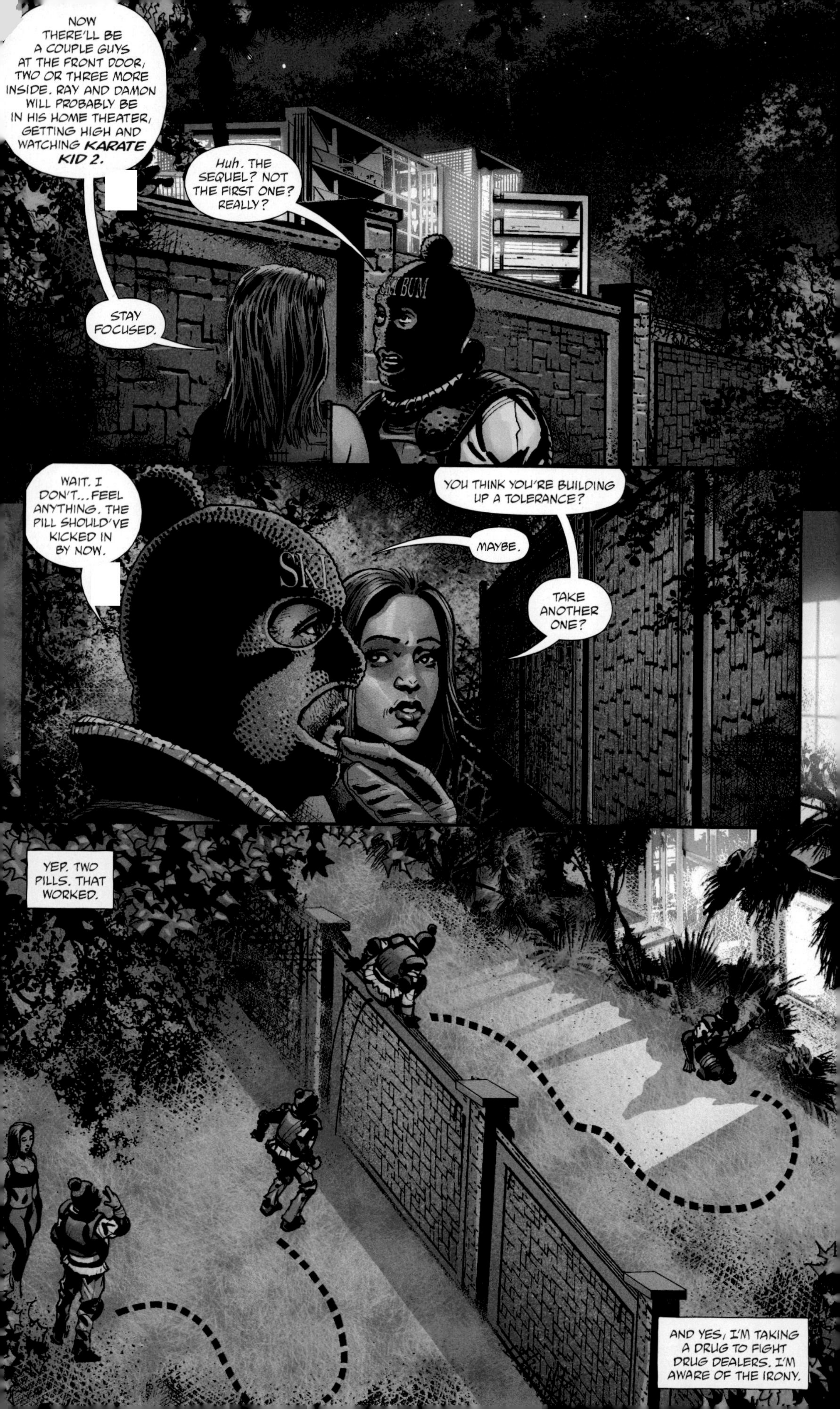
NOW THERE'LL BE A COUPLE GUYS AT THE FRONT DOOR, TWO OR THREE MORE INSIDE. RAY AND DAMON WILL PROBABLY BE IN HIS HOME THEATER, GETTING HIGH AND WATCHING KARATE KID 2.
Huh. THE SEQUEL? NOT THE FIRST ONE? REALLY?
STAY FOCUSED.
SKI BUM
WAIT. I DON'T...FEEL ANYTHING. THE PILL SHOULD'VE KICKED IN BY NOW.
YOU THINK YOU'RE BUILDING UP A TOLERANCE?
MAYBE.
TAKE ANOTHER ONE?
YEP. TWO PILLS. THAT WORKED.
AND YES, I'M TAKING A DRUG TO FIGHT DRUG DEALERS. I'M AWARE OF THE IRONY.

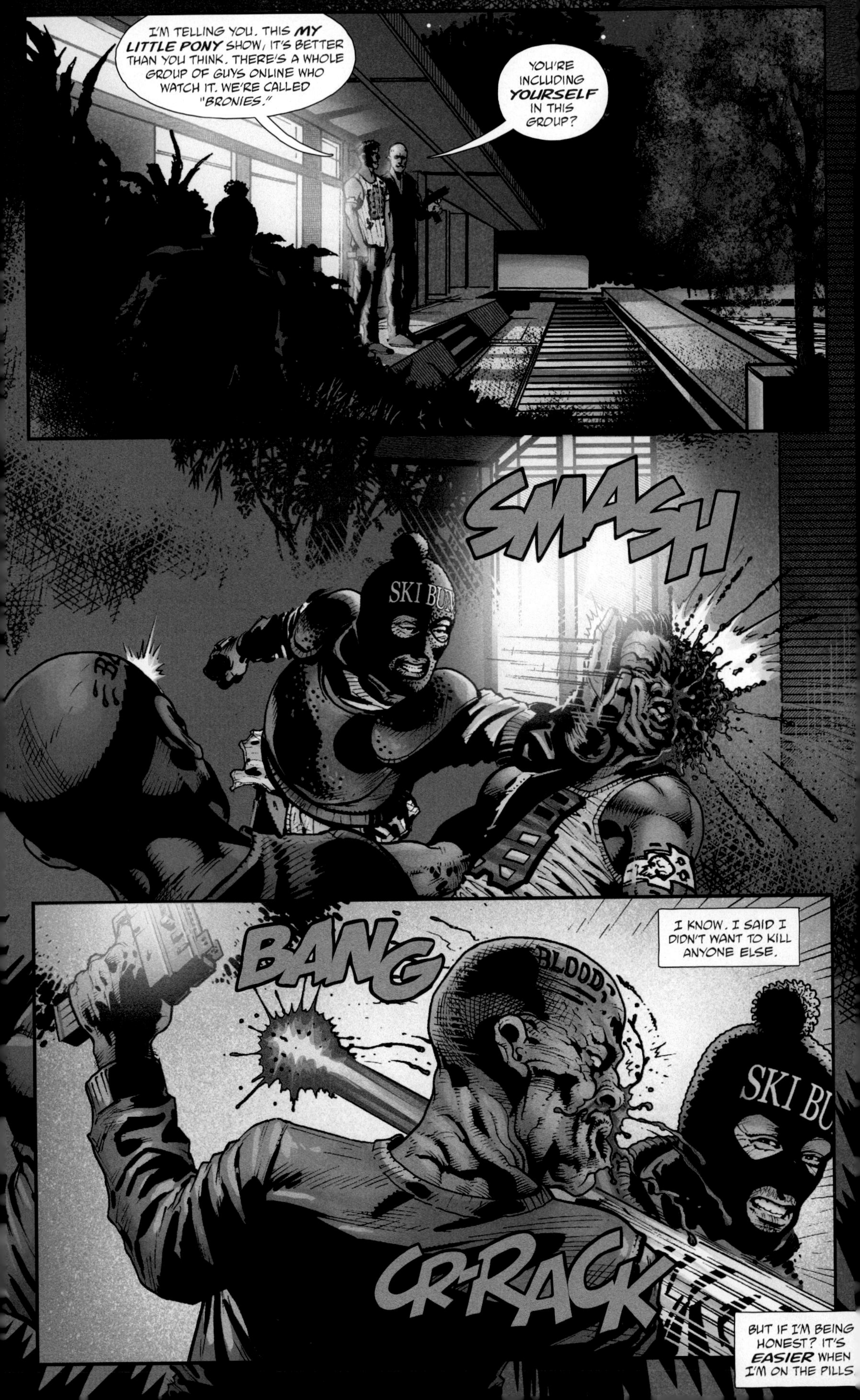

I'M TELLING YOU. THIS *MY LITTLE PONY* SHOW, IT'S BETTER THAN YOU THINK. THERE'S A WHOLE GROUP OF GUYS ONLINE WHO WATCH IT. WE'RE CALLED "BRONIES."
YOU'RE INCLUDING *YOURSELF* IN THIS GROUP?
SMASH
SKI BUN
BANG
BLOOD
I KNOW. I SAID I DIDN'T WANT TO KILL ANYONE ELSE.
SKI BU
CR-RACK
BUT IF I'M BEING HONEST? IT'S *EASIER* WHEN I'M ON THE PILLS.

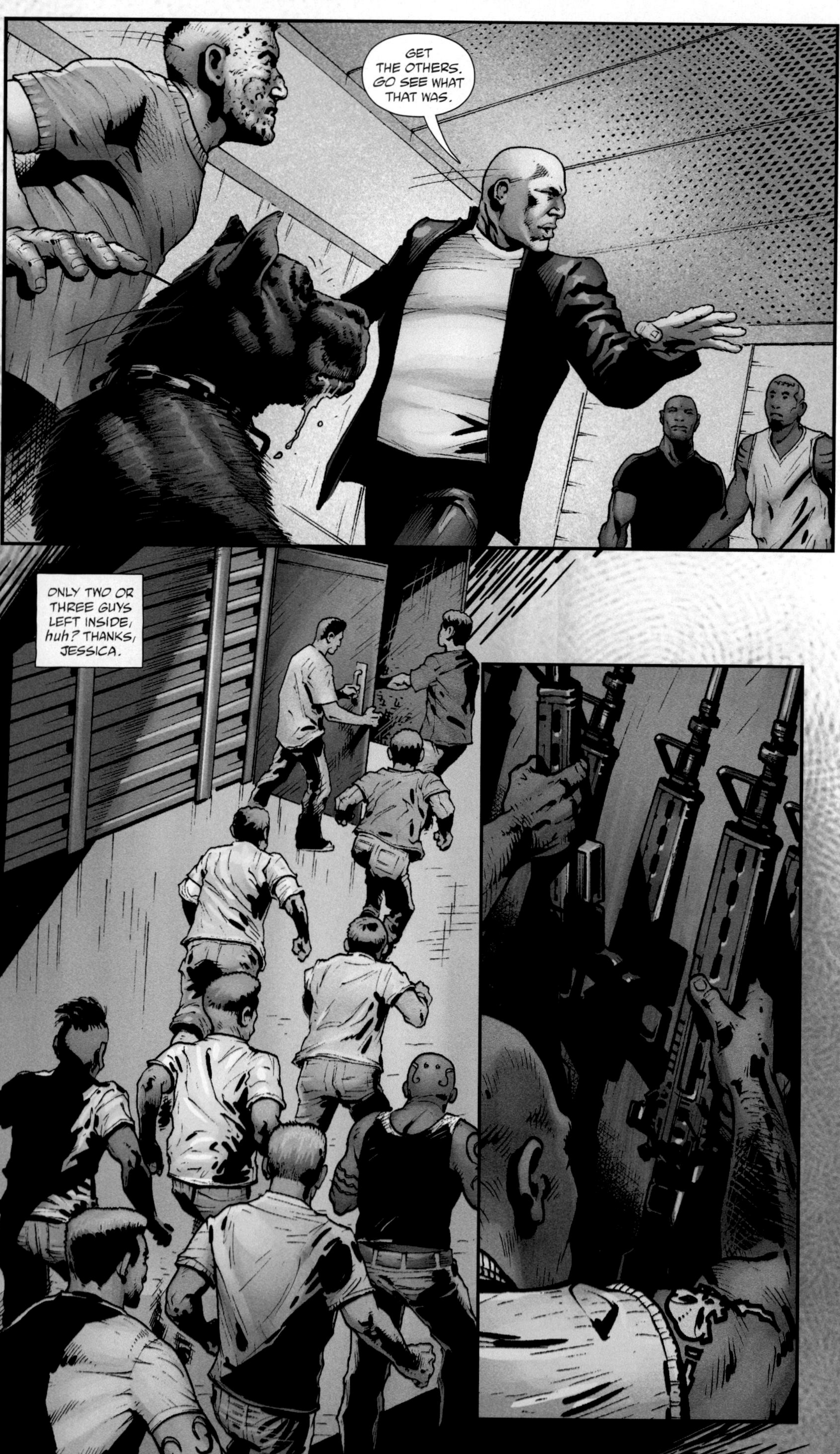
GET THE OTHERS. GO SEE WHAT THAT WAS.
ONLY TWO OR THREE GUYS LEFT INSIDE, *huh?* THANKS, JESSICA.

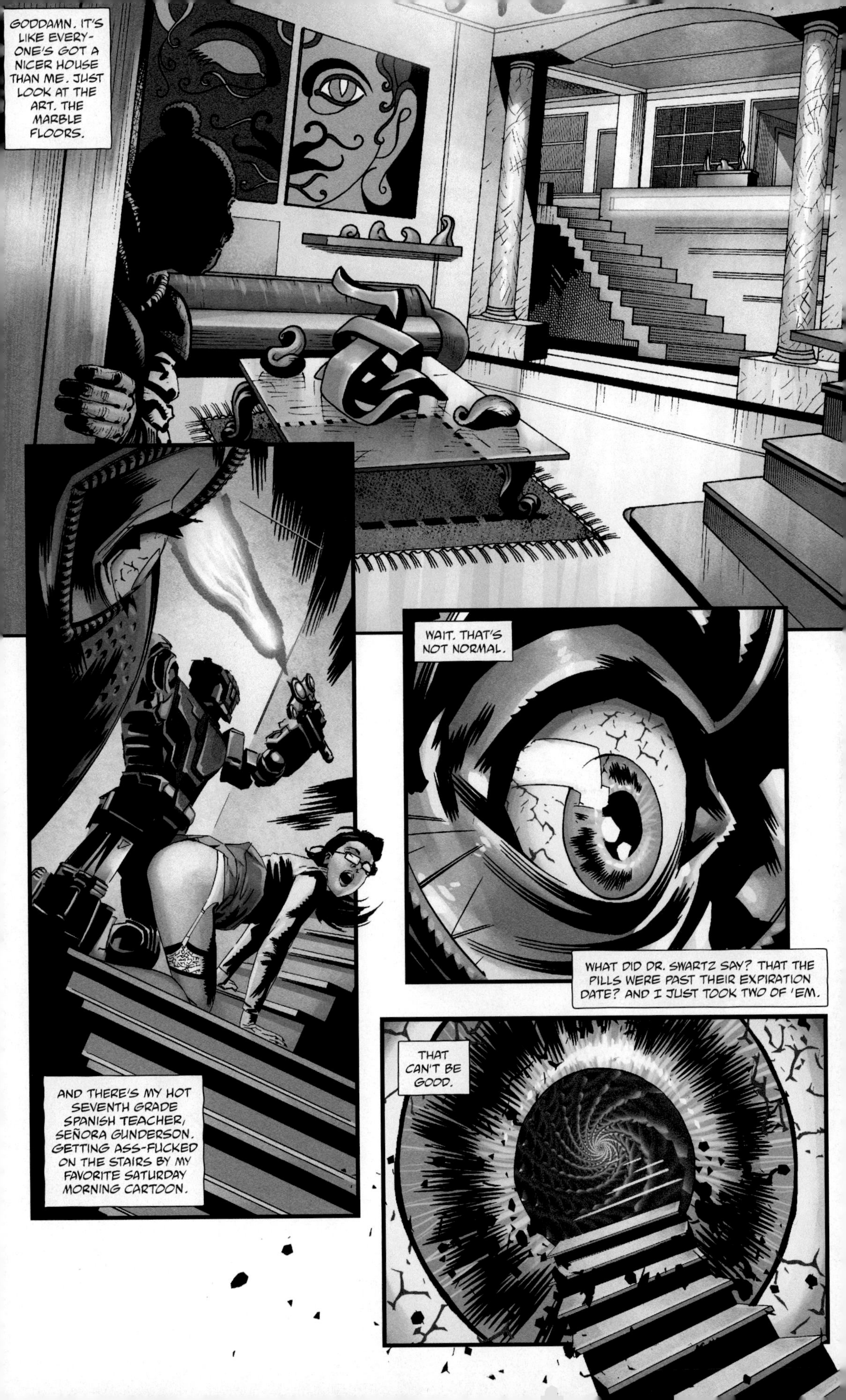
GODDAMN. IT'S LIKE EVERY-ONE'S GOT A NICER HOUSE THAN ME. JUST LOOK AT THE ART. THE MARBLE FLOORS.
AND THERE'S MY HOT SEVENTH GRADE SPANISH TEACHER, SEÑORA GUNDERSON, GETTING ASS-FUCKED ON THE STAIRS BY MY FAVORITE SATURDAY MORNING CARTOON.
WAIT. THAT'S NOT NORMAL.
WHAT DID DR. SWARTZ SAY? THAT THE PILLS WERE PAST THEIR EXPIRATION DATE? AND I JUST TOOK TWO OF 'EM.
THAT CAN'T BE GOOD.

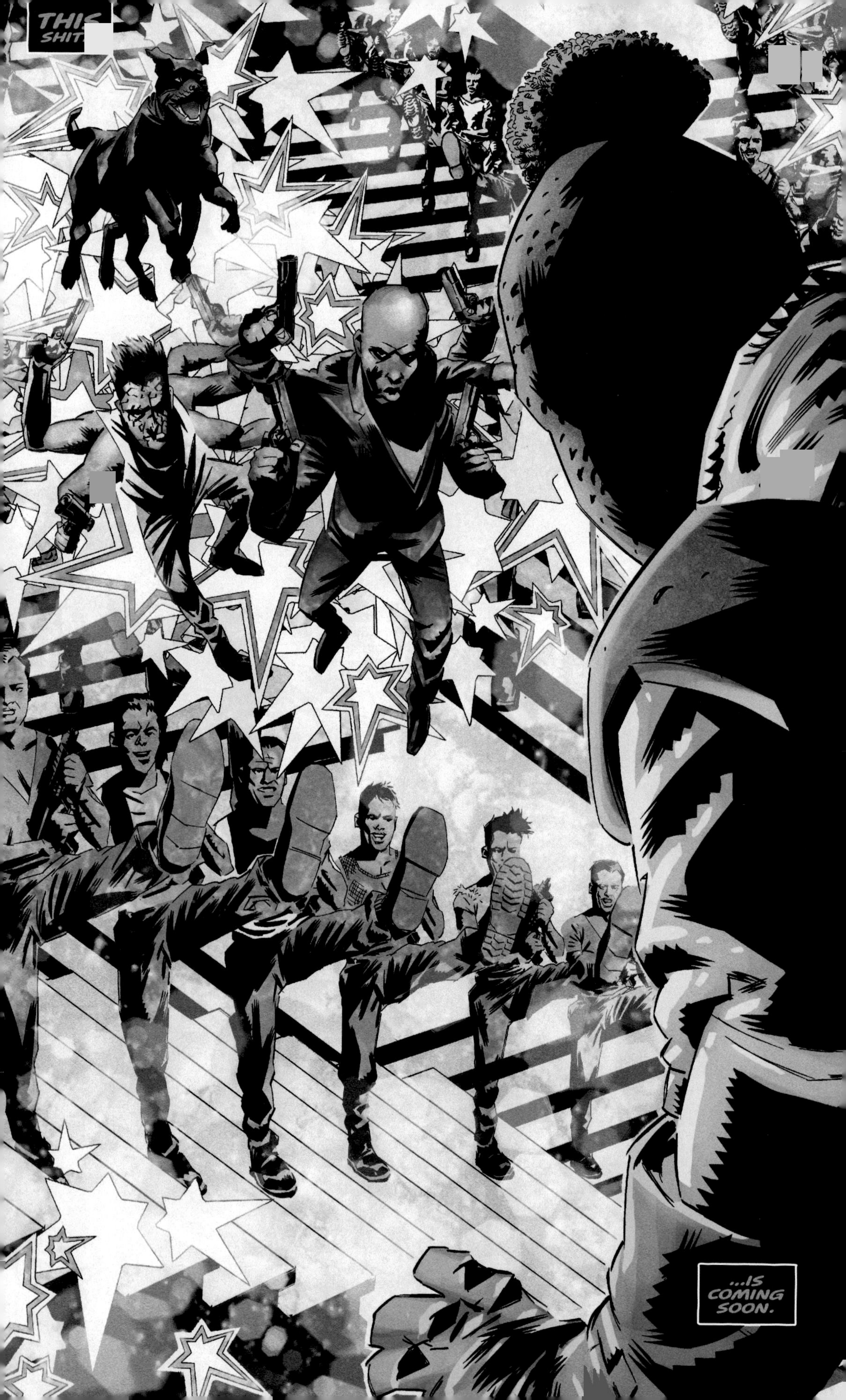
THIS SHIT
...IS COMING SOON.

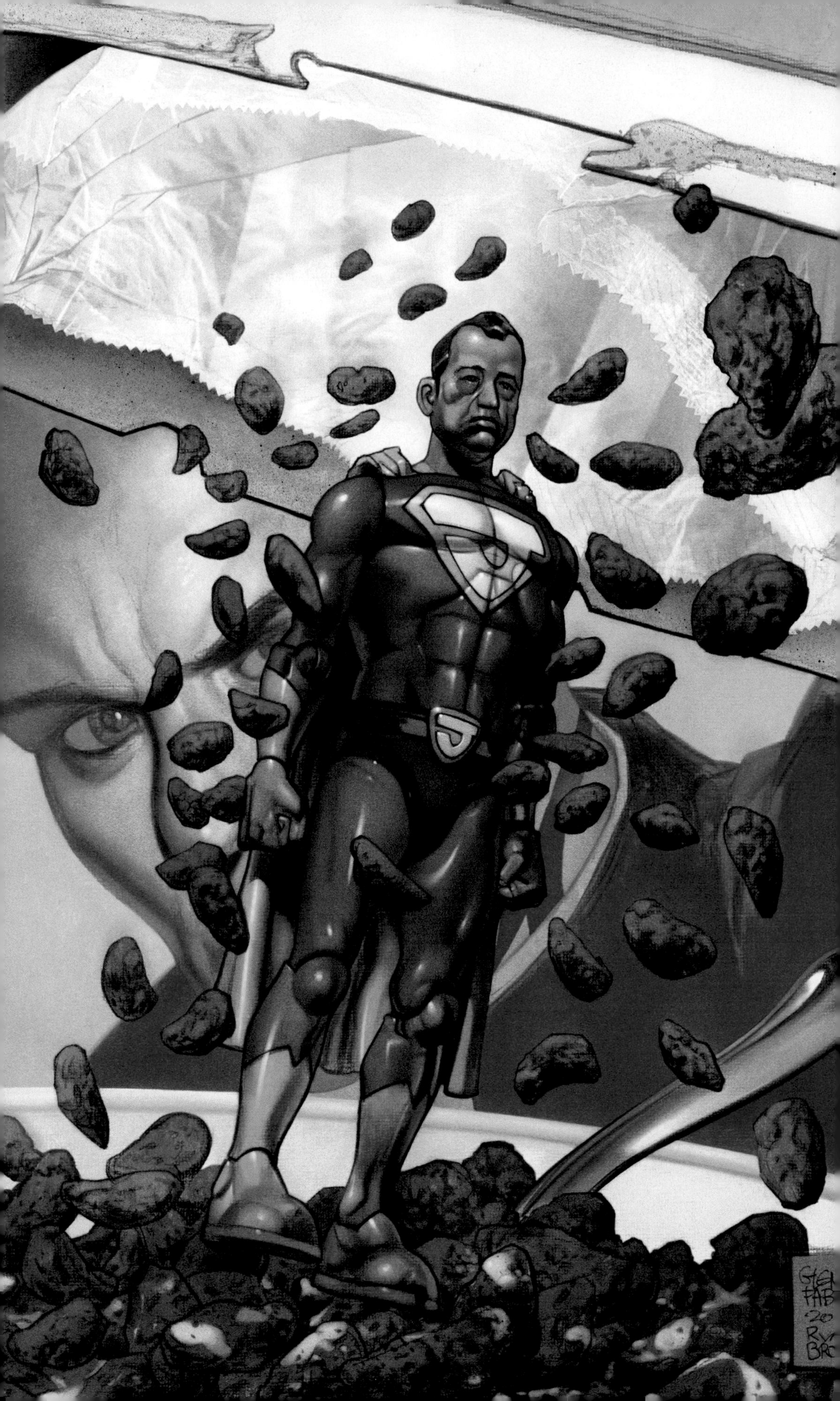

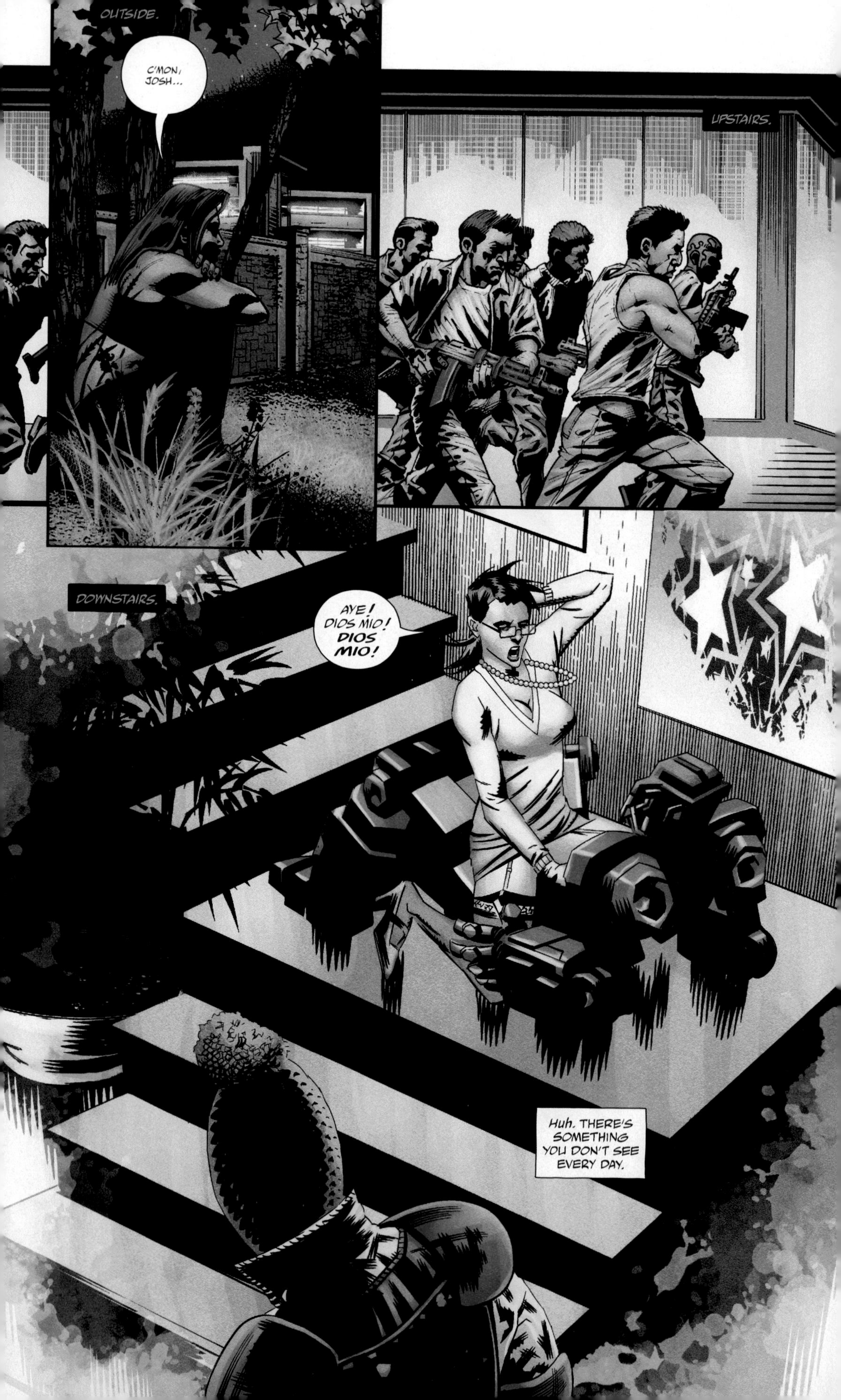
OUTSIDE.
C'MON, JOSH...
UPSTAIRS.
DOWNSTAIRS.
AYE! DIOS MIO! DIOS MIO!
Huh. THERE'S SOMETHING YOU DON'T SEE EVERY DAY.

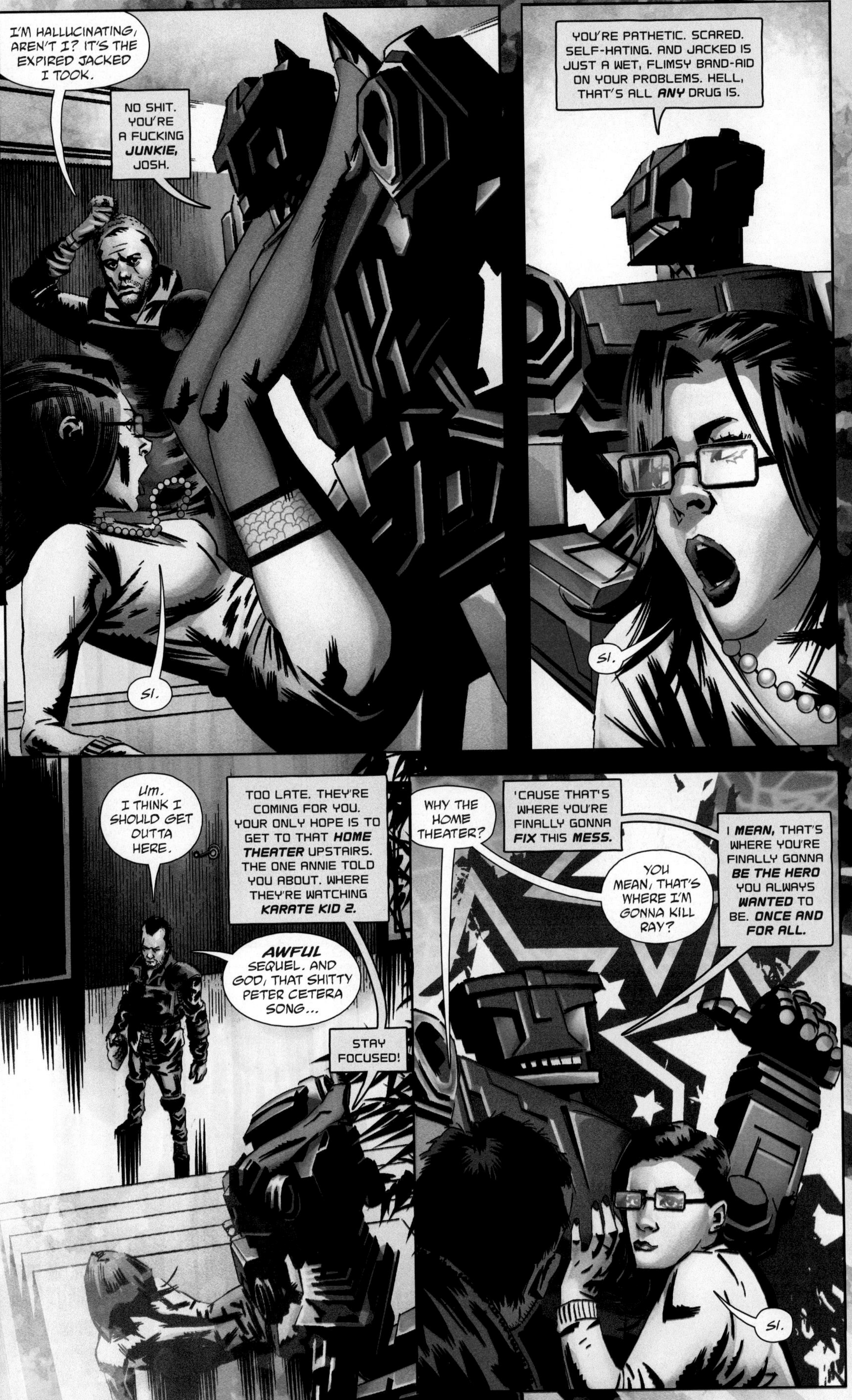
I'M HALLUCINATING, AREN'T I? IT'S THE EXPIRED JACKED I TOOK.
NO SHIT. YOU'RE A FUCKING JUNKIE, JOSH.
SI.
YOU'RE PATHETIC. SCARED. SELF-HATING. AND JACKED IS JUST A WET, FLIMSY BAND-AID ON YOUR PROBLEMS. HELL, THAT'S ALL ANY DRUG IS.
SI.
UM. I THINK I SHOULD GET OUTTA HERE.
TOO LATE. THEY'RE COMING FOR YOU. YOUR ONLY HOPE IS TO GET TO THAT HOME THEATER UPSTAIRS. THE ONE ANNIE TOLD YOU ABOUT. WHERE THEY'RE WATCHING KARATE KID 2.
AWFUL SEQUEL. AND GOD, THAT SHITTY PETER CETERA SONG...
STAY FOCUSED!
WHY THE HOME THEATER?
'CAUSE THAT'S WHERE YOU'RE FINALLY GONNA FIX THIS MESS.
YOU MEAN, THAT'S WHERE I'M GONNA KILL RAY?
I MEAN, THAT'S WHERE YOU'RE FINALLY GONNA BE THE HERO YOU ALWAYS WANTED TO BE. ONCE AND FOR ALL.
SI.

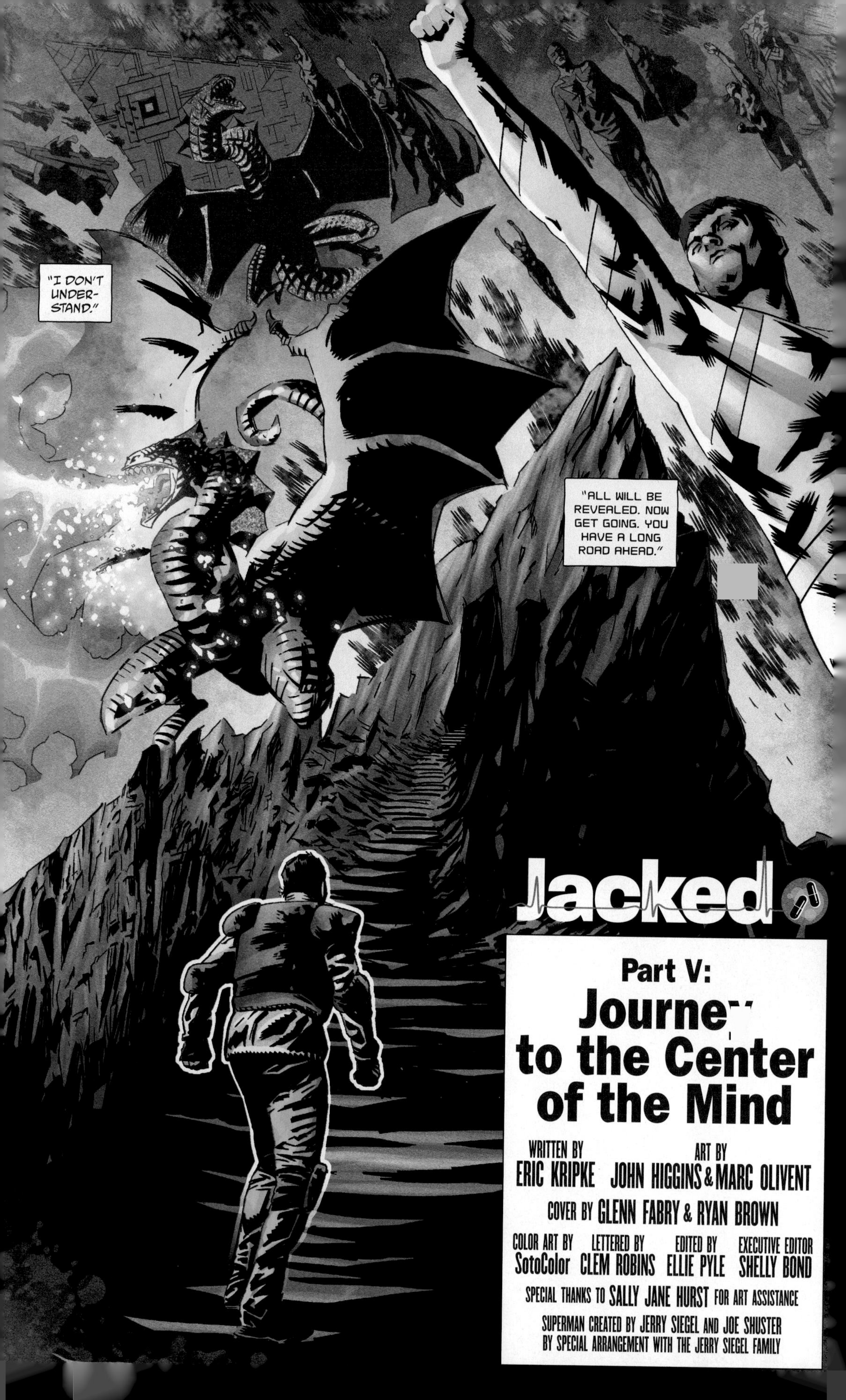
"I DON'T UNDER-STAND."
"ALL WILL BE REVEALED. NOW GET GOING. YOU HAVE A LONG ROAD AHEAD."
Jacked
Part V:
Journey to the Center of the Mind
WRITTEN BY ERIC KRIPKE
ART BY JOHN HIGGINS & MARC OLIVENT
COVER BY GLENN FABRY & RYAN BROWN
COLOR ART BY SotoColor
LETTERED BY CLEM ROBINS
EDITED BY ELLIE PYLE
EXECUTIVE EDITOR SHELLY BOND
SPECIAL THANKS TO SALLY JANE HURST FOR ART ASSISTANCE
SUPERMAN CREATED BY JERRY SIEGEL AND JOE SHUSTER
BY SPECIAL ARRANGEMENT WITH THE JERRY SIEGEL FAMILY

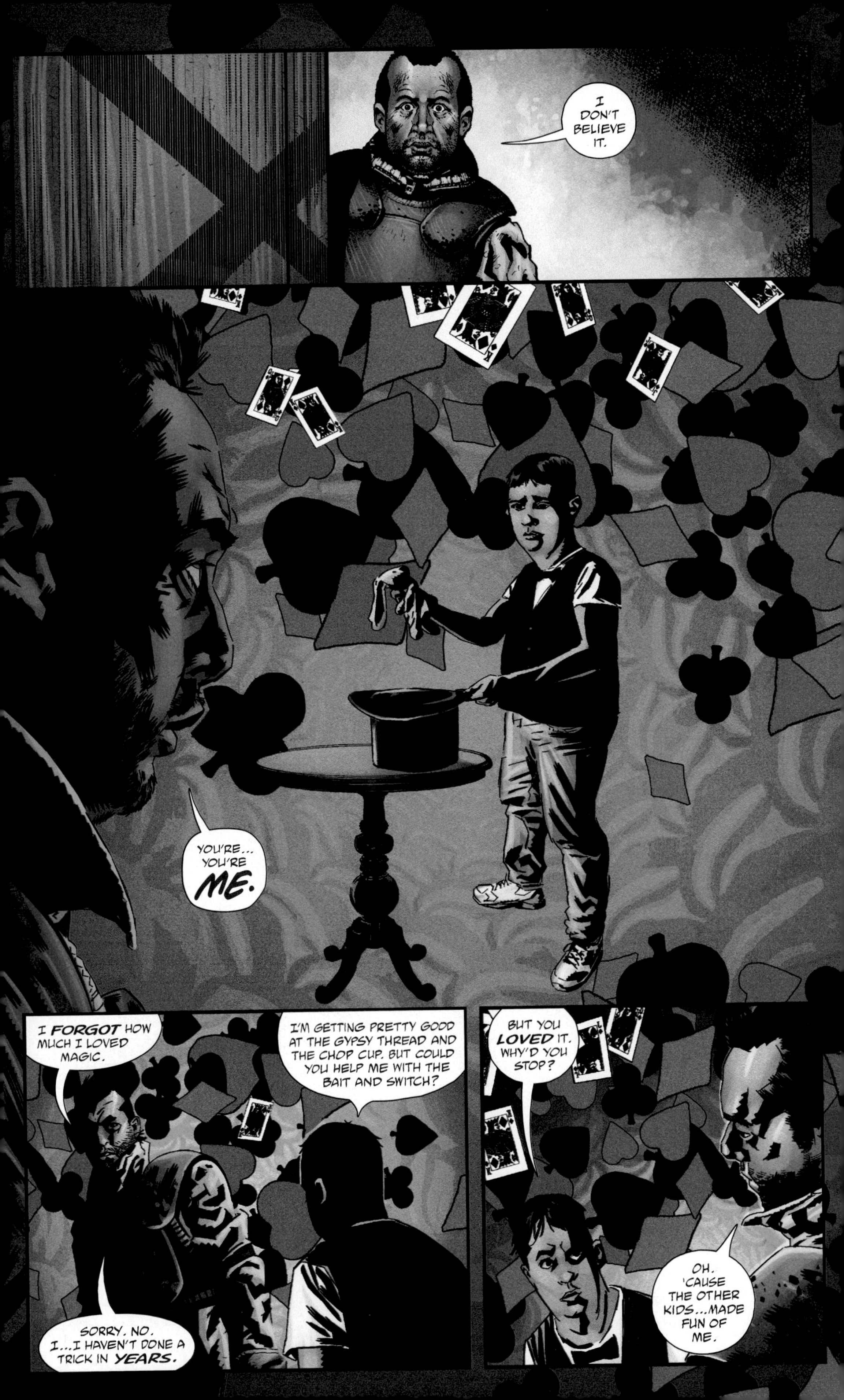
I DON'T BELIEVE IT.
YOU'RE... YOU'RE ME.
I FORGOT HOW MUCH I LOVED MAGIC.
I'M GETTING PRETTY GOOD AT THE GYPSY THREAD AND THE CHOP CUP. BUT COULD YOU HELP ME WITH THE BAIT AND SWITCH?
SORRY. NO. I...I HAVEN'T DONE A TRICK IN YEARS.
BUT YOU LOVED IT. WHY'D YOU STOP?
OH. 'CAUSE THE OTHER KIDS...MADE FUN OF ME.

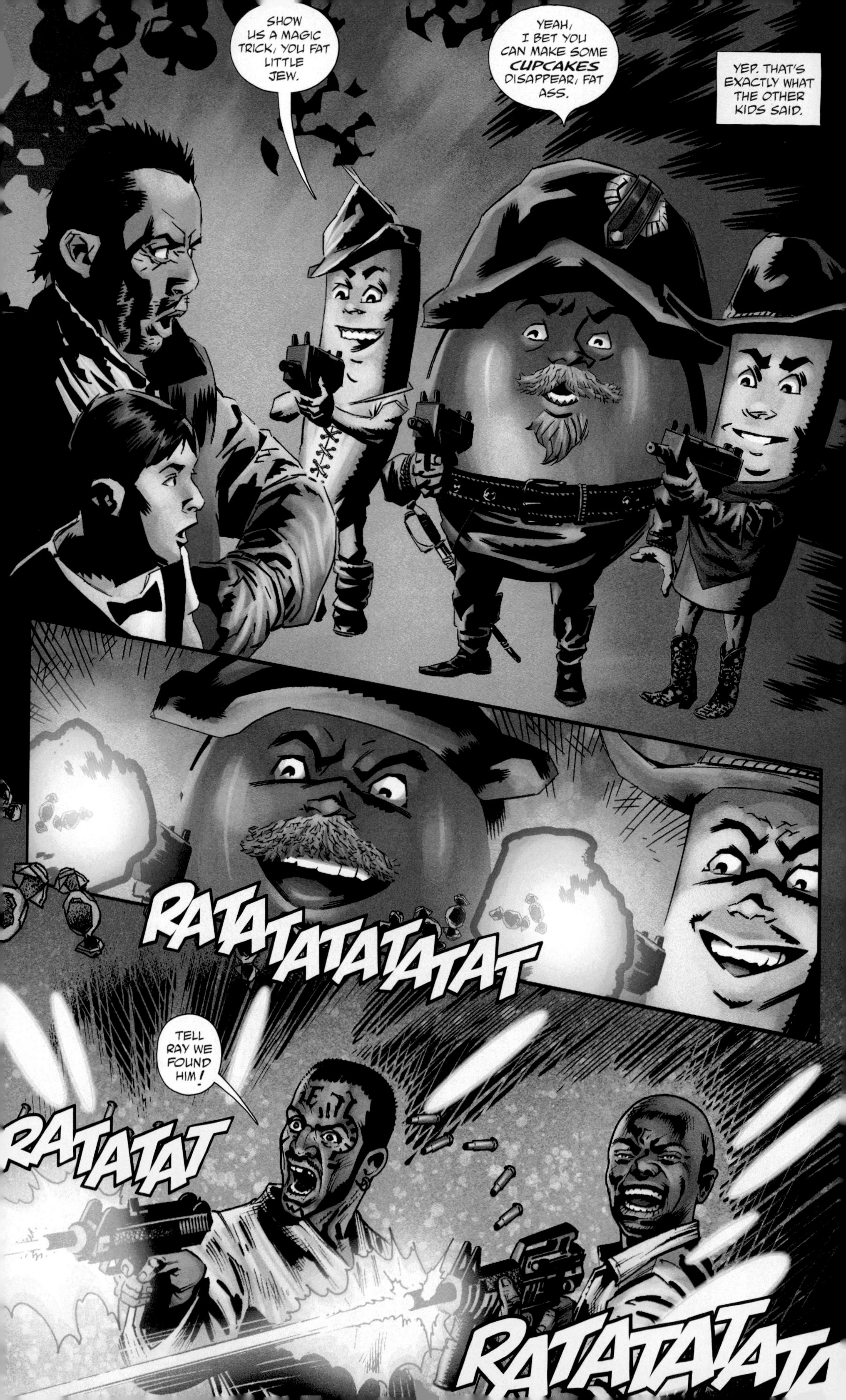

SHOW US A MAGIC TRICK, YOU FAT LITTLE JEW.
YEAH, I BET YOU CAN MAKE SOME CUPCAKES DISAPPEAR, FAT ASS.
YEP. THAT'S EXACTLY WHAT THE OTHER KIDS SAID.
RATATATATATATAT
TELL RAY WE FOUND HIM!
RATATAT
RATATATATATA

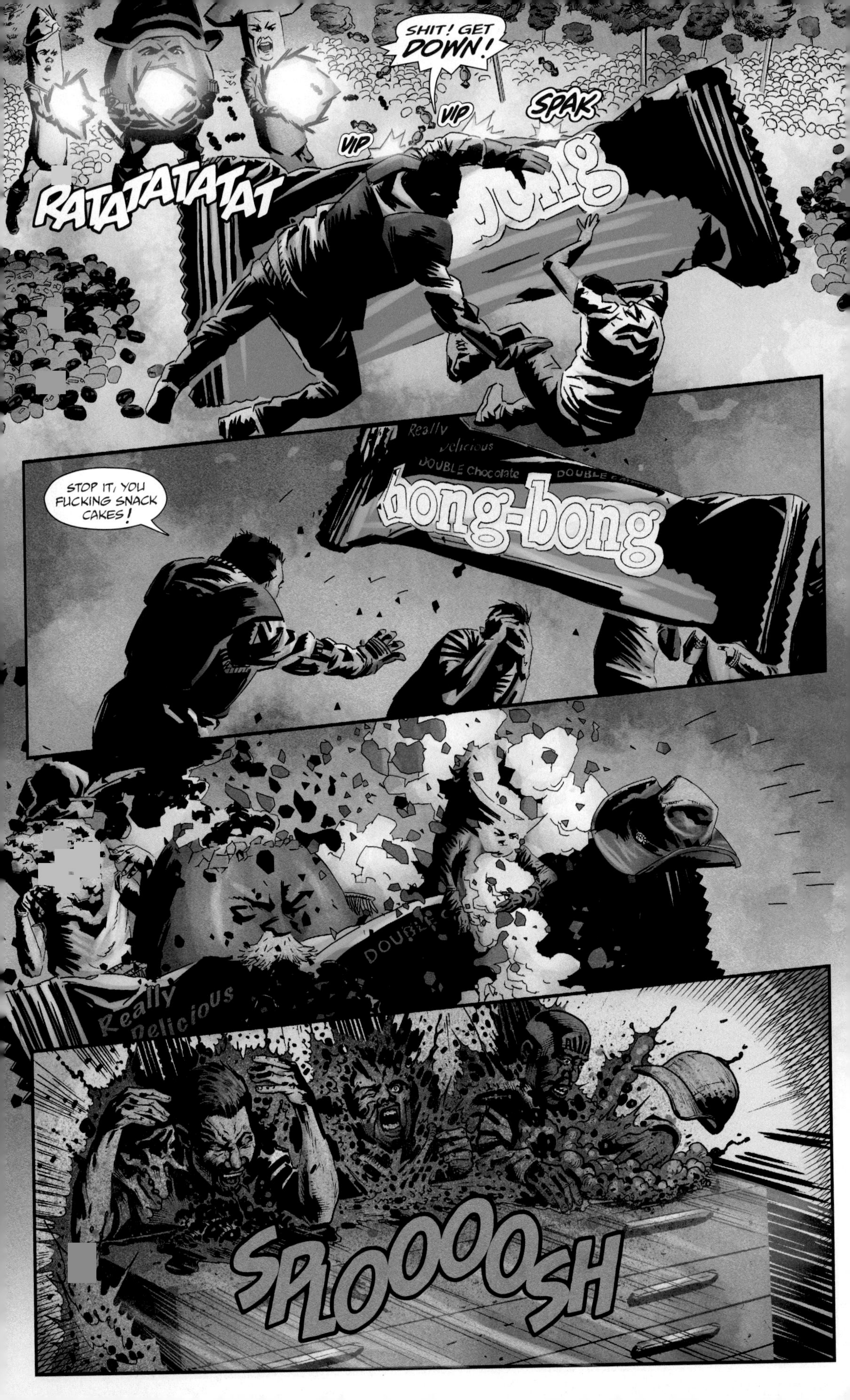
SHIT! GET DOWN!
VIP
VIP
SPAK
RATATATATAT
Really
Delicious
DOUBLE Chocolate
bong-bong
STOP IT, YOU FUCKING SNACK CAKES!
Really Delicious
SPLOOOOSH

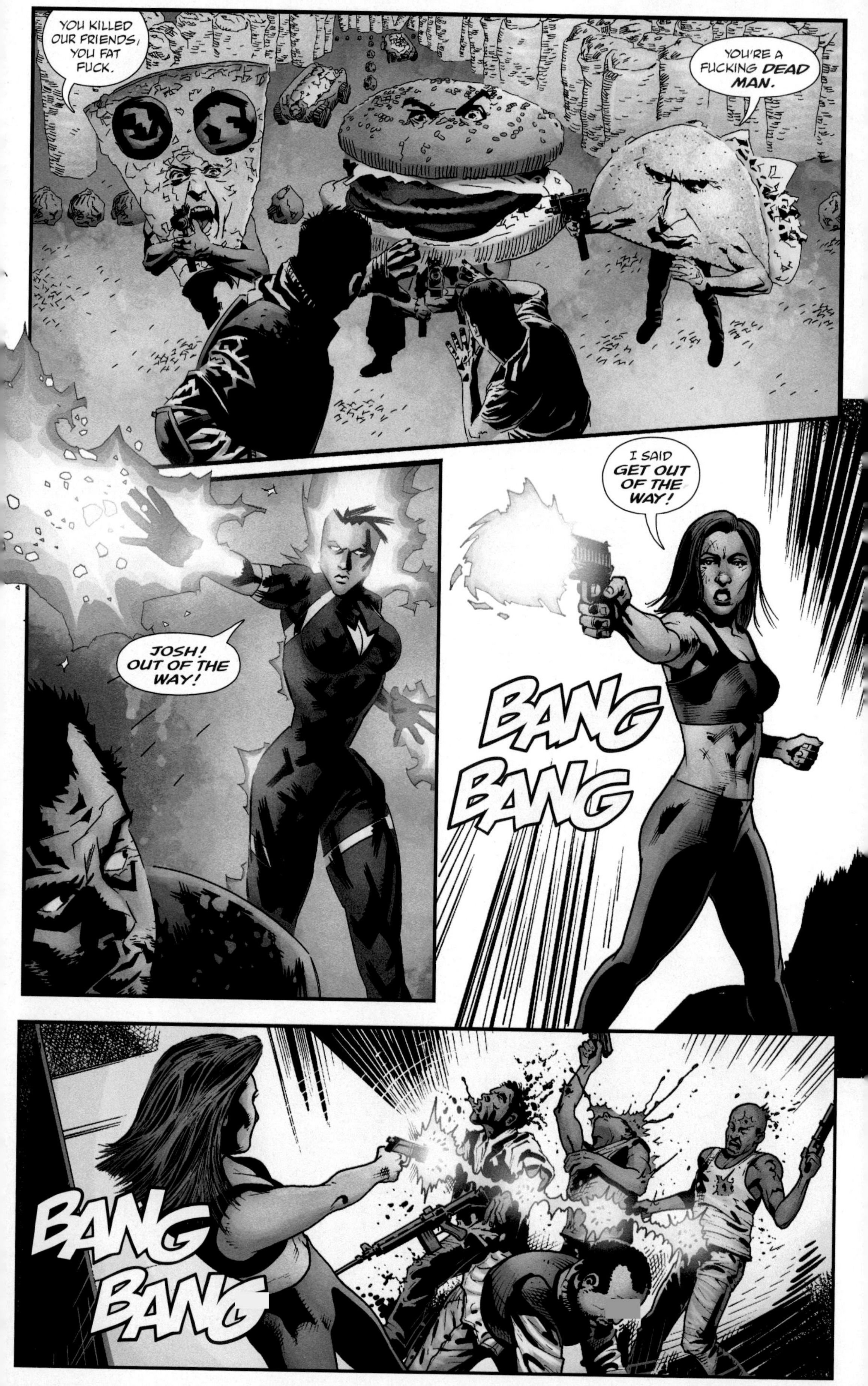
YOU KILLED OUR FRIENDS, YOU FAT FUCK.
YOU'RE A FUCKING DEAD MAN.
JOSH! OUT OF THE WAY!
I SAID GET OUT OF THE WAY!
BANG BANG
BANG BANG

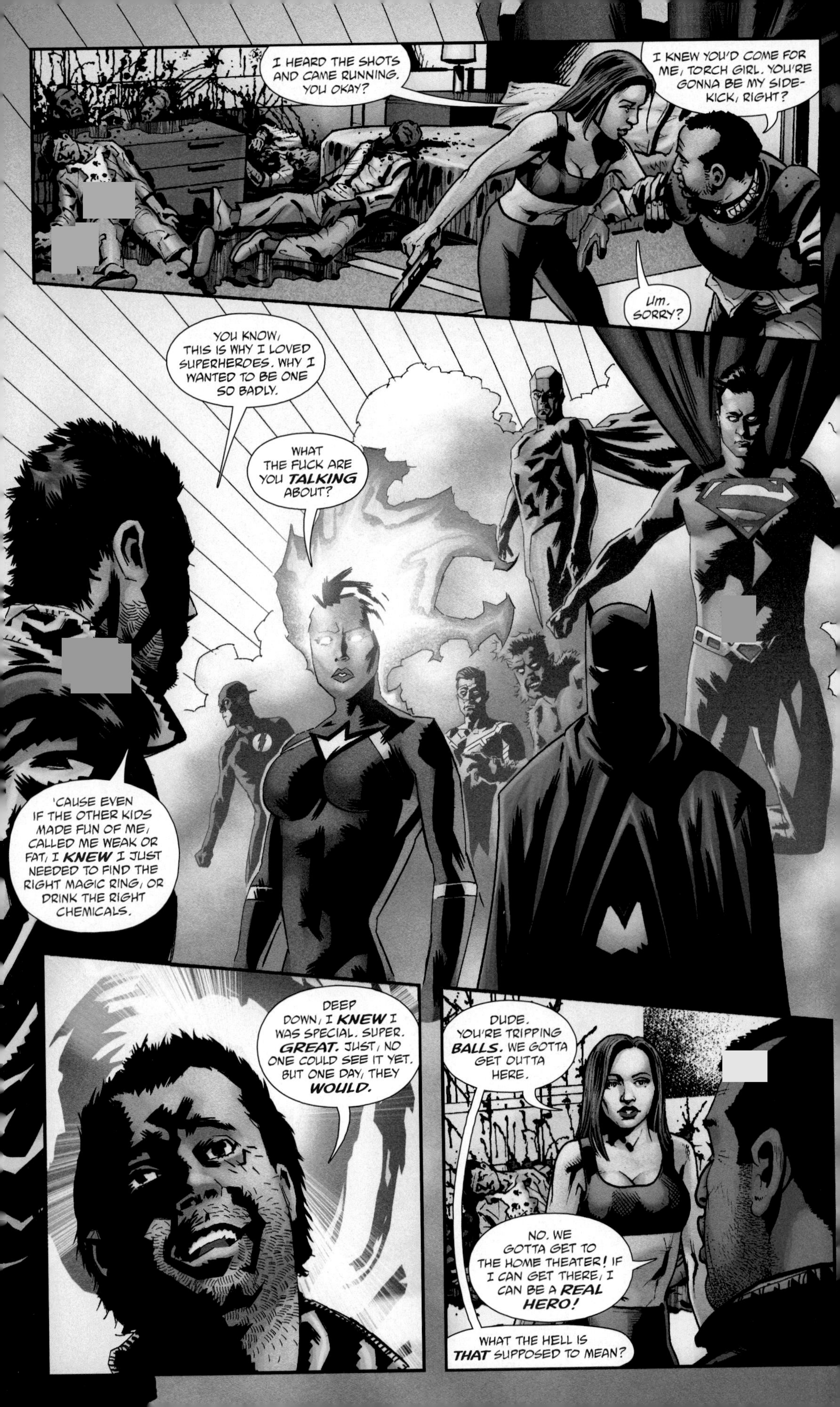

I HEARD THE SHOTS AND CAME RUNNING. YOU OKAY?
I KNEW YOU'D COME FOR ME, TORCH GIRL. YOU'RE GONNA BE MY SIDE-KICK, RIGHT?
UM. SORRY?
YOU KNOW, THIS IS WHY I LOVED SUPERHEROES. WHY I WANTED TO BE ONE SO BADLY.
WHAT THE FUCK ARE YOU **TALKING** ABOUT?
'CAUSE EVEN IF THE OTHER KIDS MADE FUN OF ME, CALLED ME WEAK OR FAT, I **KNEW** I JUST NEEDED TO FIND THE RIGHT MAGIC RING, OR DRINK THE RIGHT CHEMICALS.
DEEP DOWN, I **KNEW** I WAS SPECIAL. SUPER. **GREAT.** JUST, NO ONE COULD SEE IT YET. BUT ONE DAY, THEY **WOULD.**
DUDE. YOU'RE TRIPPING **BALLS.** WE GOTTA GET OUTTA HERE.
NO. WE GOTTA GET TO THE HOME THEATER! IF I CAN GET THERE, I CAN BE A **REAL HERO!**
WHAT THE HELL IS **THAT** SUPPOSED TO MEAN?

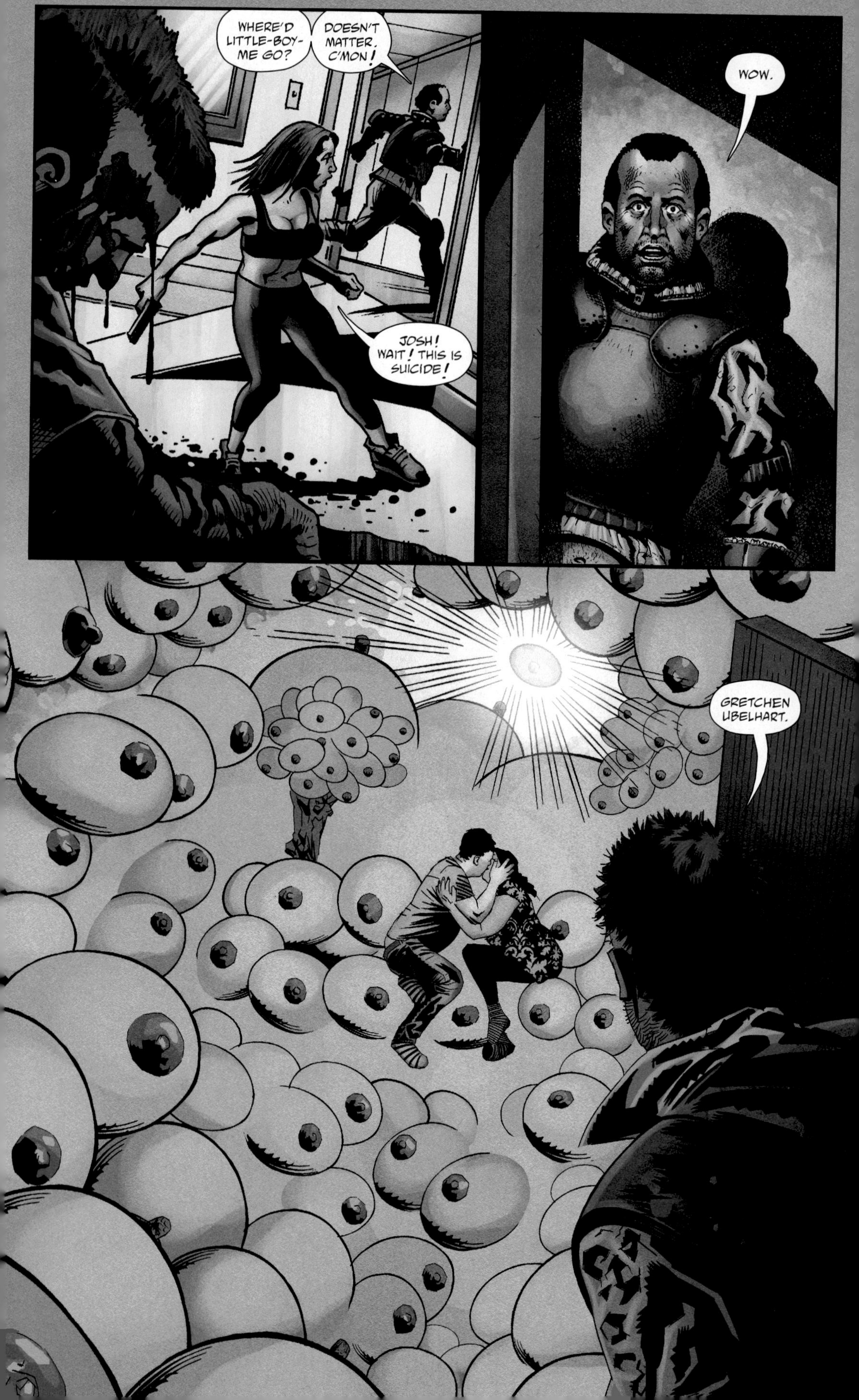
WHERE'D LITTLE-BOY-ME GO?
DOESN'T MATTER. C'MON!
JOSH! WAIT! THIS IS SUICIDE!
WOW.
GRETCHEN UBELHART.

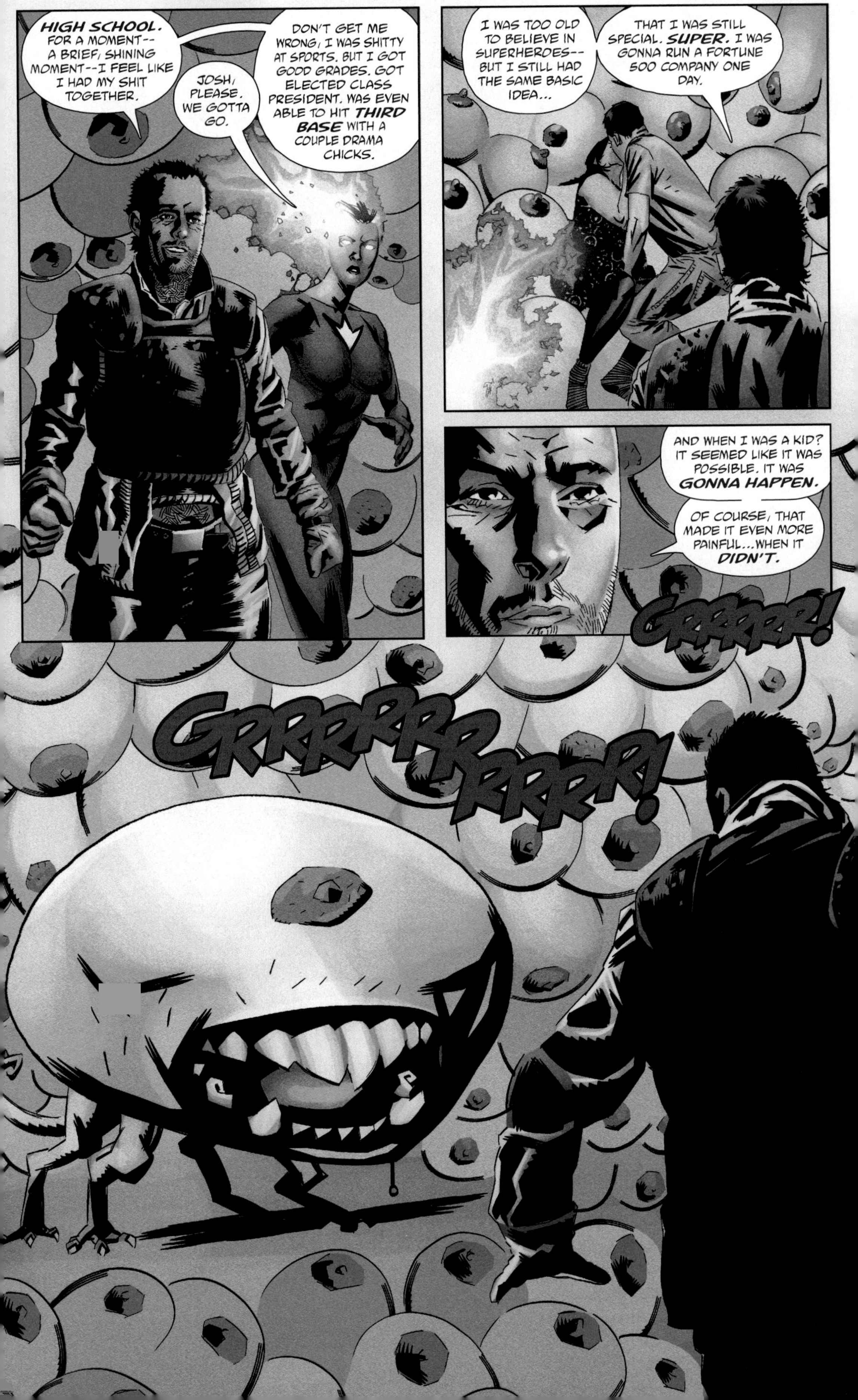
HIGH SCHOOL. FOR A MOMENT--A BRIEF, SHINING MOMENT--I FEEL LIKE I HAD MY SHIT TOGETHER.
JOSH, PLEASE. WE GOTTA GO.
DON'T GET ME WRONG, I WAS SHITTY AT SPORTS. BUT I GOT GOOD GRADES. GOT ELECTED CLASS PRESIDENT. WAS EVEN ABLE TO HIT THIRD BASE WITH A COUPLE DRAMA CHICKS.
I WAS TOO OLD TO BELIEVE IN SUPERHEROES--BUT I STILL HAD THE SAME BASIC IDEA...
THAT I WAS STILL SPECIAL. SUPER. I WAS GONNA RUN A FORTUNE 500 COMPANY ONE DAY.
AND WHEN I WAS A KID? IT SEEMED LIKE IT WAS POSSIBLE. IT WAS GONNA HAPPEN.
OF COURSE, THAT MADE IT EVEN MORE PAINFUL...WHEN IT DIDN'T.
GRRRRR!
GRRRRRRRRRR!

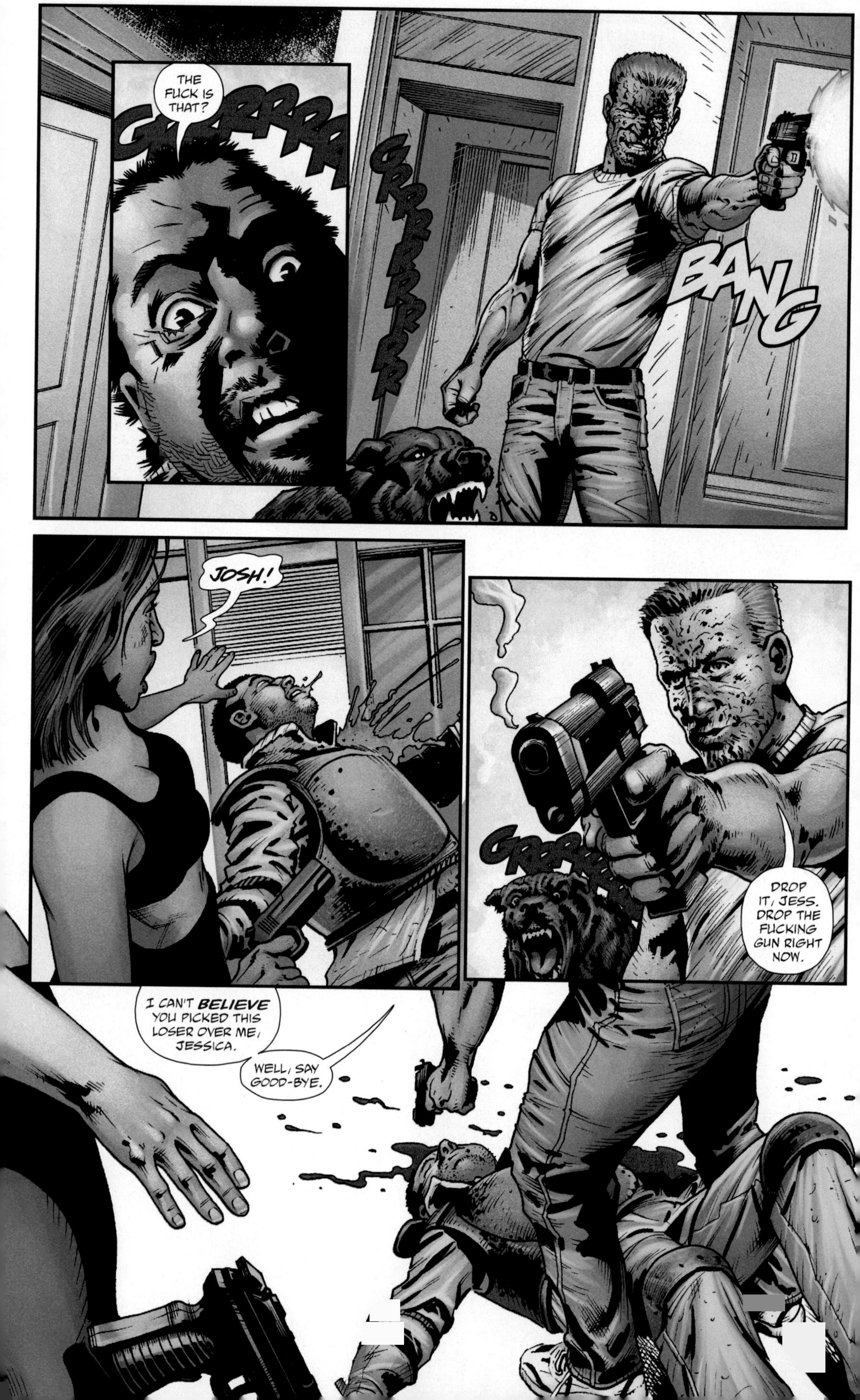

GRRRRR
THE FUCK IS THAT?
GRRRRRRRRR
BANG
JOSH!
GRRR
DROP IT, JESS. DROP THE FUCKING GUN RIGHT NOW.
I CAN'T BELIEVE YOU PICKED THIS LOSER OVER ME, JESSICA.
WELL, SAY GOOD-BYE.

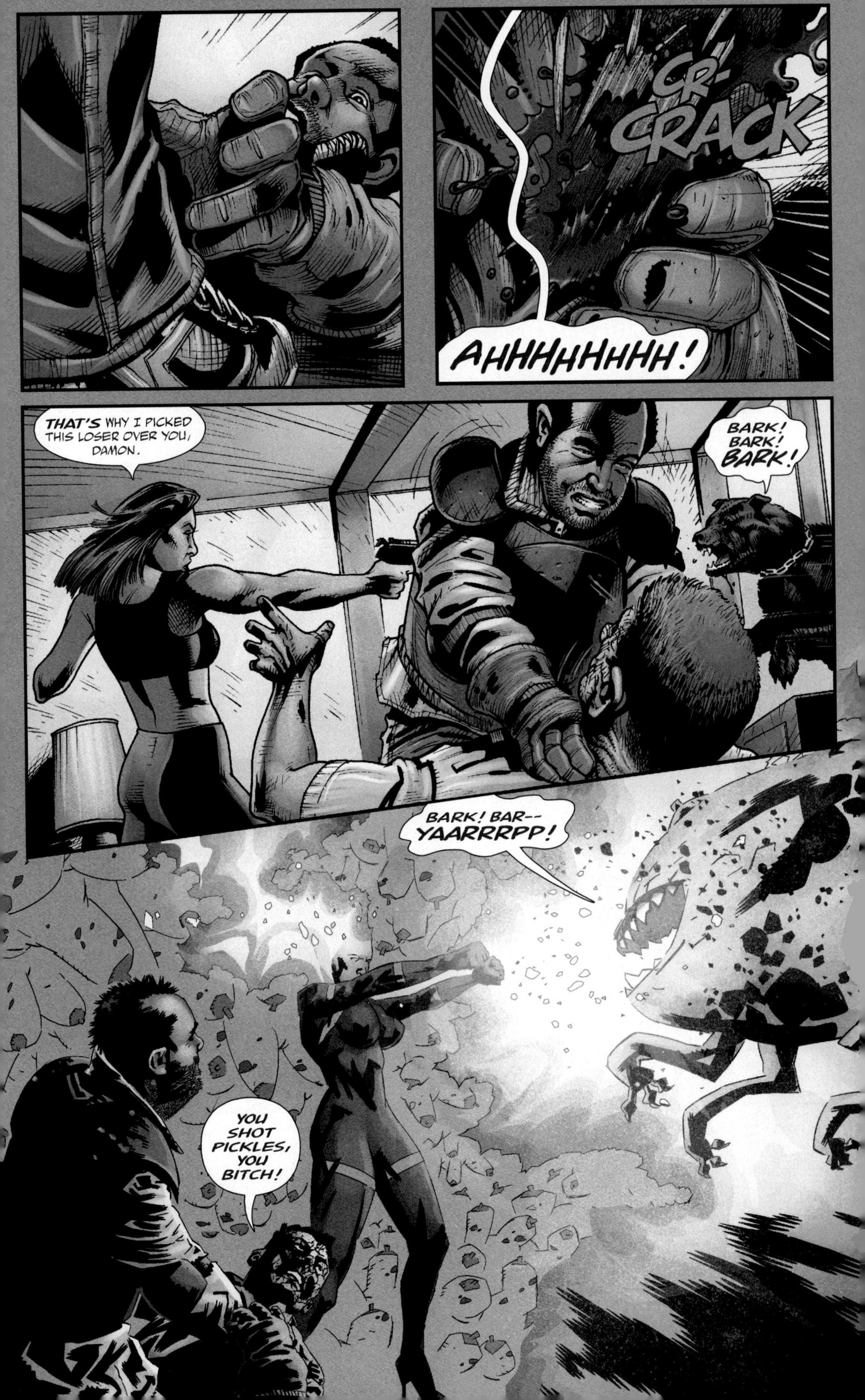
CR-CRACK
AHHHHHHHH!
THAT'S WHY I PICKED THIS LOSER OVER YOU, DAMON.
BARK! BARK! BARK!
BARK! BAR-- YAARRRPP!
YOU SHOT PICKLES, YOU BITCH!

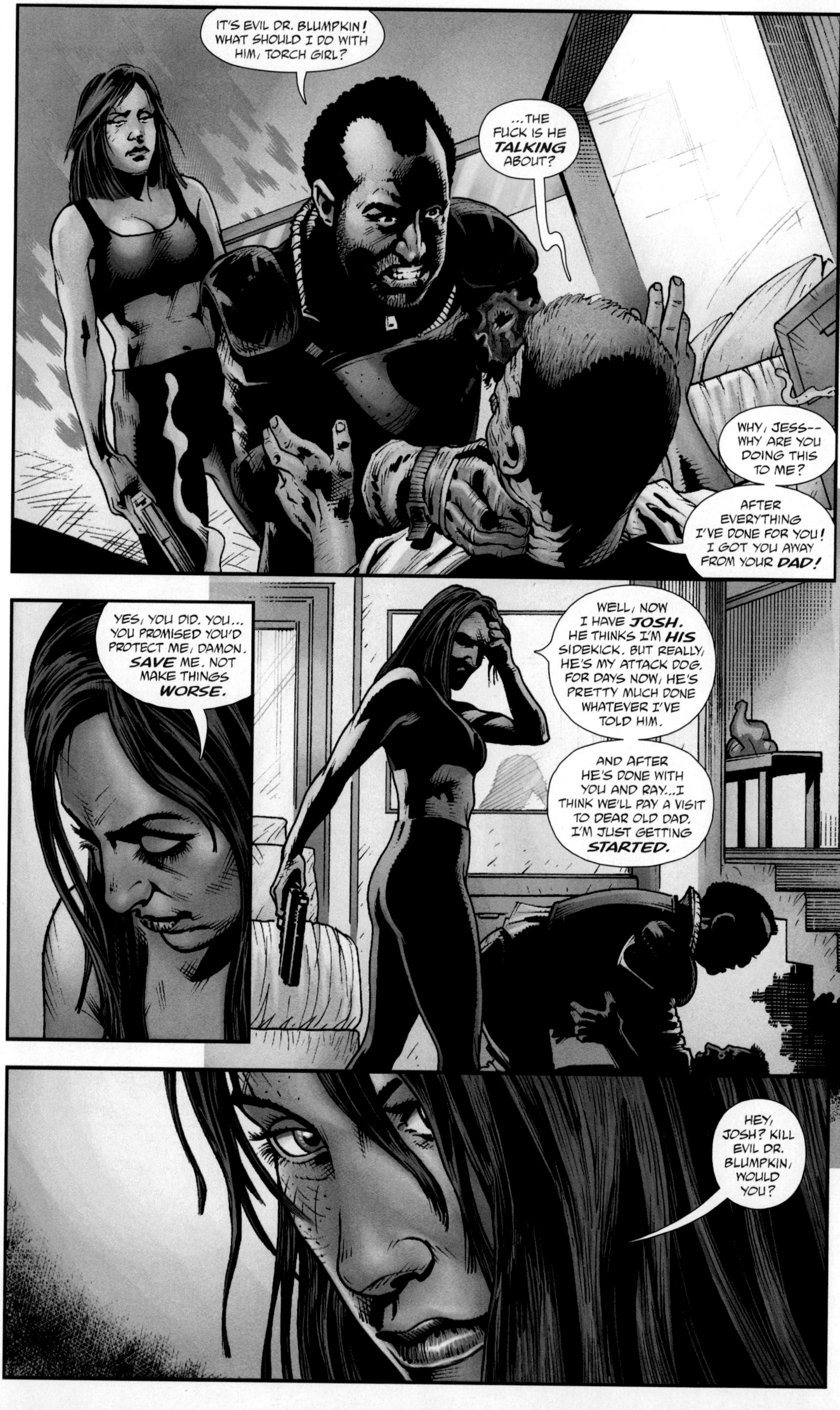
IT'S EVIL DR. BLUMPKIN! WHAT SHOULD I DO WITH HIM, TORCH GIRL?
...THE FUCK IS HE TALKING ABOUT?
WHY, JESS-- WHY ARE YOU DOING THIS TO ME?
AFTER EVERYTHING I'VE DONE FOR YOU! I GOT YOU AWAY FROM YOUR DAD!
YES, YOU DID. YOU... YOU PROMISED YOU'D PROTECT ME, DAMON. SAVE ME. NOT MAKE THINGS WORSE.
WELL, NOW I HAVE JOSH. HE THINKS I'M HIS SIDEKICK. BUT REALLY, HE'S MY ATTACK DOG. FOR DAYS NOW, HE'S PRETTY MUCH DONE WHATEVER I'VE TOLD HIM.
AND AFTER HE'S DONE WITH YOU AND RAY...I THINK WE'LL PAY A VISIT TO DEAR OLD DAD. I'M JUST GETTING STARTED.
HEY, JOSH? KILL EVIL DR. BLUMPKIN, WOULD YOU?

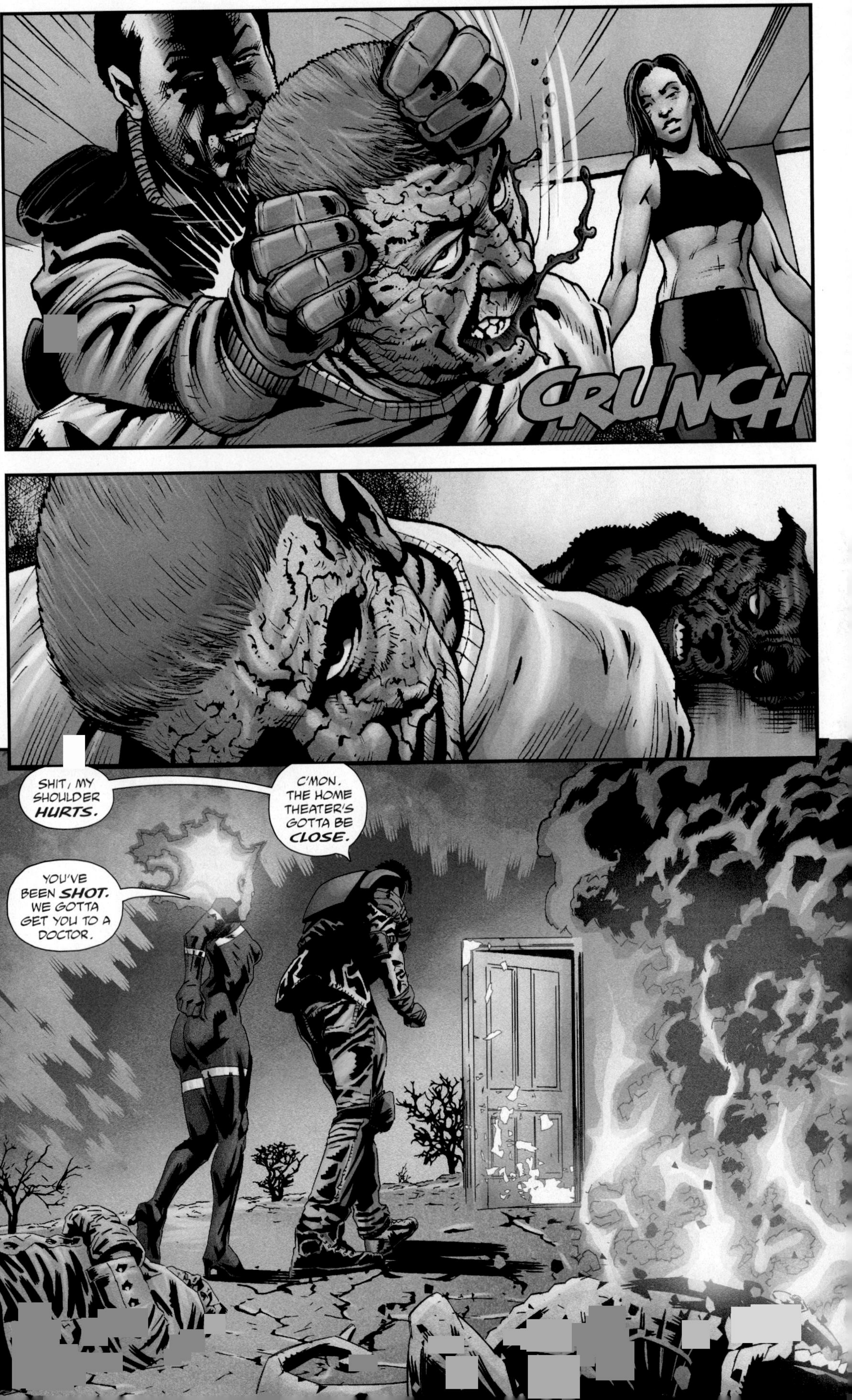
CRUNCH
SHIT, MY SHOULDER HURTS.
C'MON. THE HOME THEATER'S GOTTA BE CLOSE.
YOU'VE BEEN SHOT. WE GOTTA GET YOU TO A DOCTOR.

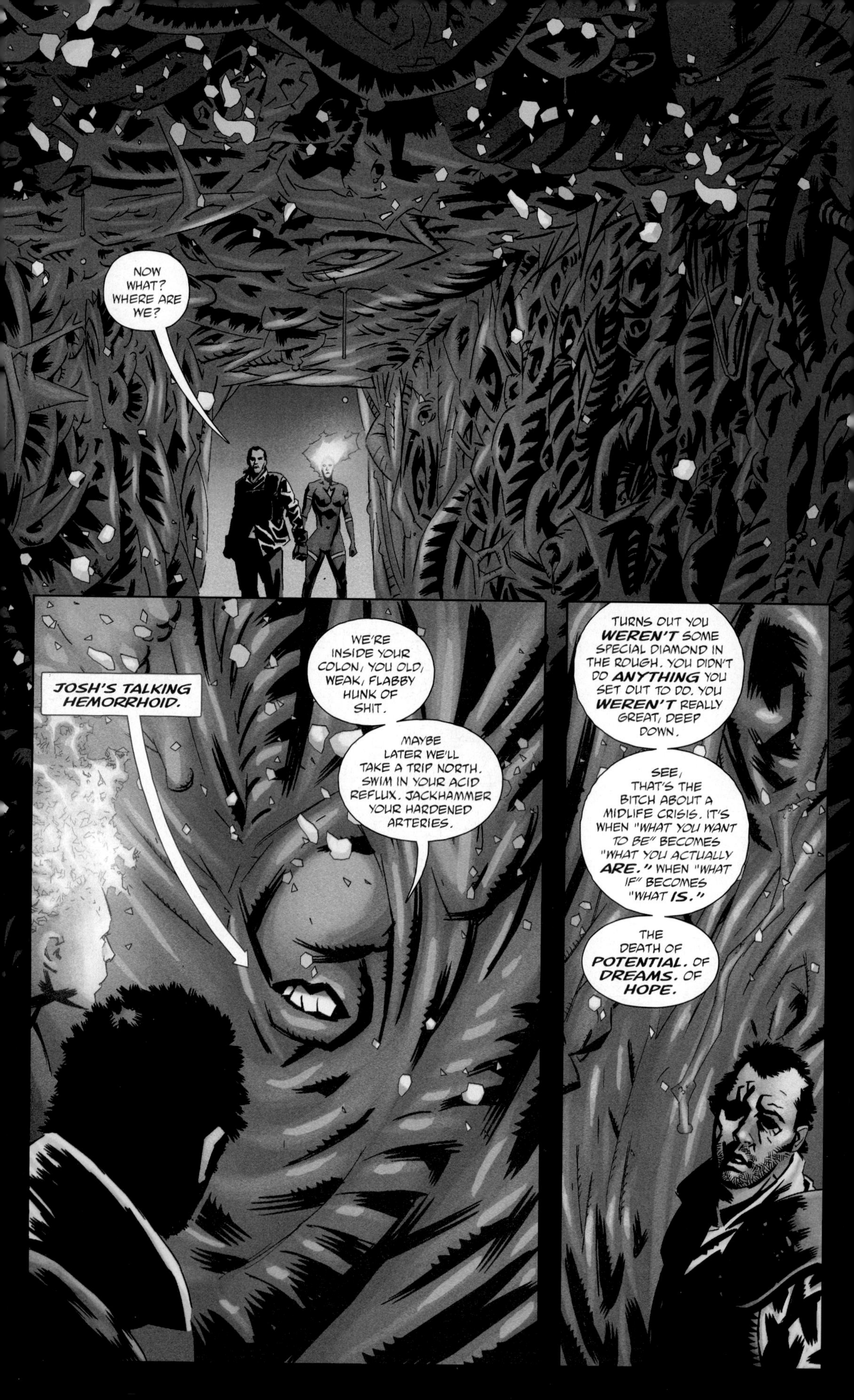
NOW WHAT? WHERE ARE WE?
JOSH'S TALKING HEMORRHOID.
WE'RE INSIDE YOUR COLON, YOU OLD, WEAK, FLABBY HUNK OF SHIT.
MAYBE LATER WE'LL TAKE A TRIP NORTH. SWIM IN YOUR ACID REFLUX. JACKHAMMER YOUR HARDENED ARTERIES.
TURNS OUT YOU WEREN'T SOME SPECIAL DIAMOND IN THE ROUGH. YOU DIDN'T DO ANYTHING YOU SET OUT TO DO. YOU WEREN'T REALLY GREAT, DEEP DOWN.
SEE, THAT'S THE BITCH ABOUT A MIDLIFE CRISIS. IT'S WHEN "WHAT YOU WANT TO BE" BECOMES "WHAT YOU ACTUALLY ARE." WHEN "WHAT IF" BECOMES "WHAT IS."
THE DEATH OF POTENTIAL. OF DREAMS. OF HOPE.

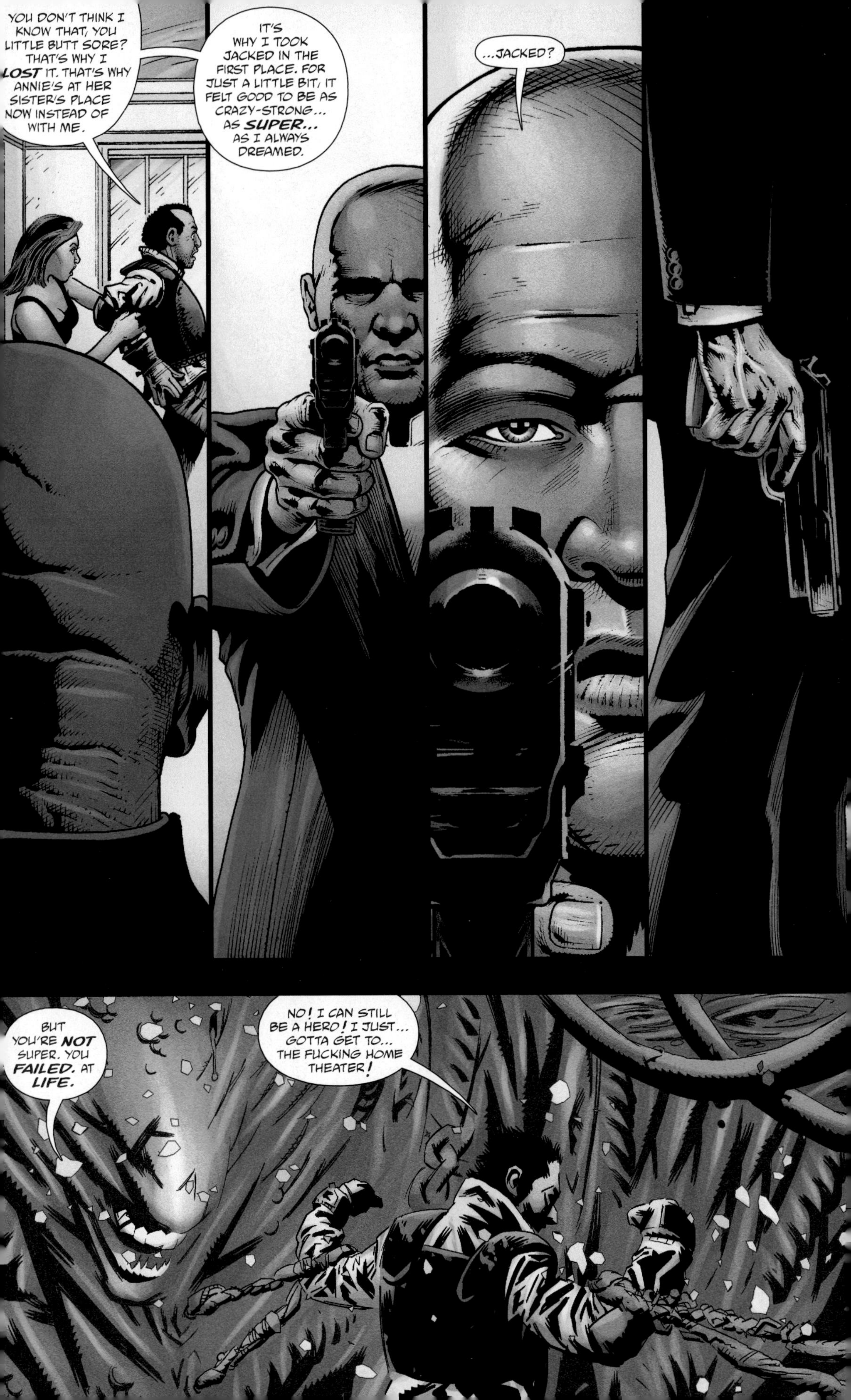
YOU DON'T THINK I KNOW THAT, YOU LITTLE BUTT SORE? THAT'S WHY I **LOST** IT. THAT'S WHY ANNIE'S AT HER SISTER'S PLACE NOW INSTEAD OF WITH ME.
IT'S WHY I TOOK JACKED IN THE FIRST PLACE. FOR JUST A LITTLE BIT, IT FELT GOOD TO BE AS CRAZY-STRONG... AS **SUPER...** AS I ALWAYS DREAMED.
...JACKED?
BUT YOU'RE **NOT** SUPER. YOU **FAILED.** AT **LIFE.**
NO! I CAN STILL BE A HERO! I JUST... GOTTA GET TO... THE FUCKING HOME THEATER!

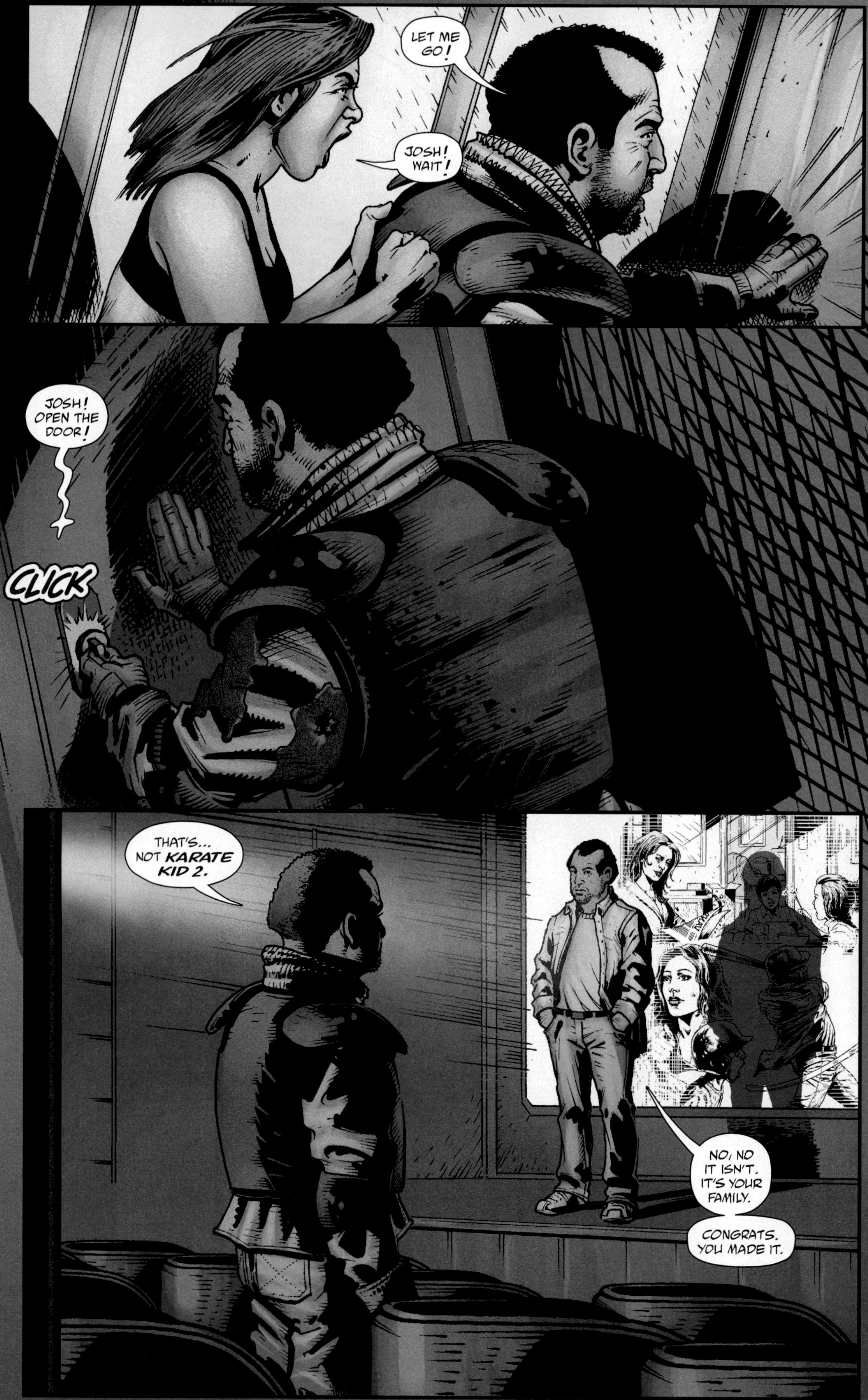
LET ME GO!
JOSH! WAIT!
JOSH! OPEN THE DOOR!
CLICK
THAT'S... NOT KARATE KID 2.
NO, NO IT ISN'T. IT'S YOUR FAMILY.
CONGRATS. YOU MADE IT.

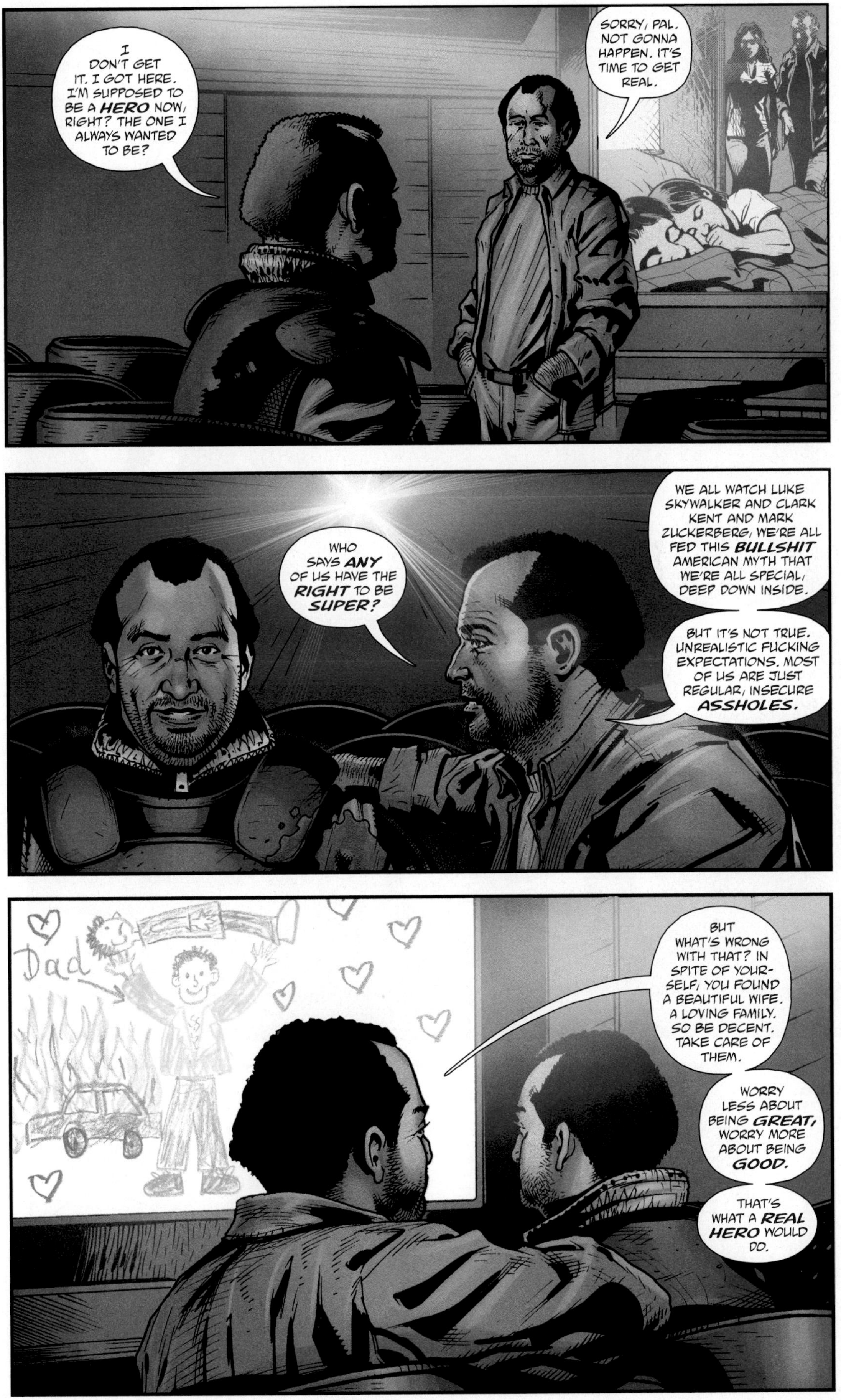
I DON'T GET IT. I GOT HERE. I'M SUPPOSED TO BE A HERO NOW, RIGHT? THE ONE I ALWAYS WANTED TO BE?
SORRY, PAL. NOT GONNA HAPPEN. IT'S TIME TO GET REAL.
WHO SAYS ANY OF US HAVE THE RIGHT TO BE SUPER?
WE ALL WATCH LUKE SKYWALKER AND CLARK KENT AND MARK ZUCKERBERG, WE'RE ALL FED THIS BULLSHIT AMERICAN MYTH THAT WE'RE ALL SPECIAL, DEEP DOWN INSIDE.
BUT IT'S NOT TRUE. UNREALISTIC FUCKING EXPECTATIONS. MOST OF US ARE JUST REGULAR, INSECURE ASSHOLES.
Dad
BUT WHAT'S WRONG WITH THAT? IN SPITE OF YOURSELF, YOU FOUND A BEAUTIFUL WIFE. A LOVING FAMILY. SO BE DECENT. TAKE CARE OF THEM.
WORRY LESS ABOUT BEING GREAT, WORRY MORE ABOUT BEING GOOD.
THAT'S WHAT A REAL HERO WOULD DO.

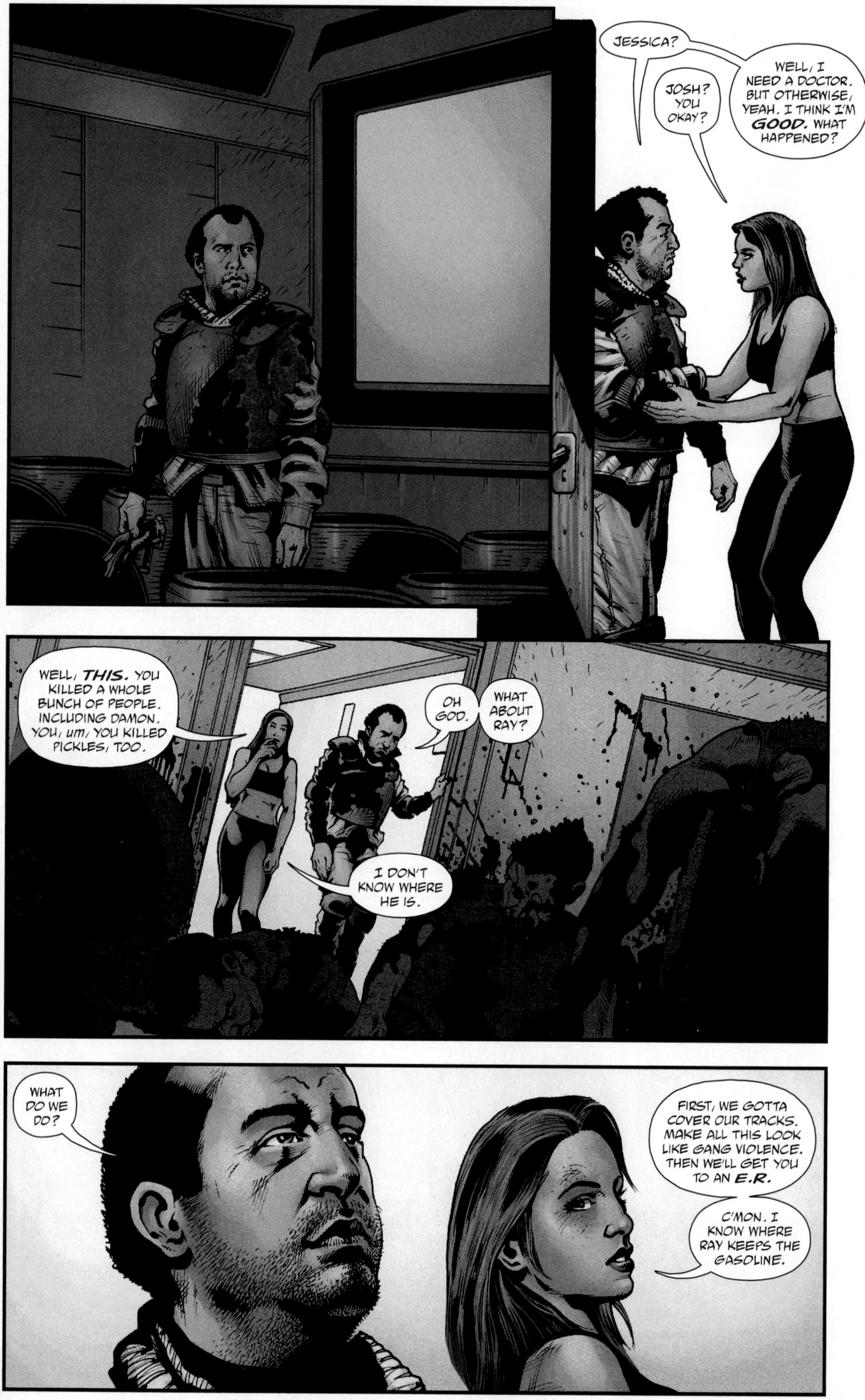

JESSICA?
JOSH? YOU OKAY?
WELL, I NEED A DOCTOR. BUT OTHERWISE, YEAH. I THINK I'M GOOD. WHAT HAPPENED?
WELL, THIS. YOU KILLED A WHOLE BUNCH OF PEOPLE. INCLUDING DAMON. YOU, um, YOU KILLED PICKLES, TOO.
OH GOD.
WHAT ABOUT RAY?
I DON'T KNOW WHERE HE IS.
WHAT DO WE DO?
FIRST, WE GOTTA COVER OUR TRACKS. MAKE ALL THIS LOOK LIKE GANG VIOLENCE. THEN WE'LL GET YOU TO AN E.R.
C'MON. I KNOW WHERE RAY KEEPS THE GASOLINE.

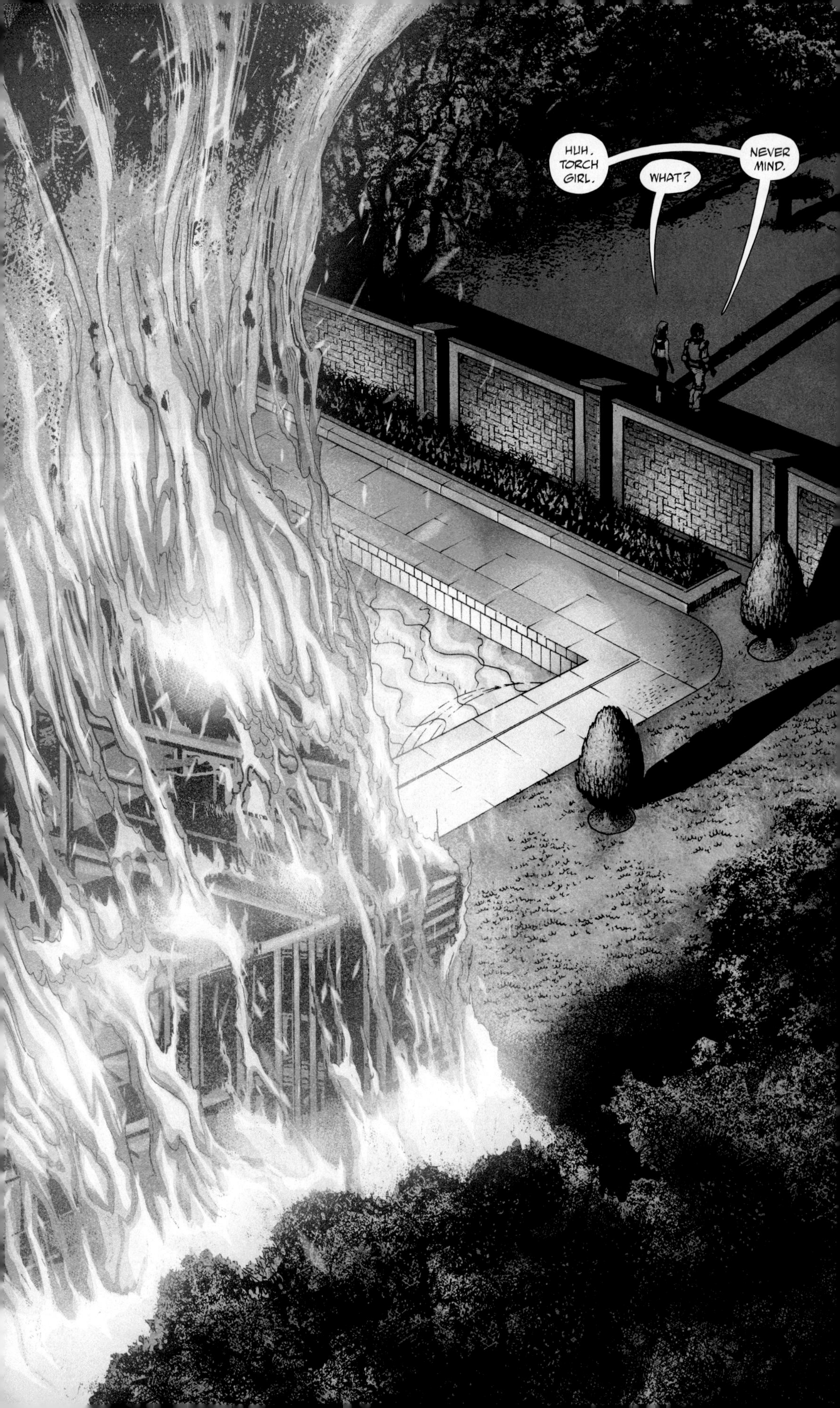
HUH. TORCH GIRL.
WHAT?
NEVER MIND.

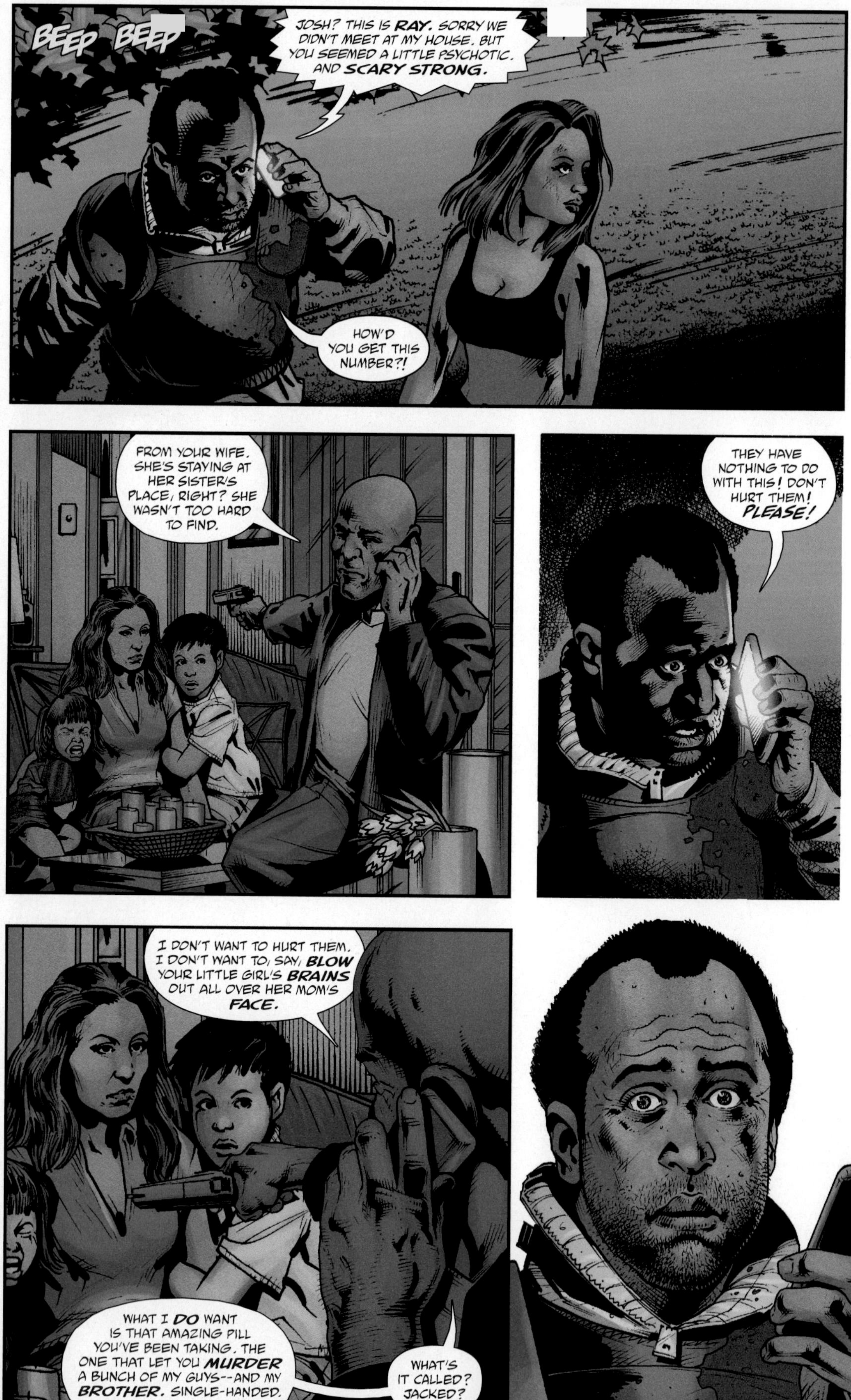
BEEP BEEP
JOSH? THIS IS RAY. SORRY WE DIDN'T MEET AT MY HOUSE. BUT YOU SEEMED A LITTLE PSYCHOTIC. AND SCARY STRONG.
HOW'D YOU GET THIS NUMBER?!
FROM YOUR WIFE. SHE'S STAYING AT HER SISTER'S PLACE, RIGHT? SHE WASN'T TOO HARD TO FIND.
THEY HAVE NOTHING TO DO WITH THIS! DON'T HURT THEM! PLEASE!
I DON'T WANT TO HURT THEM. I DON'T WANT TO, SAY, BLOW YOUR LITTLE GIRL'S BRAINS OUT ALL OVER HER MOM'S FACE.
WHAT I DO WANT IS THAT AMAZING PILL YOU'VE BEEN TAKING. THE ONE THAT LET YOU MURDER A BUNCH OF MY GUYS--AND MY BROTHER. SINGLE-HANDED.
WHAT'S IT CALLED? JACKED?

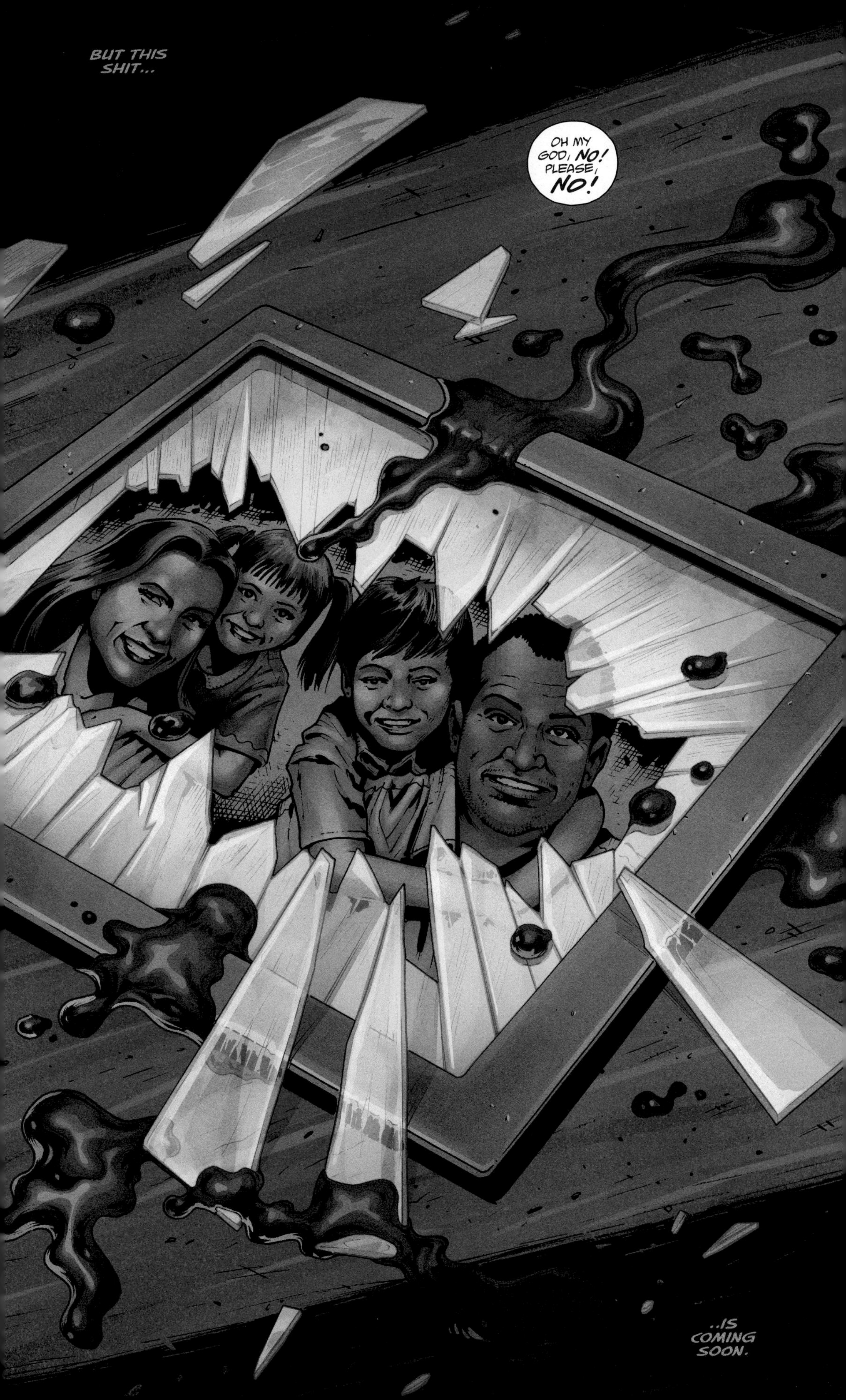
BUT THIS SHIT...
OH MY GOD, NO! PLEASE, NO!
..IS COMING SOON.

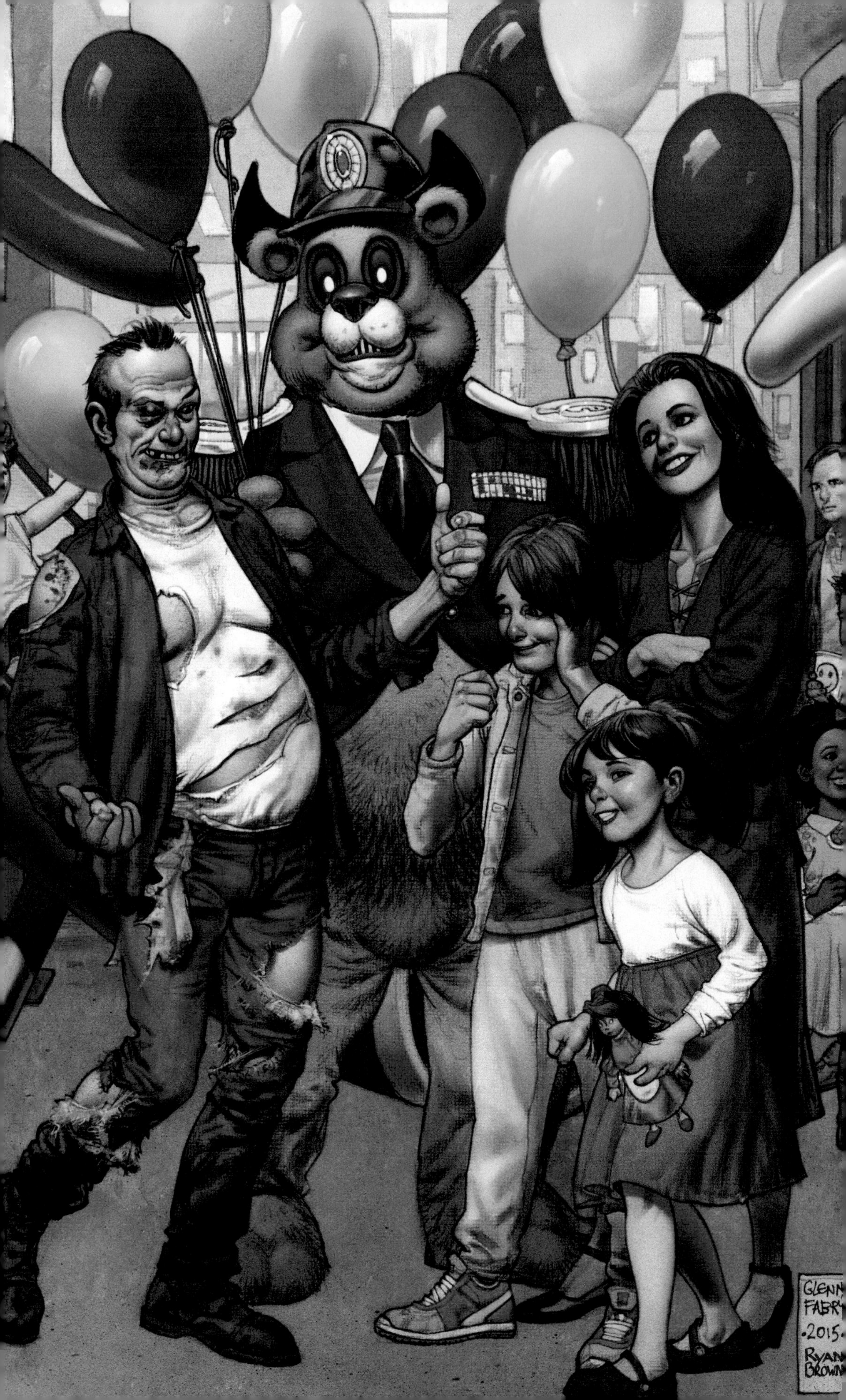
GLENN FABRY
.2015.
RYAN BROWN

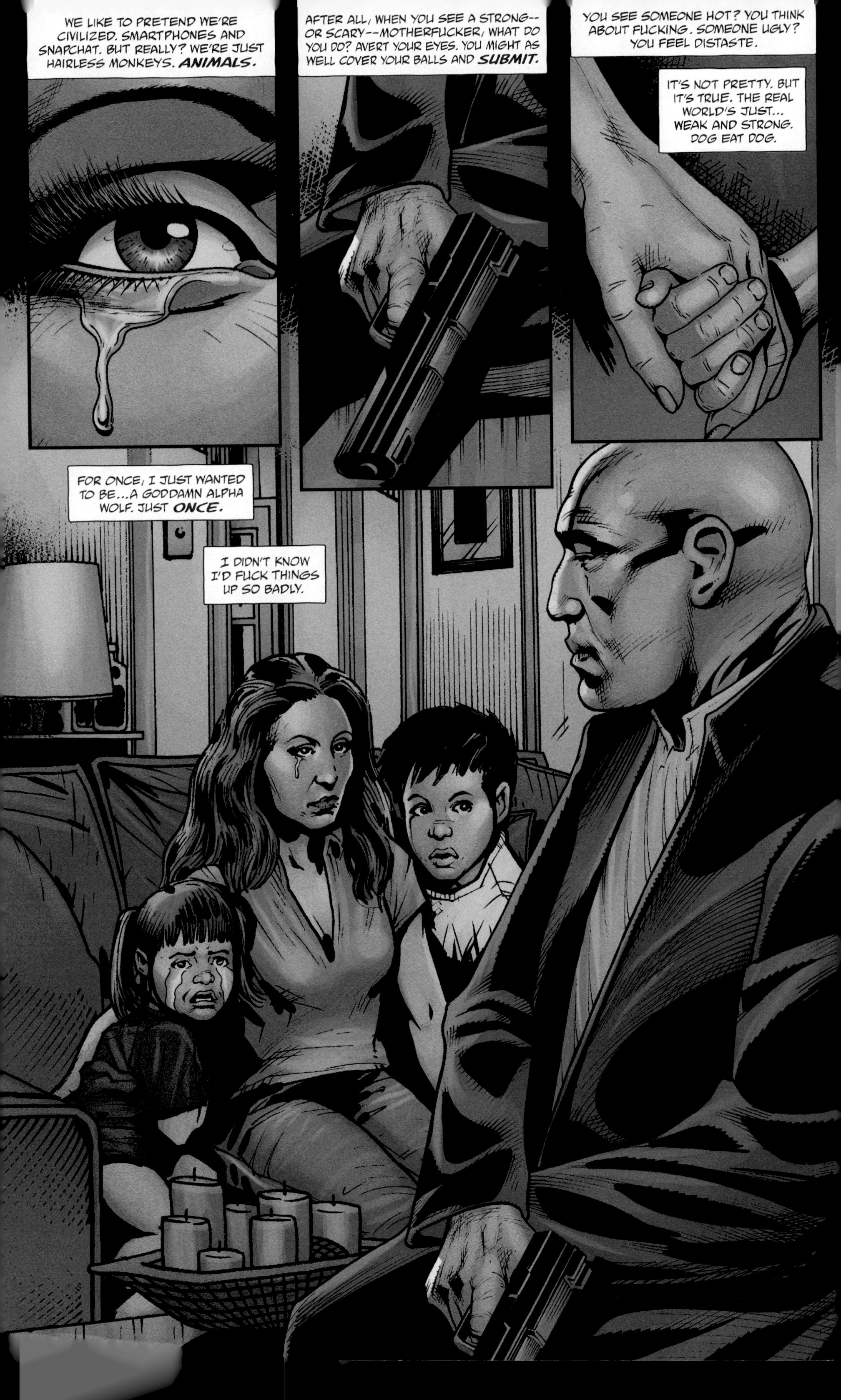
WE LIKE TO PRETEND WE'RE CIVILIZED. SMARTPHONES AND SNAPCHAT. BUT REALLY? WE'RE JUST HAIRLESS MONKEYS. ***ANIMALS.***
AFTER ALL, WHEN YOU SEE A STRONG-- OR SCARY--MOTHERFUCKER, WHAT DO YOU DO? AVERT YOUR EYES. YOU MIGHT AS WELL COVER YOUR BALLS AND ***SUBMIT.***
YOU SEE SOMEONE HOT? YOU THINK ABOUT FUCKING. SOMEONE UGLY? YOU FEEL DISTASTE.
IT'S NOT PRETTY. BUT IT'S TRUE. THE REAL WORLD'S JUST... WEAK AND STRONG. DOG EAT DOG.
FOR ONCE, I JUST WANTED TO BE...A GODDAMN ALPHA WOLF. JUST ***ONCE.***
I DIDN'T KNOW I'D FUCK THINGS UP SO BADLY.

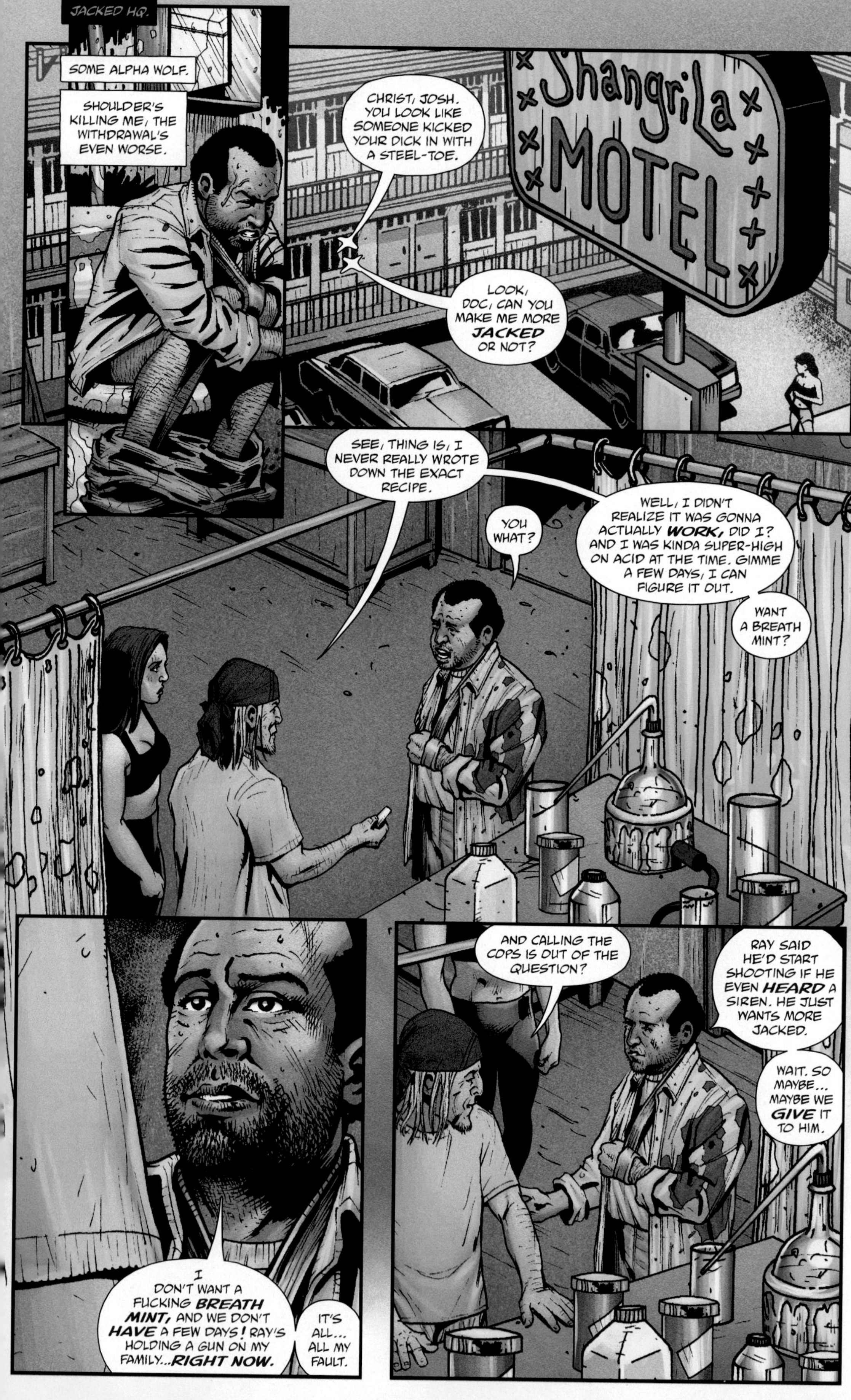
JACKED HQ.
SOME ALPHA WOLF.
SHOULDER'S KILLING ME; THE WITHDRAWAL'S EVEN WORSE.
CHRIST, JOSH. YOU LOOK LIKE SOMEONE KICKED YOUR DICK IN WITH A STEEL-TOE.
LOOK, DOC, CAN YOU MAKE ME MORE JACKED OR NOT?
Shangri La MOTEL
SEE, THING IS, I NEVER REALLY WROTE DOWN THE EXACT RECIPE.
YOU WHAT?
WELL, I DIDN'T REALIZE IT WAS GONNA ACTUALLY WORK, DID I? AND I WAS KINDA SUPER-HIGH ON ACID AT THE TIME. GIMME A FEW DAYS, I CAN FIGURE IT OUT.
WANT A BREATH MINT?
I DON'T WANT A FUCKING BREATH MINT, AND WE DON'T HAVE A FEW DAYS! RAY'S HOLDING A GUN ON MY FAMILY...RIGHT NOW.
IT'S ALL... ALL MY FAULT.
AND CALLING THE COPS IS OUT OF THE QUESTION?
RAY SAID HE'D START SHOOTING IF HE EVEN HEARD A SIREN. HE JUST WANTS MORE JACKED.
WAIT. SO MAYBE... MAYBE WE GIVE IT TO HIM.

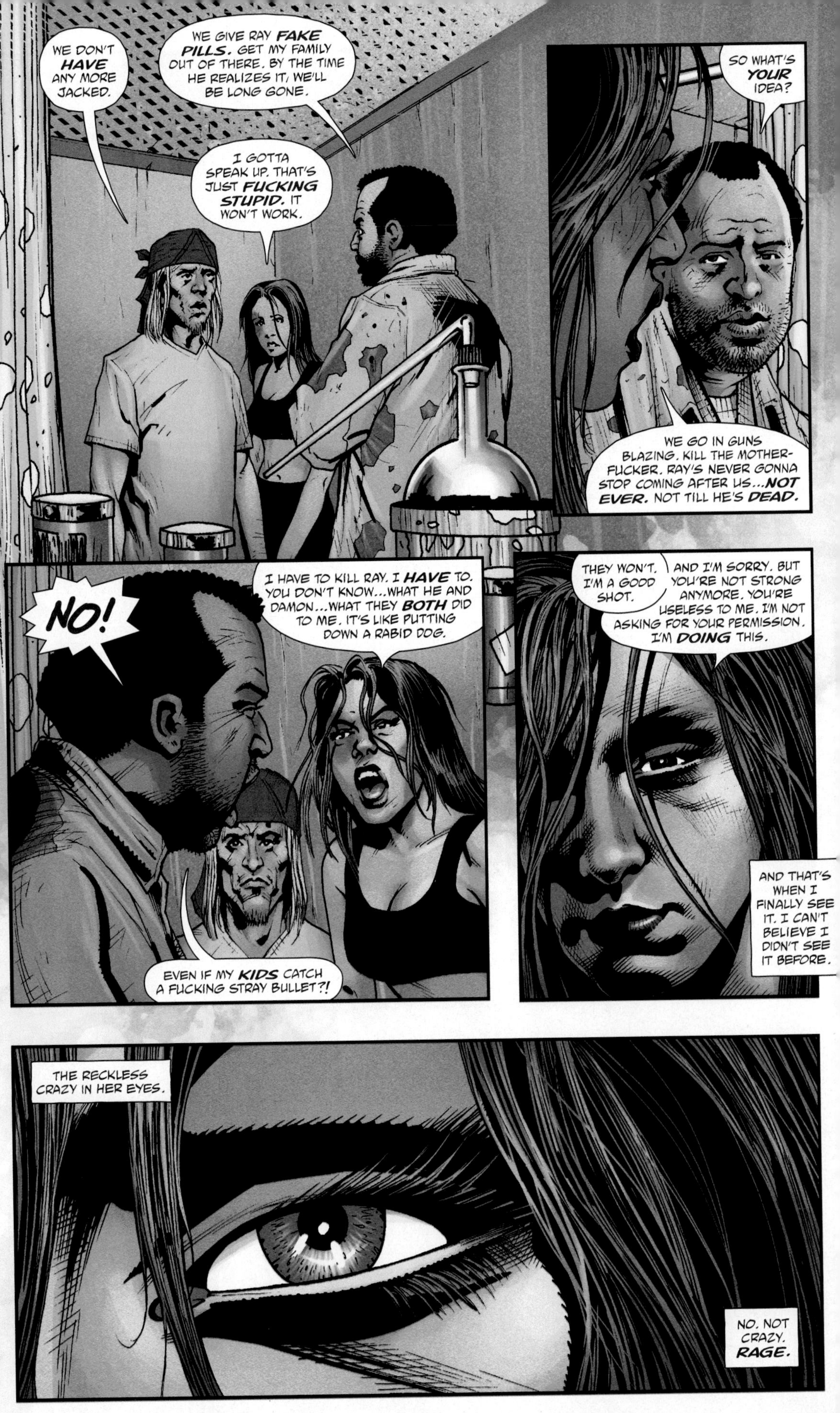

WE DON'T HAVE ANY MORE JACKED.
WE GIVE RAY FAKE PILLS. GET MY FAMILY OUT OF THERE. BY THE TIME HE REALIZES IT, WE'LL BE LONG GONE.
I GOTTA SPEAK UP. THAT'S JUST FUCKING STUPID. IT WON'T WORK.
SO WHAT'S YOUR IDEA?
WE GO IN GUNS BLAZING. KILL THE MOTHER-FUCKER. RAY'S NEVER GONNA STOP COMING AFTER US...NOT EVER. NOT TILL HE'S DEAD.
NO!
I HAVE TO KILL RAY. I HAVE TO. YOU DON'T KNOW...WHAT HE AND DAMON...WHAT THEY BOTH DID TO ME. IT'S LIKE PUTTING DOWN A RABID DOG.
EVEN IF MY KIDS CATCH A FUCKING STRAY BULLET?!
THEY WON'T. I'M A GOOD SHOT.
AND I'M SORRY. BUT YOU'RE NOT STRONG ANYMORE. YOU'RE USELESS TO ME. I'M NOT ASKING FOR YOUR PERMISSION. I'M DOING THIS.
AND THAT'S WHEN I FINALLY SEE IT. I CAN'T BELIEVE I DIDN'T SEE IT BEFORE.
THE RECKLESS CRAZY IN HER EYES.
NO. NOT CRAZY. RAGE.

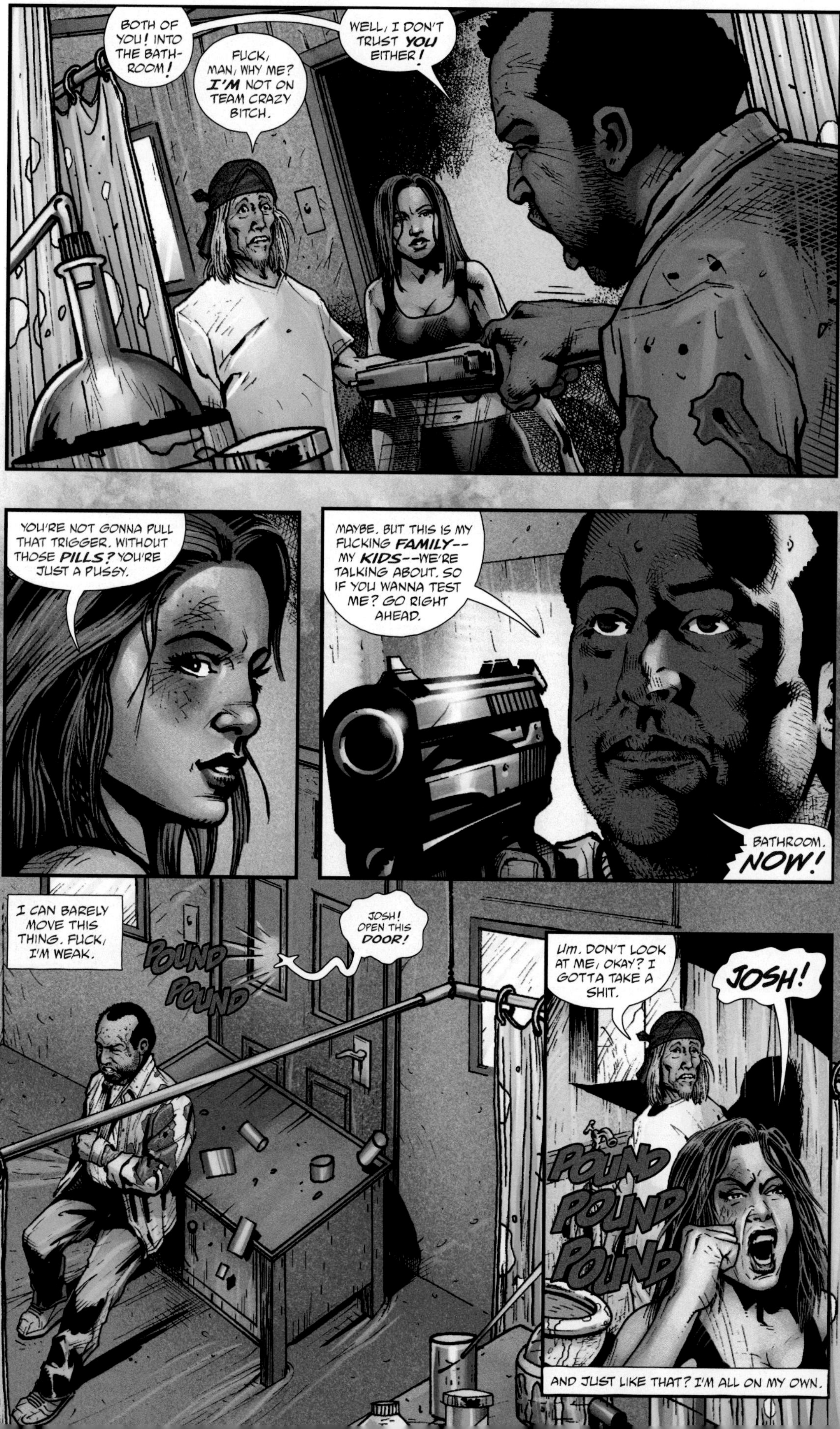
BOTH OF YOU! INTO THE BATH-ROOM!
FUCK, MAN, WHY ME? I'M NOT ON TEAM CRAZY BITCH.
WELL, I DON'T TRUST YOU EITHER!
YOU'RE NOT GONNA PULL THAT TRIGGER. WITHOUT THOSE PILLS? YOU'RE JUST A PUSSY.
MAYBE. BUT THIS IS MY FUCKING FAMILY-- MY KIDS--WE'RE TALKING ABOUT. SO IF YOU WANNA TEST ME? GO RIGHT AHEAD.
BATHROOM. NOW!
I CAN BARELY MOVE THIS THING. FUCK, I'M WEAK.
POUND POUND
JOSH! OPEN THIS DOOR!
UM. DON'T LOOK AT ME, OKAY? I GOTTA TAKE A SHIT.
JOSH!
POUND POUND POUND
AND JUST LIKE THAT? I'M ALL ON MY OWN.

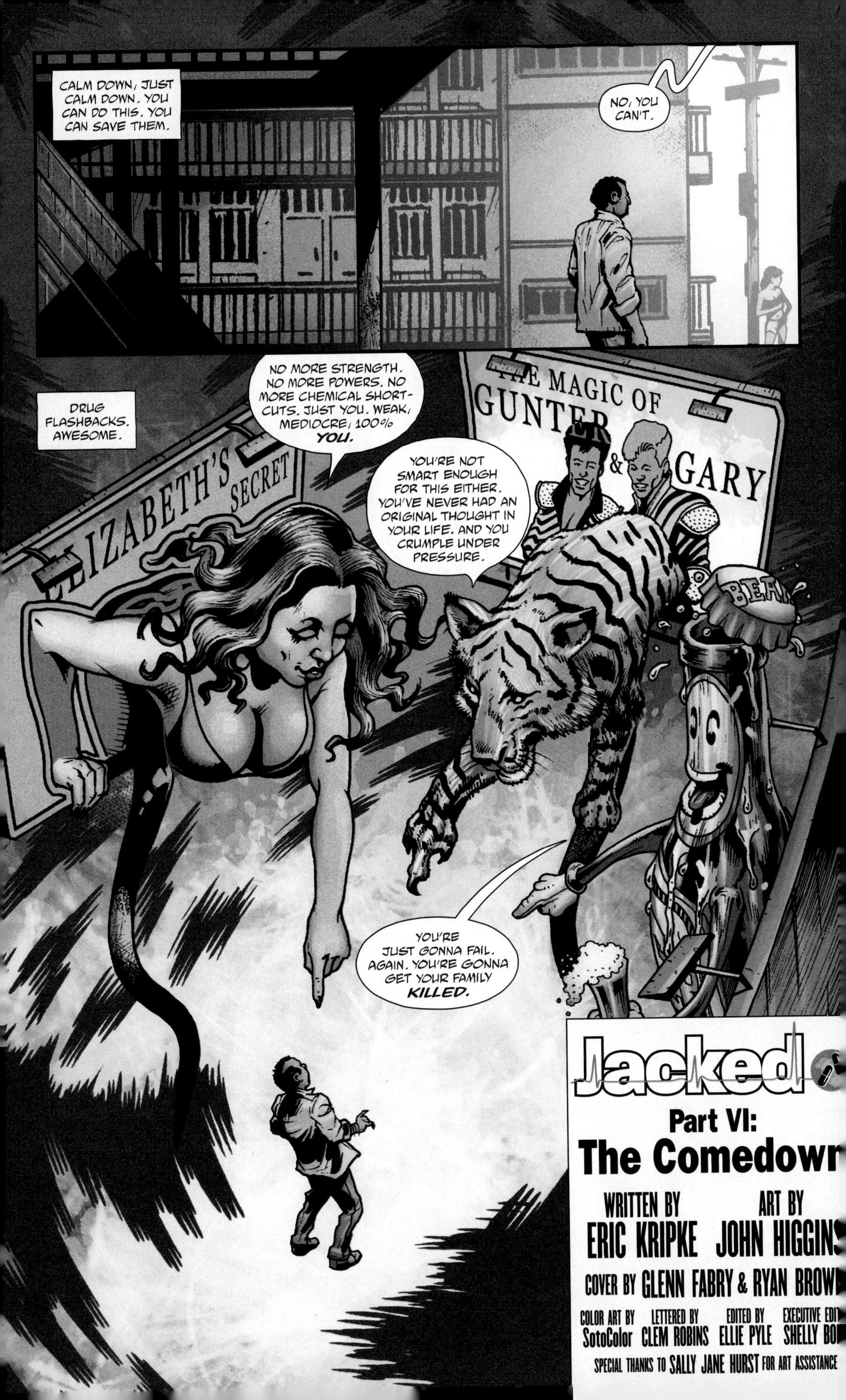
CALM DOWN, JUST CALM DOWN. YOU CAN DO THIS. YOU CAN SAVE THEM.
NO, YOU CAN'T.
DRUG FLASHBACKS. AWESOME.
NO MORE STRENGTH. NO MORE POWERS. NO MORE CHEMICAL SHORT-CUTS. JUST YOU. WEAK, MEDIOCRE, 100% **YOU.**
ELIZABETH'S SECRET
THE MAGIC OF GUNTER & GARY
YOU'RE NOT SMART ENOUGH FOR THIS EITHER. YOU'VE NEVER HAD AN ORIGINAL THOUGHT IN YOUR LIFE. AND YOU CRUMPLE UNDER PRESSURE.
YOU'RE JUST GONNA FAIL. AGAIN. YOU'RE GONNA GET YOUR FAMILY **KILLED.**
Jacked
Part VI:
The Comedown
WRITTEN BY ERIC KRIPKE
ART BY JOHN HIGGIN
COVER BY GLENN FABRY & RYAN BROW
COLOR ART BY SotoColor
LETTERED BY CLEM ROBINS
EDITED BY ELLIE PYLE
EXECUTIVE EDI SHELLY BO
SPECIAL THANKS TO SALLY JANE HURST FOR ART ASSISTANCE

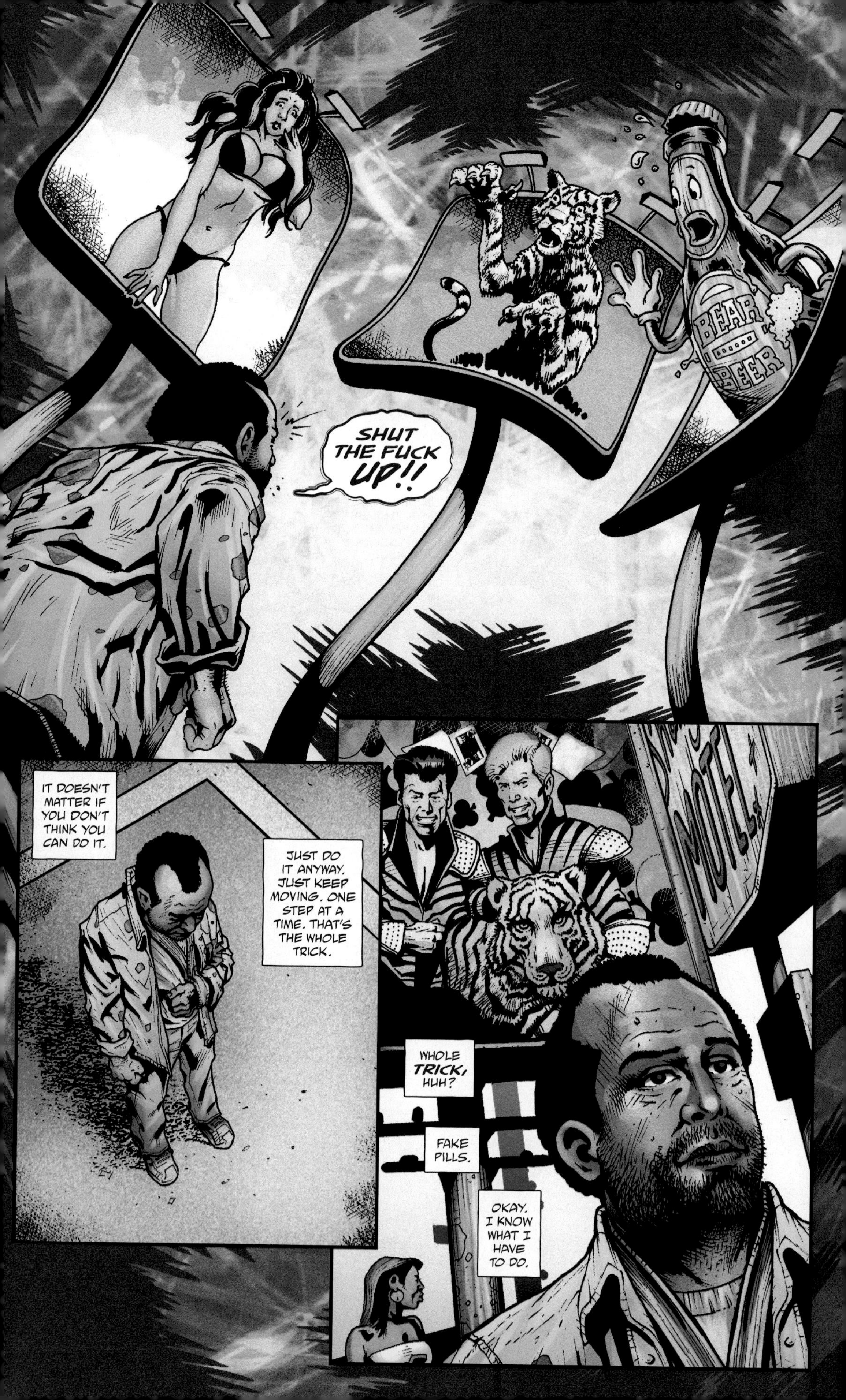
BEAR BEER
SHUT THE FUCK UP!!
IT DOESN'T MATTER IF YOU DON'T THINK YOU CAN DO IT.
JUST DO IT ANYWAY. JUST KEEP MOVING. ONE STEP AT A TIME. THAT'S THE WHOLE TRICK.
WHOLE TRICK, HUH?
FAKE PILLS.
OKAY. I KNOW WHAT I HAVE TO DO.

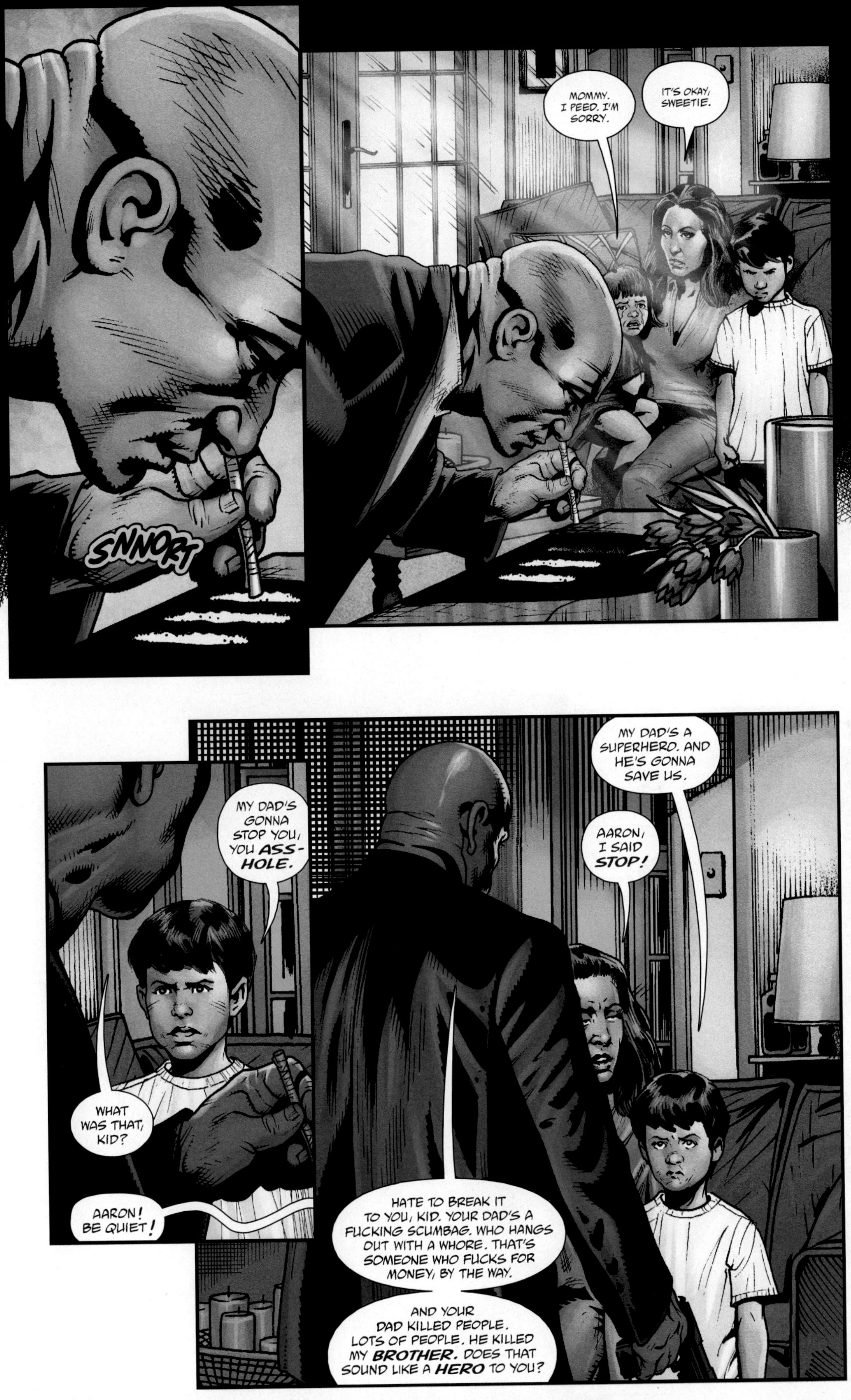
SNNORT
MOMMY. I PEED. I'M SORRY.
IT'S OKAY, SWEETIE.
MY DAD'S A SUPERHERO. AND HE'S GONNA SAVE US.
MY DAD'S GONNA STOP YOU, YOU **ASS-HOLE.**
WHAT WAS THAT, KID?
AARON! BE QUIET!
AARON, I SAID **STOP!**
HATE TO BREAK IT TO YOU, KID. YOUR DAD'S A FUCKING SCUMBAG. WHO HANGS OUT WITH A WHORE. THAT'S SOMEONE WHO FUCKS FOR MONEY, BY THE WAY.
AND YOUR DAD KILLED PEOPLE. LOTS OF PEOPLE. HE KILLED MY **BROTHER.** DOES THAT SOUND LIKE A **HERO** TO YOU?

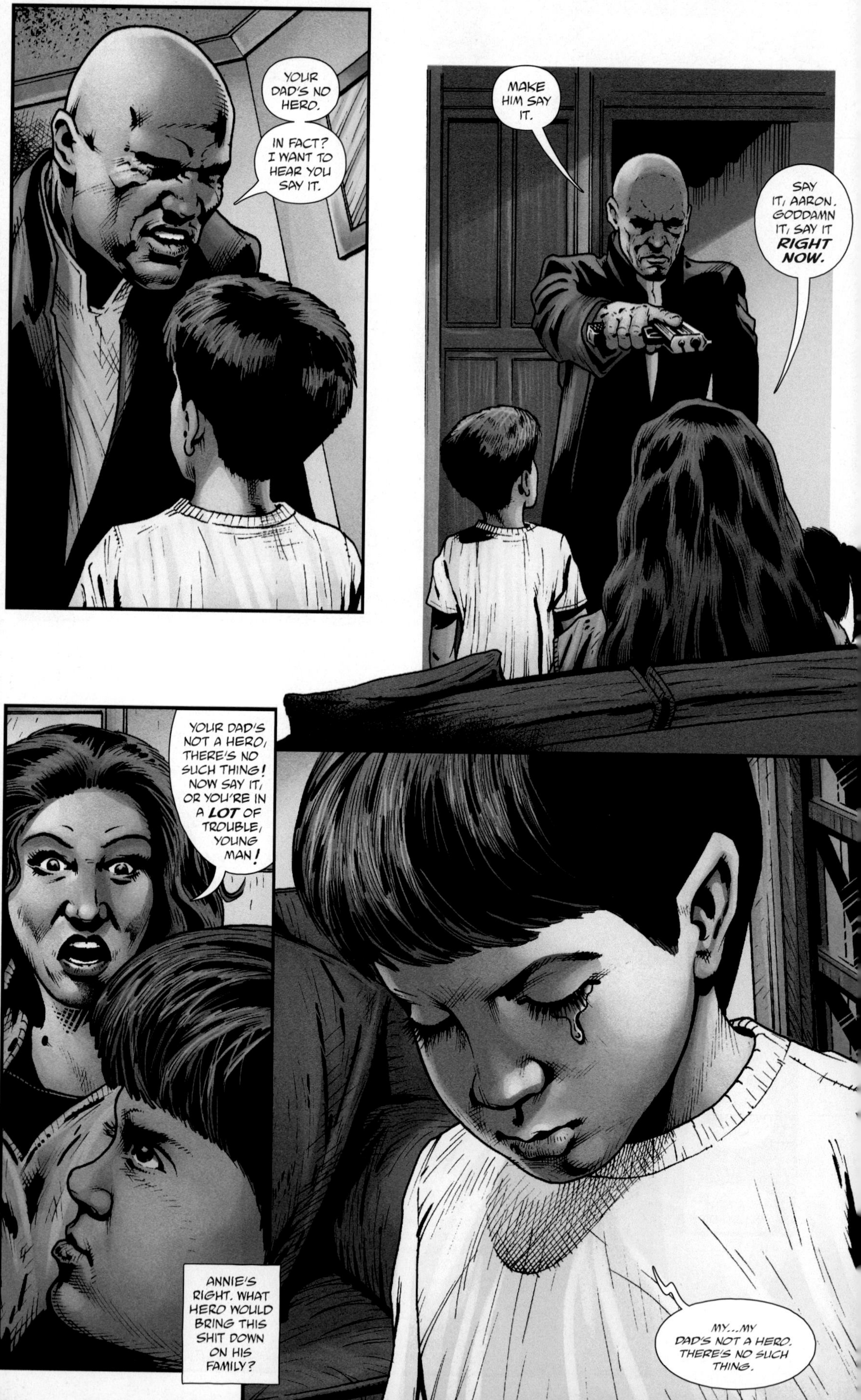
YOUR DAD'S NO HERO.
IN FACT? I WANT TO HEAR YOU SAY IT.
MAKE HIM SAY IT.
SAY IT, AARON. GODDAMN IT, SAY IT **RIGHT NOW.**
YOUR DAD'S NOT A HERO, THERE'S NO SUCH THING! NOW SAY IT, OR YOU'RE IN A **LOT** OF TROUBLE, YOUNG MAN!
ANNIE'S RIGHT. WHAT HERO WOULD BRING THIS SHIT DOWN ON HIS FAMILY?
MY...MY DAD'S NOT A HERO. THERE'S NO SUCH THING.

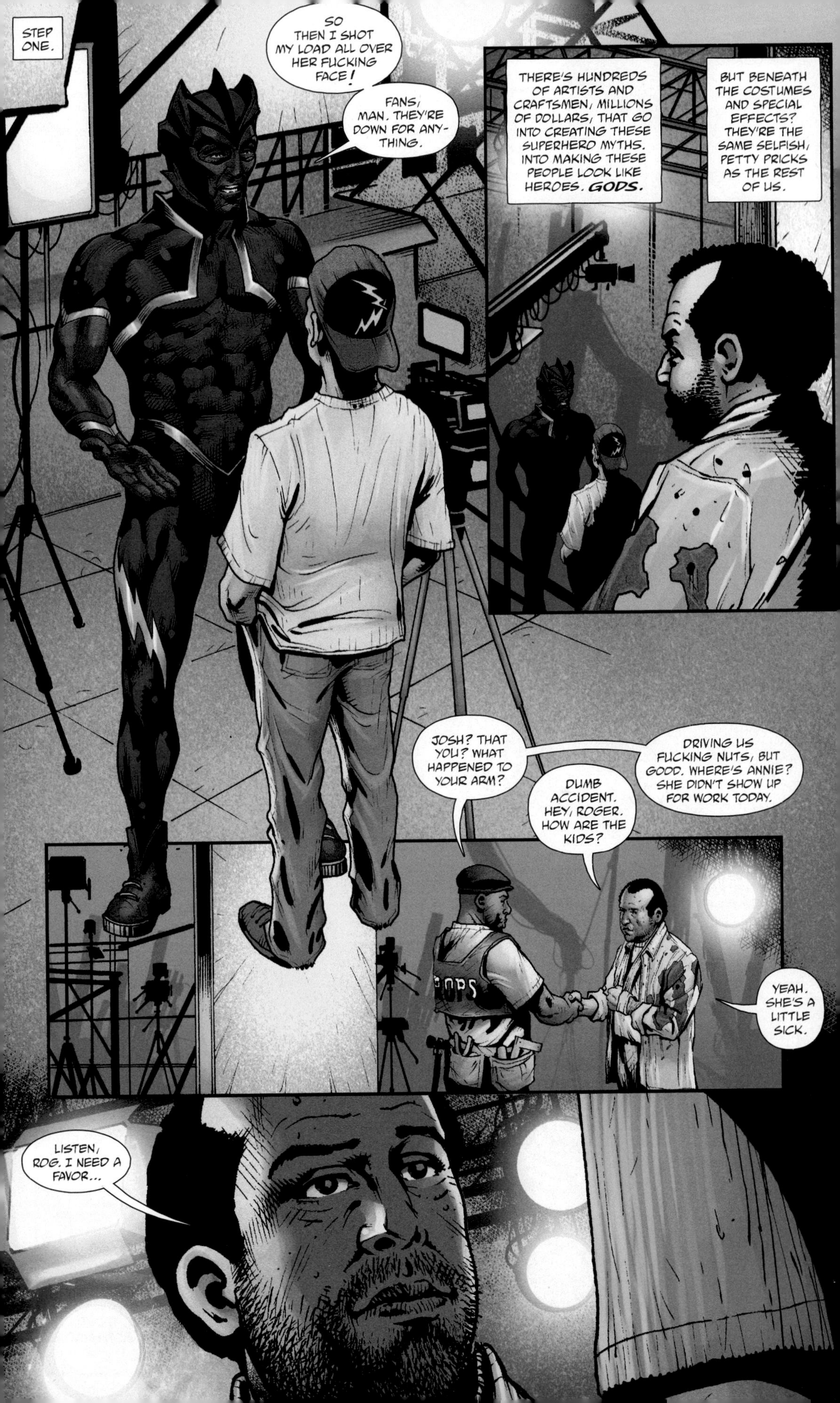
STEP ONE.
SO THEN I SHOT MY LOAD ALL OVER HER FUCKING FACE!
FANS, MAN. THEY'RE DOWN FOR ANY-THING.
THERE'S HUNDREDS OF ARTISTS AND CRAFTSMEN, MILLIONS OF DOLLARS, THAT GO INTO CREATING THESE SUPERHERO MYTHS. INTO MAKING THESE PEOPLE LOOK LIKE HEROES. GODS.
BUT BENEATH THE COSTUMES AND SPECIAL EFFECTS? THEY'RE THE SAME SELFISH, PETTY PRICKS AS THE REST OF US.
JOSH? THAT YOU? WHAT HAPPENED TO YOUR ARM?
DUMB ACCIDENT. HEY, ROGER. HOW ARE THE KIDS?
DRIVING US FUCKING NUTS, BUT GOOD. WHERE'S ANNIE? SHE DIDN'T SHOW UP FOR WORK TODAY.
YEAH. SHE'S A LITTLE SICK.
LISTEN, ROG. I NEED A FAVOR...

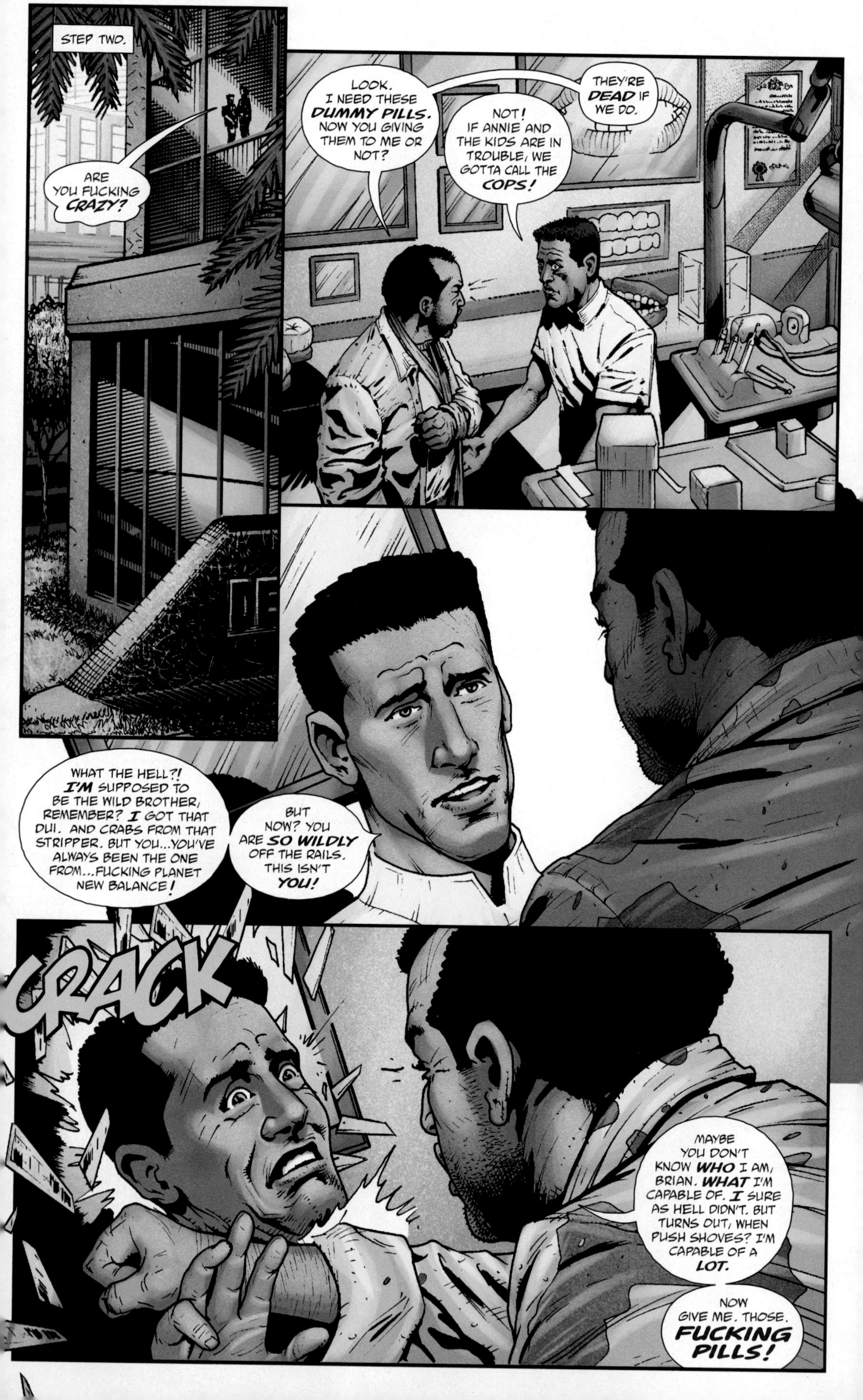
STEP TWO.
ARE YOU FUCKING CRAZY?
LOOK. I NEED THESE DUMMY PILLS. NOW YOU GIVING THEM TO ME OR NOT?
THEY'RE DEAD IF WE DO.
NOT! IF ANNIE AND THE KIDS ARE IN TROUBLE, WE GOTTA CALL THE COPS!
WHAT THE HELL?! I'M SUPPOSED TO BE THE WILD BROTHER, REMEMBER? I GOT THAT DUI. AND CRABS FROM THAT STRIPPER. BUT YOU...YOU'VE ALWAYS BEEN THE ONE FROM...FUCKING PLANET NEW BALANCE!
BUT NOW? YOU ARE SO WILDLY OFF THE RAILS. THIS ISN'T YOU!
CRACK
MAYBE YOU DON'T KNOW WHO I AM, BRIAN. WHAT I'M CAPABLE OF. I SURE AS HELL DIDN'T. BUT TURNS OUT, WHEN PUSH SHOVES? I'M CAPABLE OF A LOT.
NOW GIVE ME. THOSE. FUCKING PILLS!

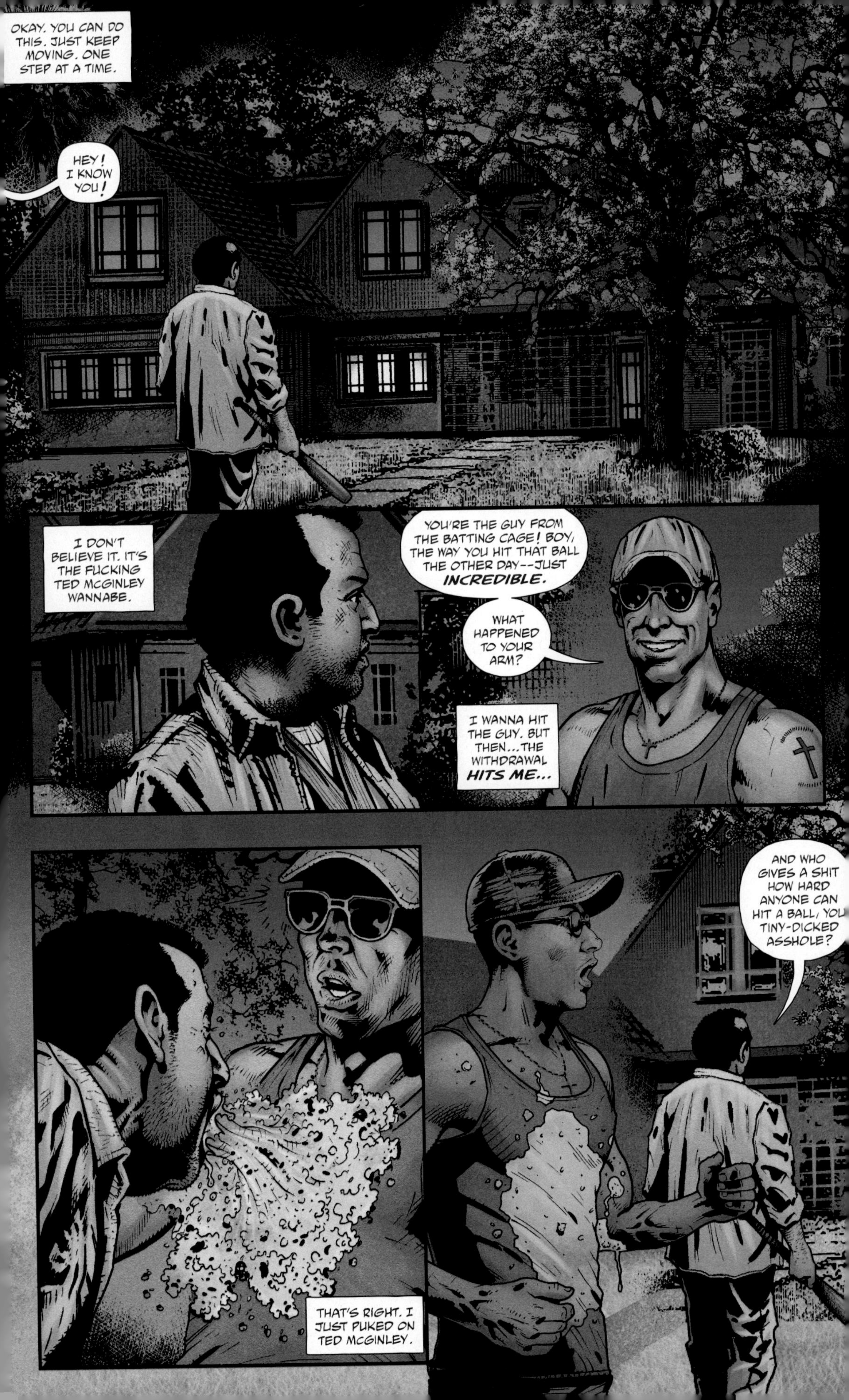

OKAY. YOU CAN DO THIS. JUST KEEP MOVING. ONE STEP AT A TIME.
HEY! I KNOW YOU!
I DON'T BELIEVE IT. IT'S THE FUCKING TED MCGINLEY WANNABE.
YOU'RE THE GUY FROM THE BATTING CAGE! BOY, THE WAY YOU HIT THAT BALL THE OTHER DAY--JUST INCREDIBLE.
WHAT HAPPENED TO YOUR ARM?
I WANNA HIT THE GUY. BUT THEN... THE WITHDRAWAL HITS ME...
THAT'S RIGHT. I JUST PUKED ON TED MCGINLEY.
AND WHO GIVES A SHIT HOW HARD ANYONE CAN HIT A BALL, YOU TINY-DICKED ASSHOLE?

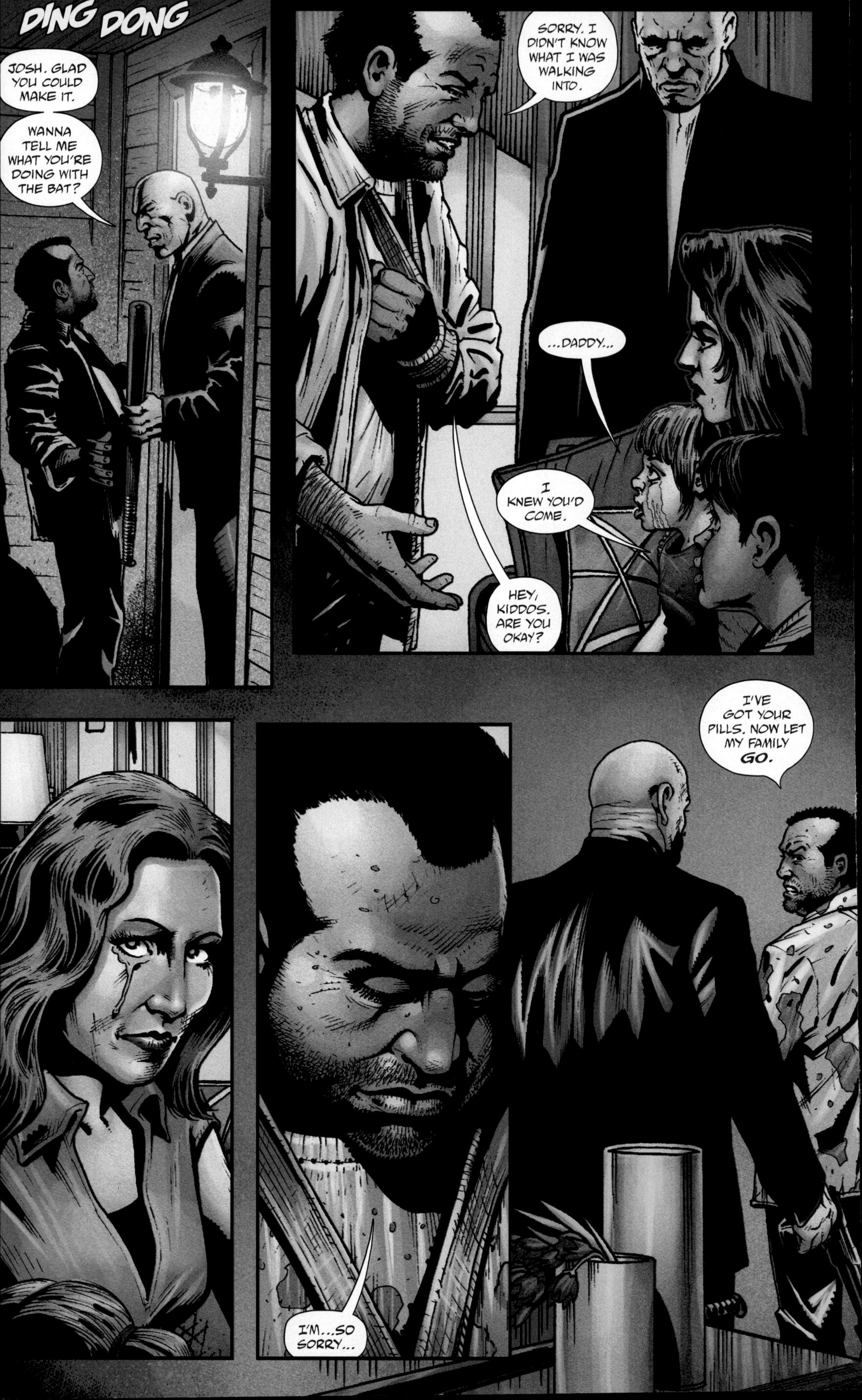
DING DONG
JOSH. GLAD YOU COULD MAKE IT.
WANNA TELL ME WHAT YOU'RE DOING WITH THE BAT?
SORRY. I DIDN'T KNOW WHAT I WAS WALKING INTO.
...DADDY...
I KNEW YOU'D COME.
HEY, KIDDOS. ARE YOU OKAY?
I'VE GOT YOUR PILLS. NOW LET MY FAMILY GO.
I'M...SO SORRY...

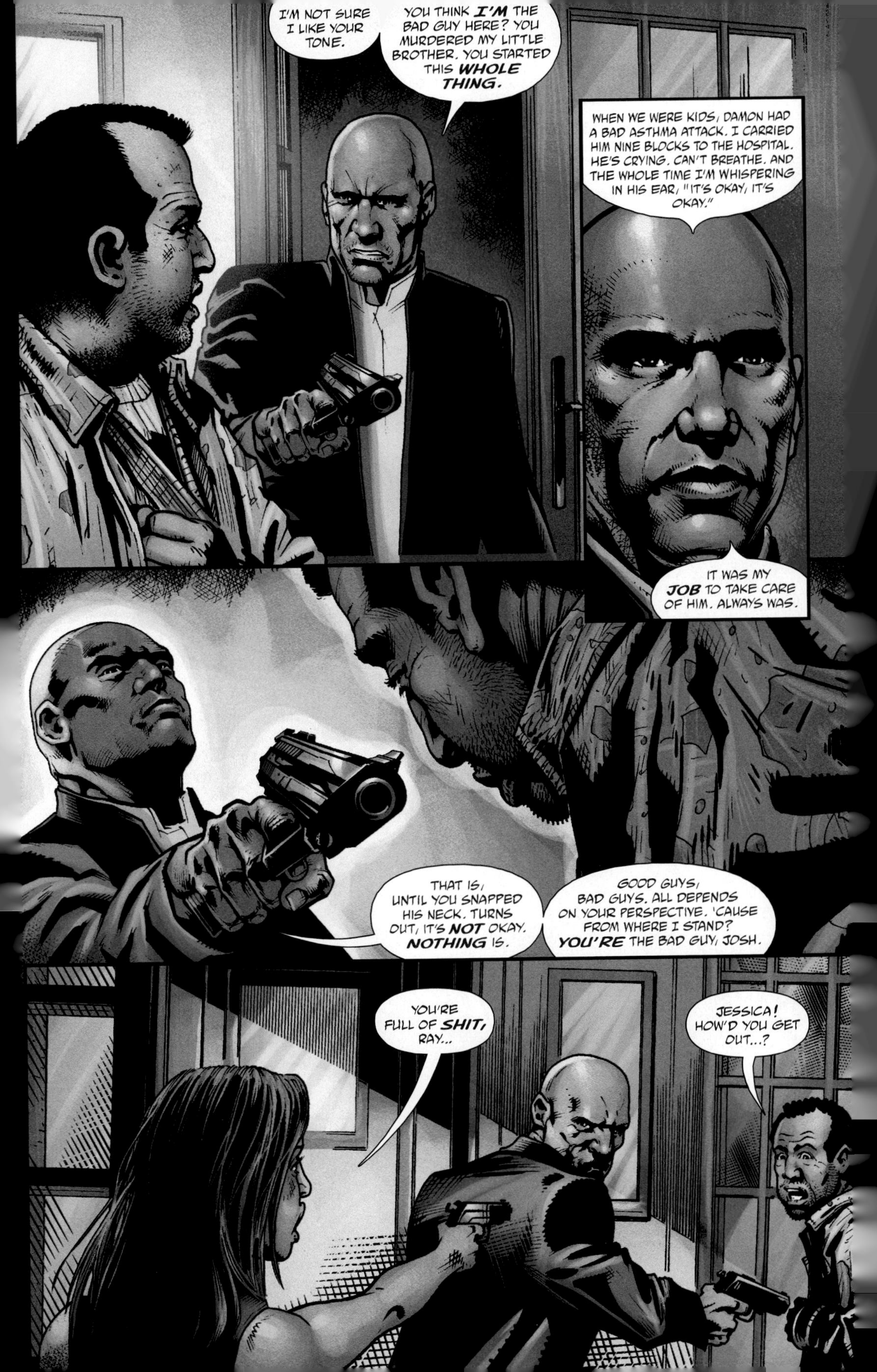
I'M NOT SURE I LIKE YOUR TONE.
YOU THINK I'M THE BAD GUY HERE? YOU MURDERED MY LITTLE BROTHER. YOU STARTED THIS WHOLE THING.
WHEN WE WERE KIDS, DAMON HAD A BAD ASTHMA ATTACK. I CARRIED HIM NINE BLOCKS TO THE HOSPITAL. HE'S CRYING. CAN'T BREATHE. AND THE WHOLE TIME I'M WHISPERING IN HIS EAR, "IT'S OKAY, IT'S OKAY."
IT WAS MY JOB TO TAKE CARE OF HIM. ALWAYS WAS.
THAT IS, UNTIL YOU SNAPPED HIS NECK. TURNS OUT, IT'S NOT OKAY. NOTHING IS.
GOOD GUYS, BAD GUYS. ALL DEPENDS ON YOUR PERSPECTIVE. 'CAUSE FROM WHERE I STAND? YOU'RE THE BAD GUY, JOSH.
YOU'RE FULL OF SHIT, RAY...
JESSICA! HOW'D YOU GET OUT...?

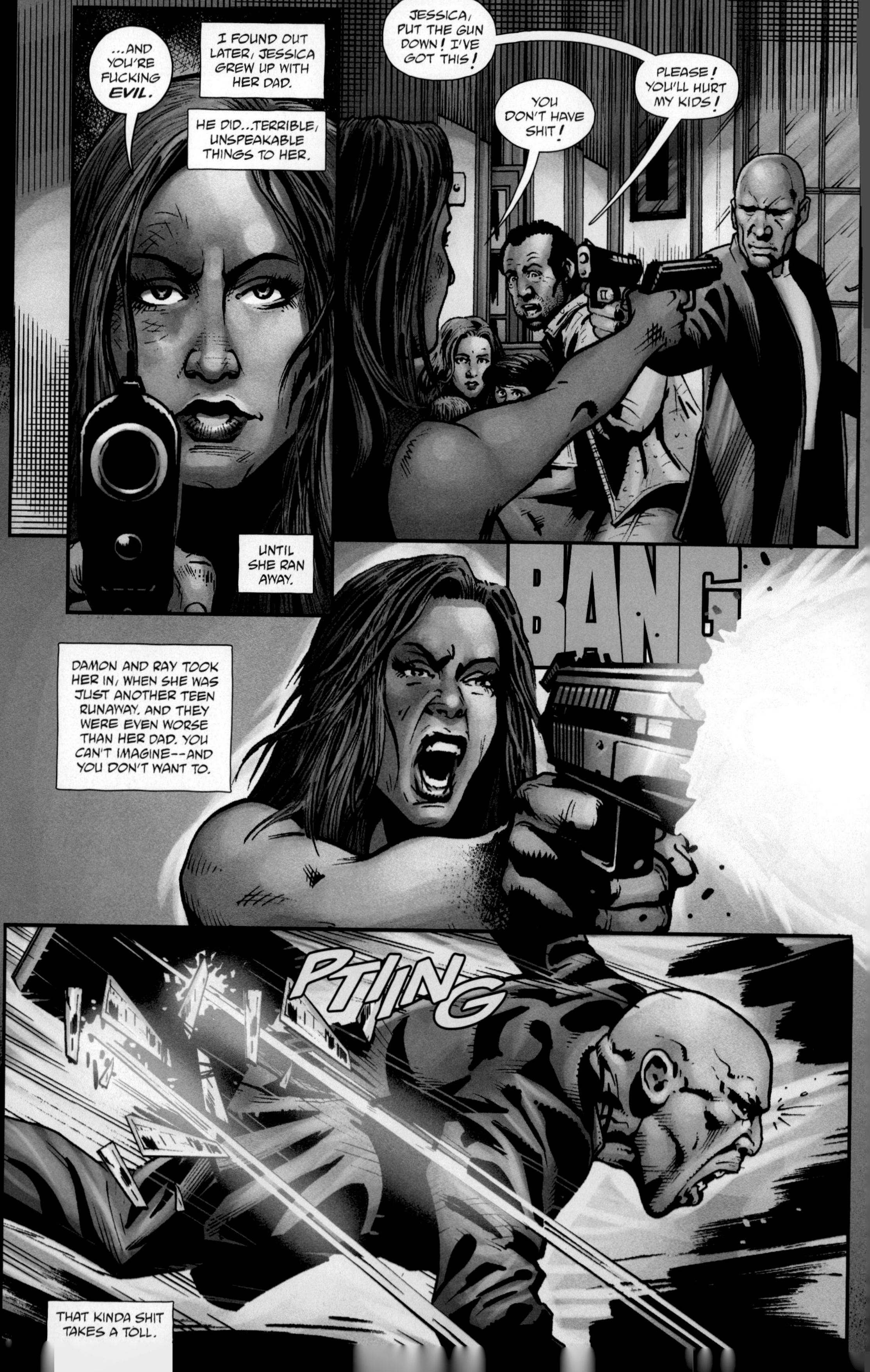
...AND YOU'RE FUCKING **EVIL.**
I FOUND OUT LATER, JESSICA GREW UP WITH HER DAD.
HE DID...TERRIBLE, UNSPEAKABLE THINGS TO HER.
JESSICA, PUT THE GUN DOWN! I'VE GOT THIS!
YOU DON'T HAVE SHIT!
PLEASE! YOU'LL HURT MY KIDS!
UNTIL SHE RAN AWAY.
BANG
DAMON AND RAY TOOK HER IN, WHEN SHE WAS JUST ANOTHER TEEN RUNAWAY, AND THEY WERE EVEN WORSE THAN HER DAD. YOU CAN'T IMAGINE--AND YOU DON'T WANT TO.
PTIING
THAT KINDA SHIT TAKES A TOLL.

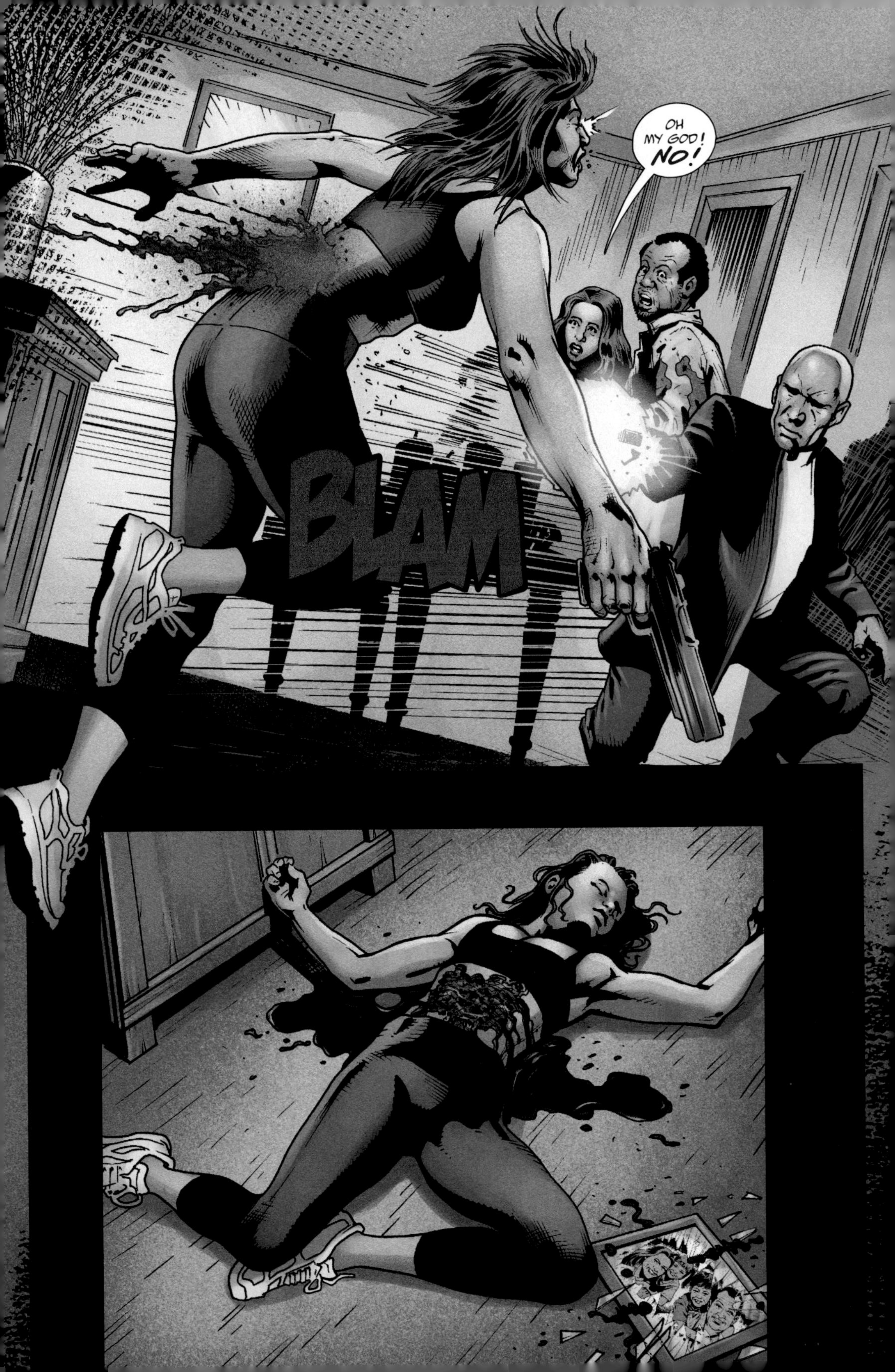
OH MY GOD! NO!
BLAM

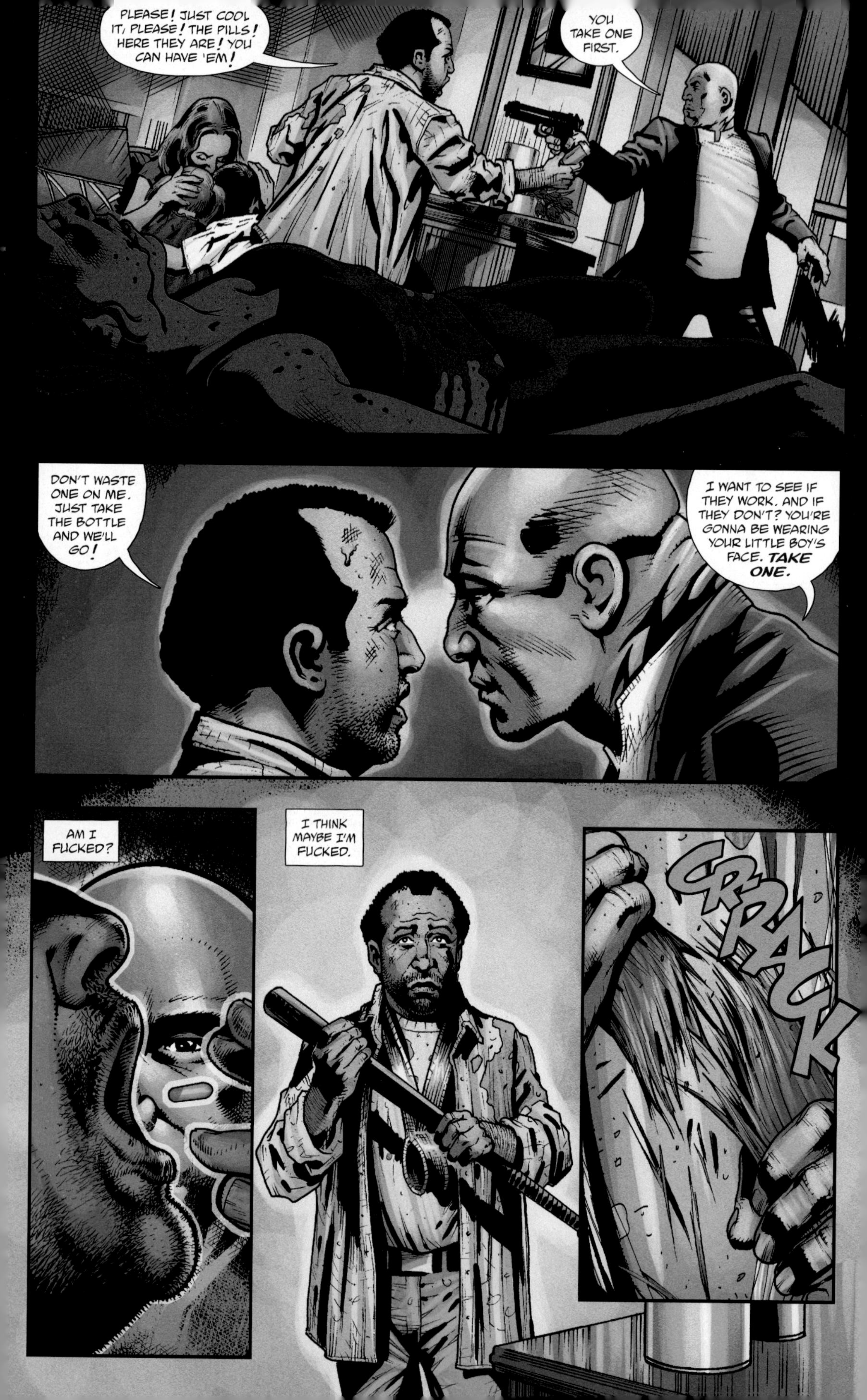
PLEASE! JUST COOL IT, PLEASE! THE PILLS! HERE THEY ARE! YOU CAN HAVE 'EM!
YOU TAKE ONE FIRST.
DON'T WASTE ONE ON ME. JUST TAKE THE BOTTLE AND WE'LL GO!
I WANT TO SEE IF THEY WORK. AND IF THEY DON'T? YOU'RE GONNA BE WEARING YOUR LITTLE BOY'S FACE. TAKE ONE.
AM I FUCKED?
I THINK MAYBE I'M FUCKED.
CRACK

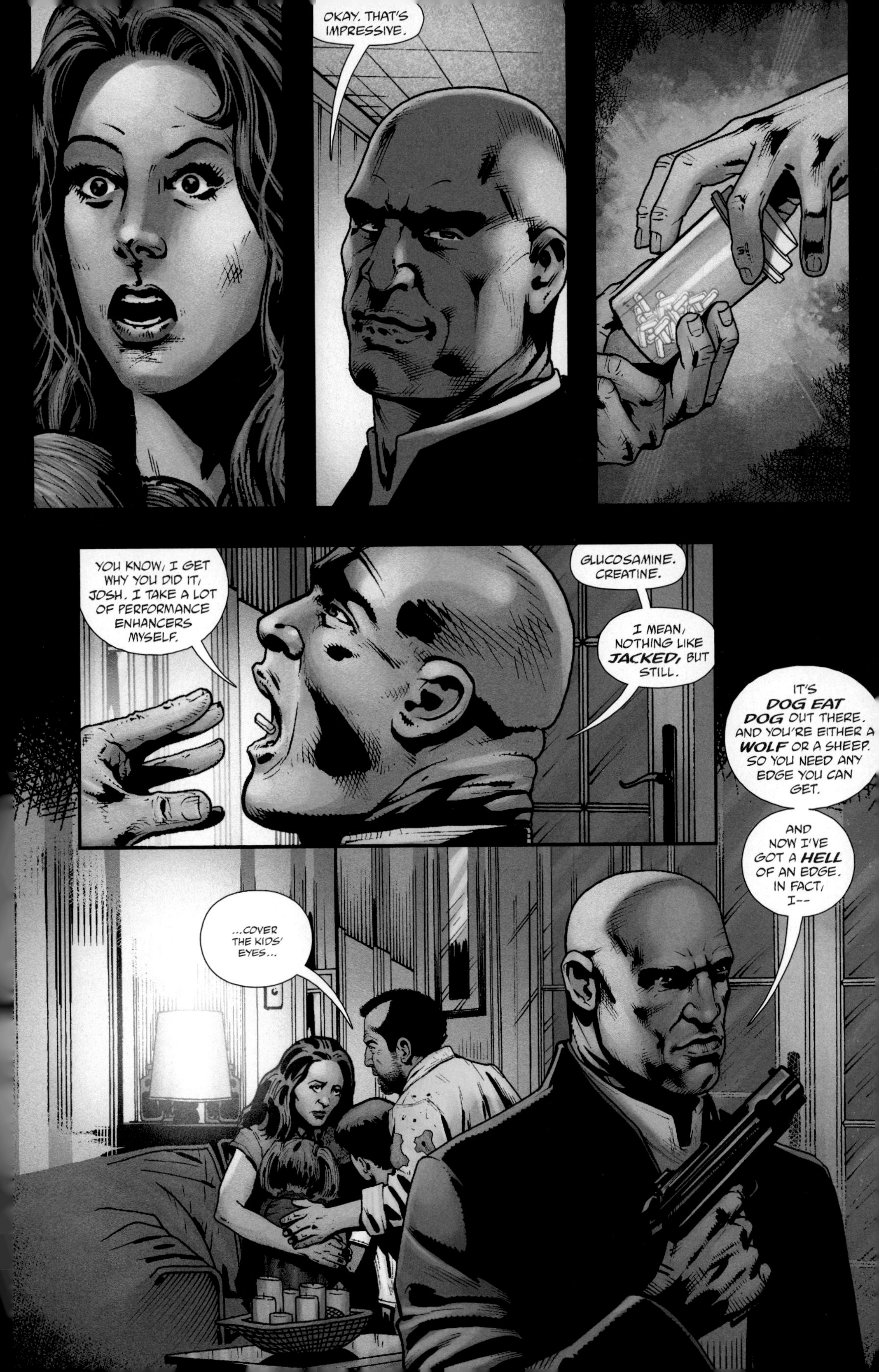
OKAY. THAT'S IMPRESSIVE.
YOU KNOW, I GET WHY YOU DID IT, JOSH. I TAKE A LOT OF PERFORMANCE ENHANCERS MYSELF.
GLUCOSAMINE. CREATINE.
I MEAN, NOTHING LIKE JACKED, BUT STILL.
IT'S DOG EAT DOG OUT THERE. AND YOU'RE EITHER A WOLF OR A SHEEP. SO YOU NEED ANY EDGE YOU CAN GET.
AND NOW I'VE GOT A HELL OF AN EDGE. IN FACT, I--
...COVER THE KIDS' EYES...

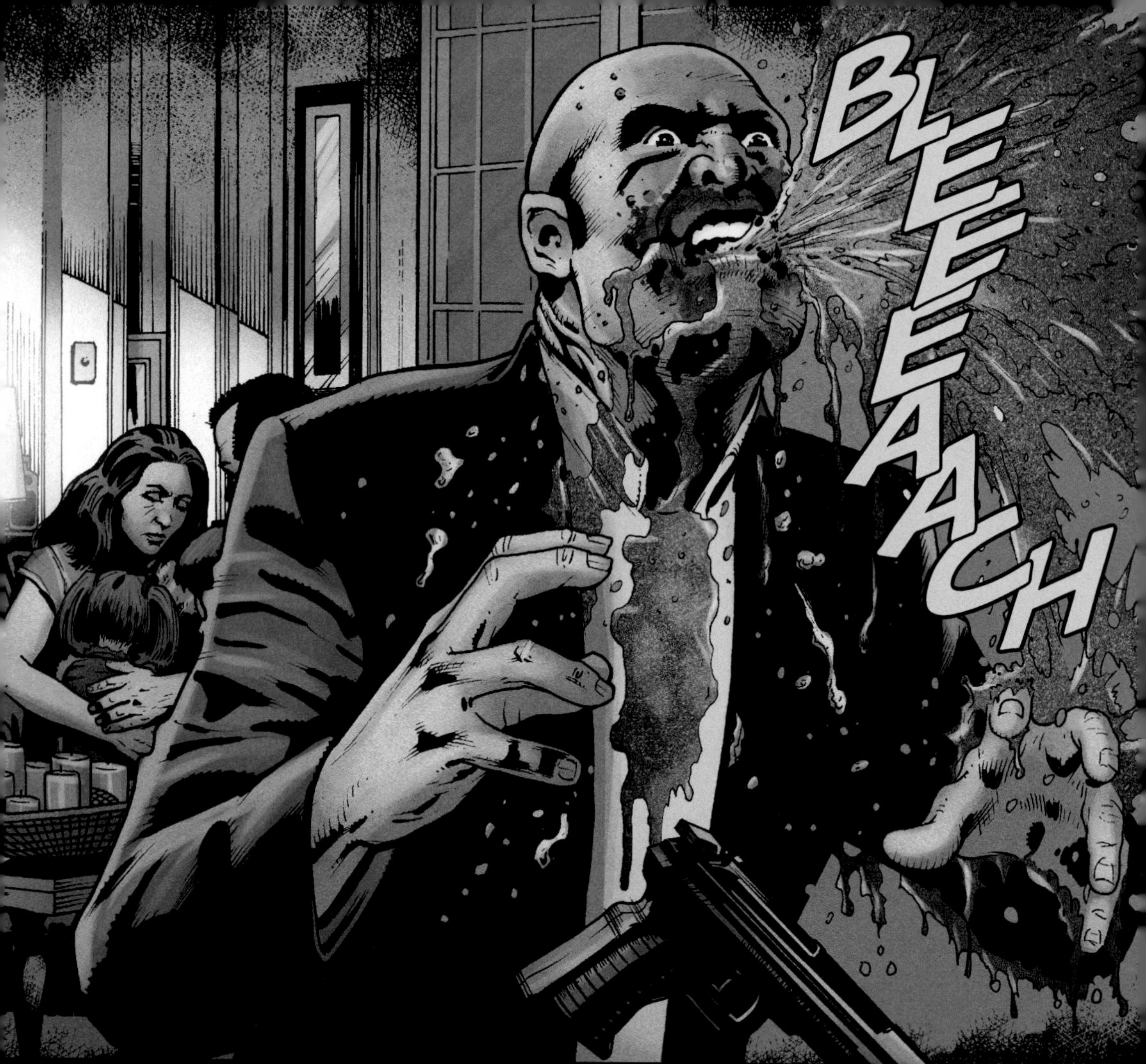
BLEEEAACH

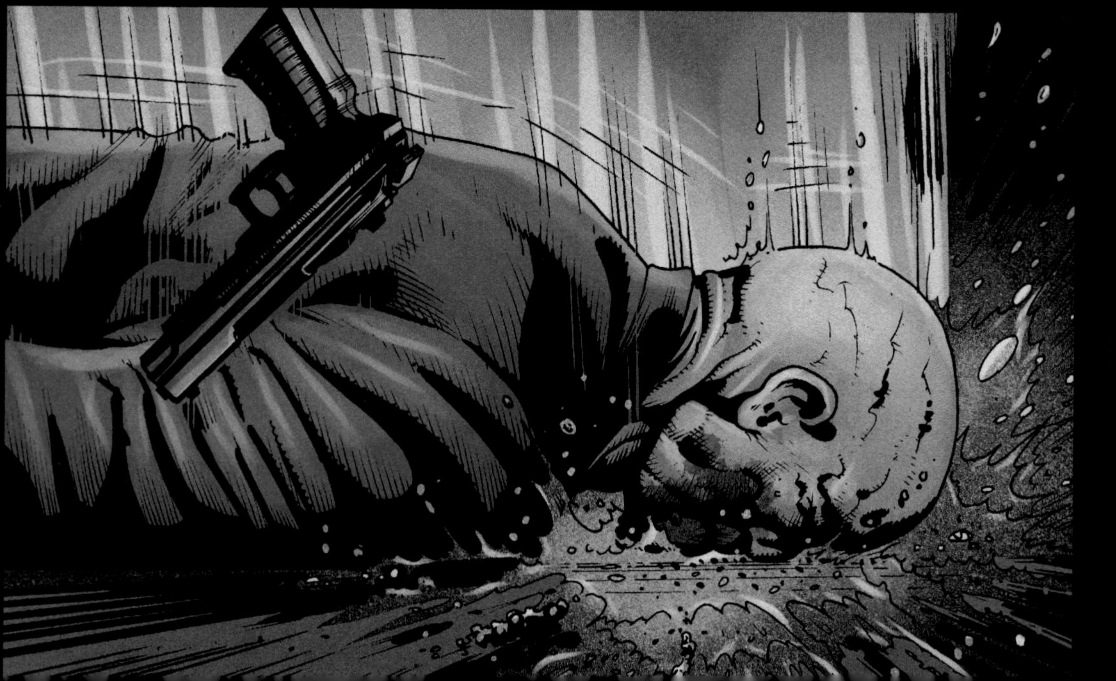

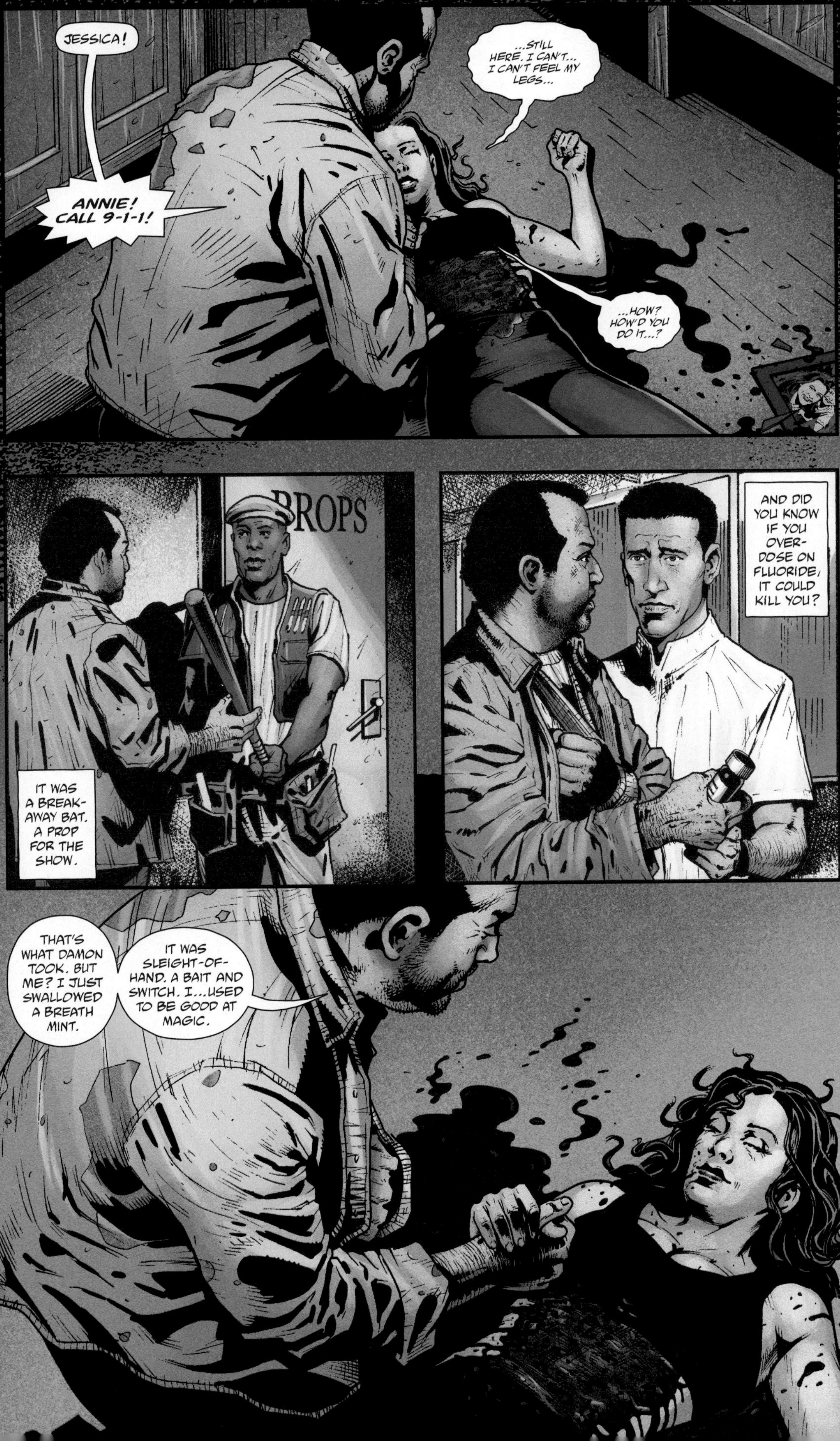
JESSICA!
...STILL HERE. I CAN'T... I CAN'T FEEL MY LEGS...
ANNIE! CALL 9-1-1!
...HOW? HOW'D YOU DO IT...?
PROPS
IT WAS A BREAK-AWAY BAT. A PROP FOR THE SHOW.
AND DID YOU KNOW IF YOU OVER-DOSE ON FLUORIDE, IT COULD KILL YOU?
THAT'S WHAT DAMON TOOK. BUT ME? I JUST SWALLOWED A BREATH MINT.
IT WAS SLEIGHT-OF-HAND. A BAIT AND SWITCH. I...USED TO BE GOOD AT MAGIC.

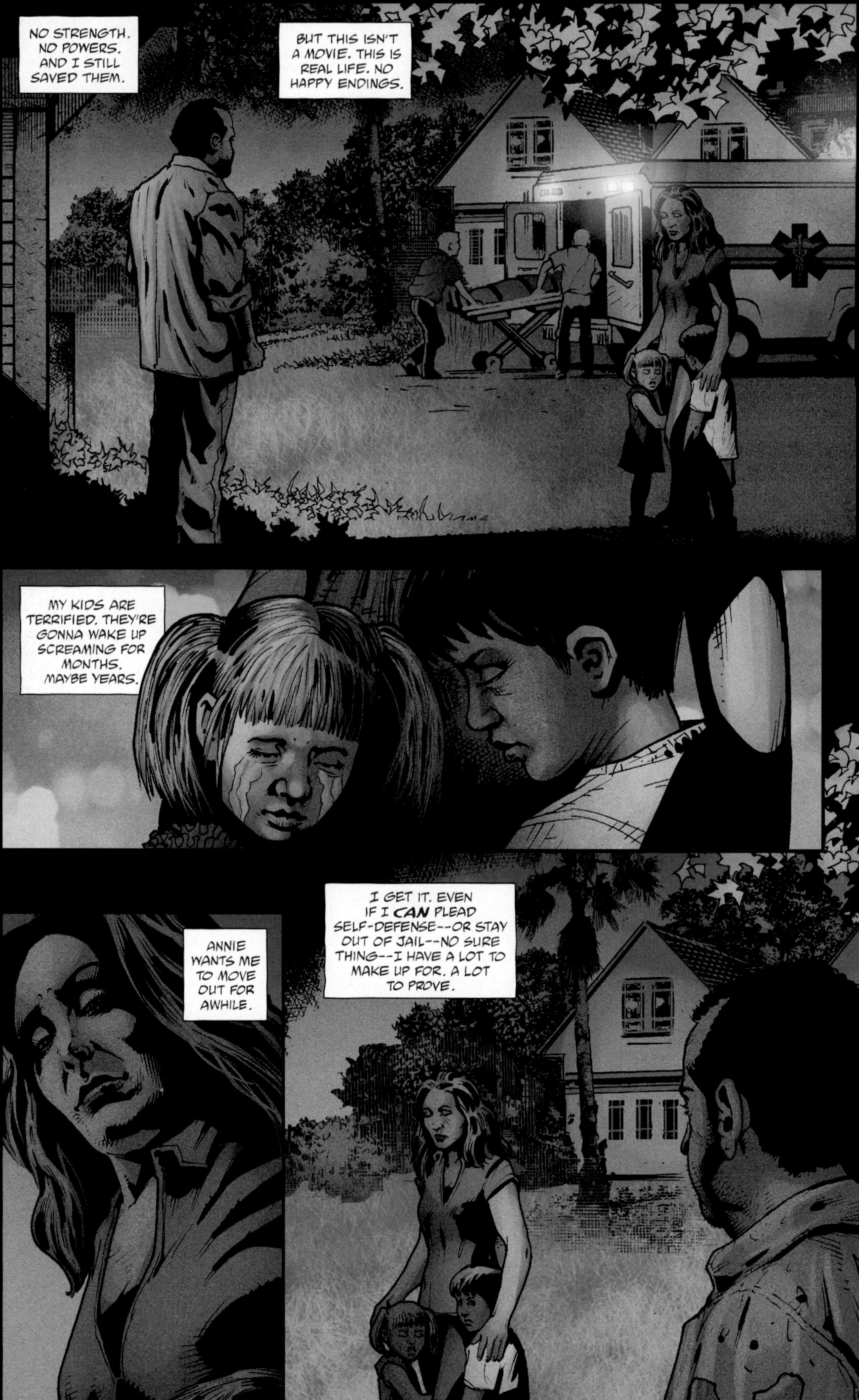
NO STRENGTH. NO POWERS. AND I STILL SAVED THEM.
BUT THIS ISN'T A MOVIE. THIS IS REAL LIFE. NO HAPPY ENDINGS.
MY KIDS ARE TERRIFIED. THEY'RE GONNA WAKE UP SCREAMING FOR MONTHS. MAYBE YEARS.
ANNIE WANTS ME TO MOVE OUT FOR AWHILE.
I GET IT. EVEN IF I CAN PLEAD SELF-DEFENSE--OR STAY OUT OF JAIL--NO SURE THING--I HAVE A LOT TO MAKE UP FOR. A LOT TO PROVE.

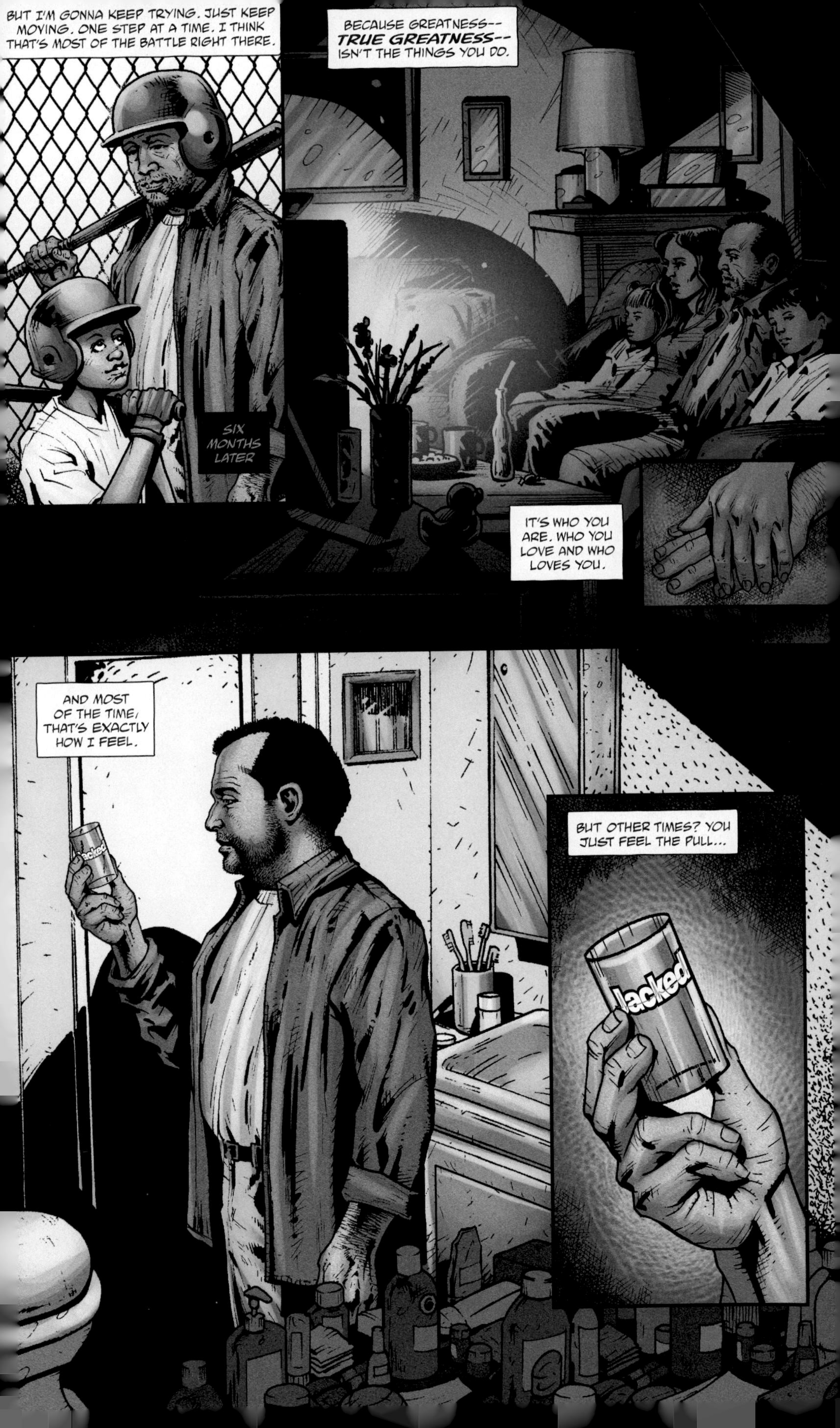

BUT I'M GONNA KEEP TRYING. JUST KEEP MOVING. ONE STEP AT A TIME. I THINK THAT'S MOST OF THE BATTLE RIGHT THERE.
SIX MONTHS LATER
BECAUSE GREATNESS-- TRUE GREATNESS-- ISN'T THE THINGS YOU DO.
IT'S WHO YOU ARE. WHO YOU LOVE AND WHO LOVES YOU.
AND MOST OF THE TIME, THAT'S EXACTLY HOW I FEEL.
Jacked
BUT OTHER TIMES? YOU JUST FEEL THE PULL...
Jacked

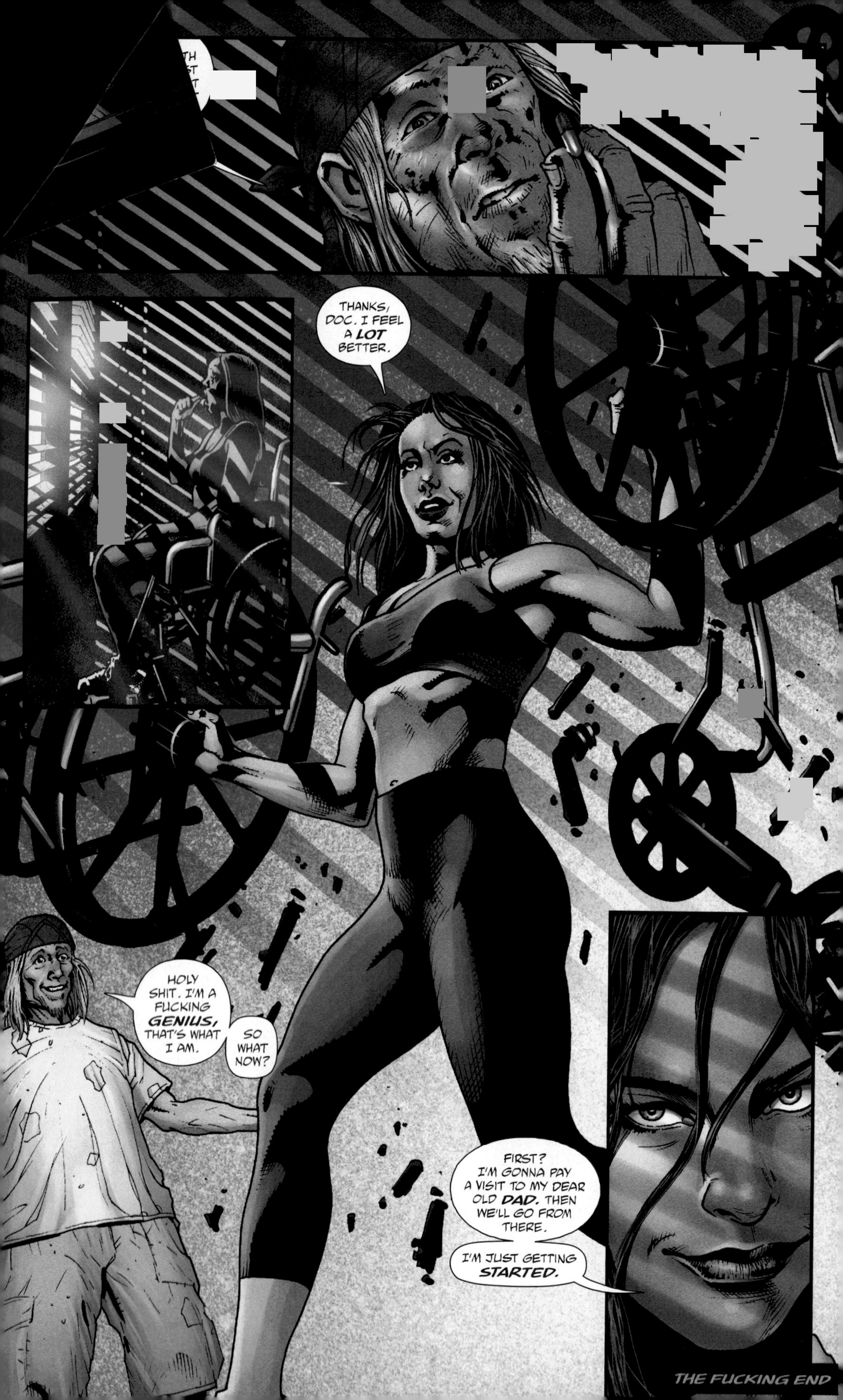

THANKS, DOC. I FEEL A LOT BETTER.
HOLY SHIT. I'M A FUCKING GENIUS, THAT'S WHAT I AM.
SO WHAT NOW?
FIRST? I'M GONNA PAY A VISIT TO MY DEAR OLD DAD. THEN WE'LL GO FROM THERE.
I'M JUST GETTING STARTED.
THE FUCKING END

"Transmet is brilliant future-shock commentary."
—SPIN MAGAZINE

"It's angry political sci-fi and it's funny as hell."
—PLAYBOY

TRANSMETROPOLITAN
VOL. 2: LUST FOR LIFE

TRANSMETROPOLITAN
VOL. 3: YEAR OF THE
BASTARD

FROM THE WRITER OF *PLANETARY*
WARREN ELLIS
with DARICK ROBERTSON

READ THE ENTIRE SERIES!

VERTIGO

"Marvelous storytelling."—PUBLISHERS WEEKLY

"Jamie Delano introduced John Constantine's solo title with breathless pace and little mercy."—PASTE MAGAZINE

FROM THE WRITER OF *ANIMAL MAN*

JAMIE DELANO

with JOHN RIDGWAY, ALFREDO ALCALA and others

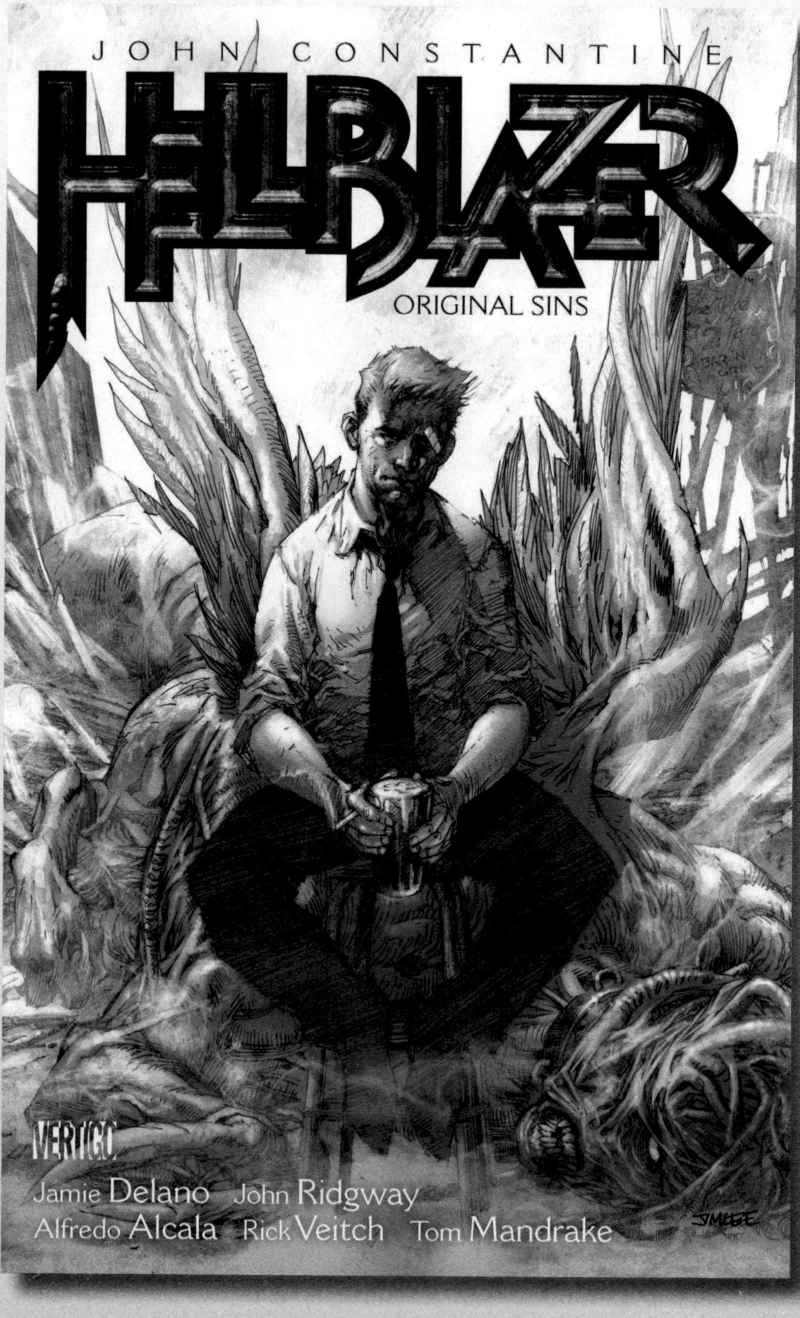
JOHN CONSTANTINE
HELLBLAZER
ORIGINAL SINS
VERTIGO
Jamie Delano John Ridgway
Alfredo Alcala Rick Veitch Tom Mandrake

JOHN CONSTANTINE, HELLBLAZER VOL. 2: THE DEVIL YOU KNOW

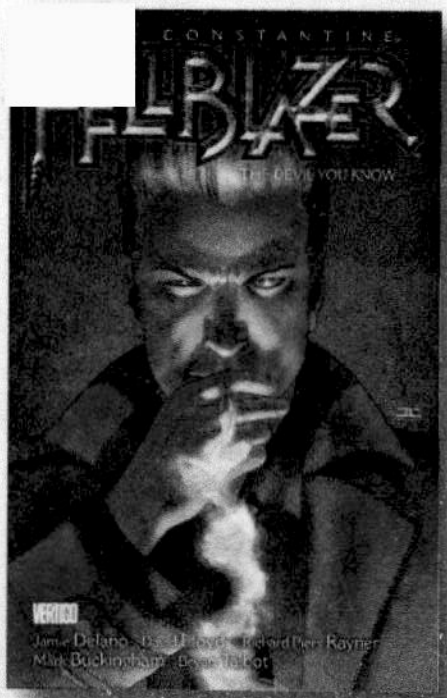

with DAVID LLOYD, MARK BUCKINGHAM and others

JOHN CONSTANTINE, HELLBLAZER VOL. 3: THE FEAR MACHINE

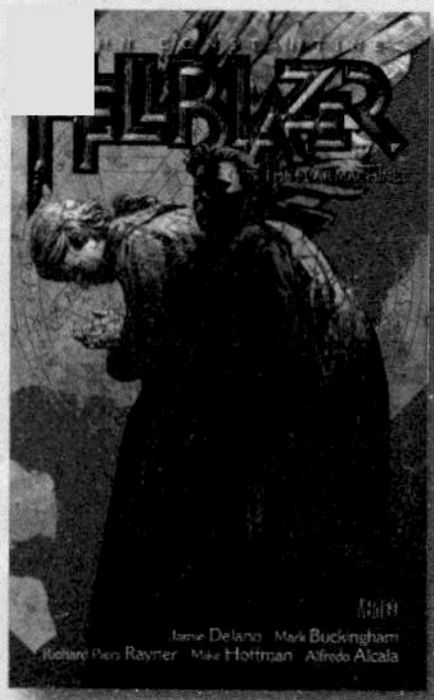

with MARK BUCKINGHAM, RICHARD PIERS RAYNER and others

JOHN CONSTANTINE, HELLBLAZER VOL. 4: THE FAMILY MAN

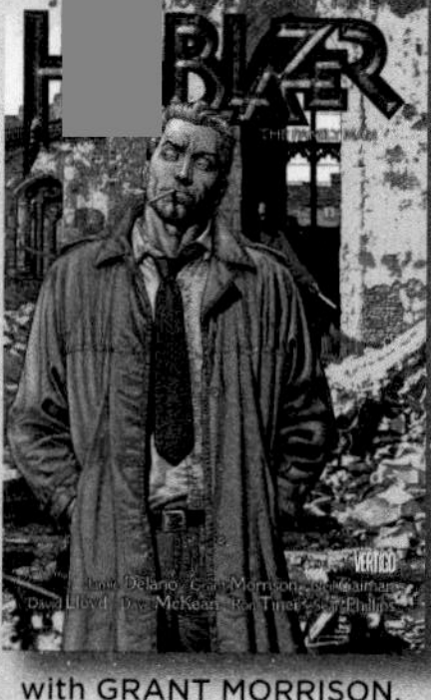

with GRANT MORRISON, NEIL GAIMAN and others